JIMMY

JIMMY

THE AUTOBIOGRAPHY OF
JIMMY FLOYD HASSELBAINK

HarperSport

An Imprint of HarperCollins*Publishers*

First published in UK in 2005 by
HarperSport
an imprint of HarperCollins*Publishers*
London

© Image Onside B.V. 2005

1

A CIP catalogue record for this book
is available from the British Library

ISBN 0 00 721387 5

Printed and bound in Great Britain
by Clays Ltd, St Ives plc

The HarperCollins website address is
www.harpercollins.co.uk

Contents

List of Illustrations

All photographs provided courtesy of Jimmy Floyd Hasselbaink and Humphry Nijman, with the exception of the following:

Page 3 (top and bottom) © Joop Boek
Page 4 (top) © Empics; (centre, left and right, bottom) © Action Images
Page 5 (top and bottom) © Action Images
Page 6 © Action Images
Page 7 (top) © Empics; (centre) © Getty Images; (bottom) © Empics
Page 8 (top left and right) © Empics; (bottom) © Action Images
Page 9 (top and bottom) © Action Images
Page 10 (top) © Action Images; (bottom) © Getty Images
Page 11 (centre) © Corbis; (bottom) © Getty Images
Page 12 (top) © Empics; (centre) © Empics; (bottom) © Action Images
Page 13 (top) © Action Images; (bottom left and right) © Action Images
Page 14 (top left) © Corbis; (top right and bottom) © Action Images
Page 15 (bottom left) © Joop Boek; (bottom right) © Popper
Page 16 © Getty Images

Acknowledgements

There are two people I need to thank, without whom this book would not have been possible.

To my mum: thank you for being there all the time and for giving me your wholehearted support. You may have been very strict with me as a child but I always appreciated your honesty, and now that I am older I can understand why you were that hard on me. No child could wish for a better mother. I love you so much.

To my agent and trusted friend Humphry: you are the only person who believed in me as a young footballer in Holland; the only one who dared to give me a chance. You are the father-figure in my life that I never had. Thank you for supporting me and keeping me on the right track. All the good things that have happened to me in my career are down to you.

Introduction

It was a very big step for me to commit to this book and expose my personality so openly. It feels a little dangerous to make myself so vulnerable. I am very curious and at the same time quite nervous about the reactions of the readers. But what's here is what happened; it's my life story.

I might have played football at the highest level, for big clubs like Leeds United, Atlético Madrid, Chelsea and Middlesbrough, and generally been seen to have had a highly successful career. But it hasn't always been smooth progress to where I am now.

Between the ages of twelve and nineteen my life was in chaos. I was mostly on the street making mischief, and getting myself a name with the local police. Several of my friends from that time are now dealing in hard drugs such as heroin and cocaine. Some of them were already smoking hash when they were sixteen. My family didn't live in a very good neighbourhood. You could say it was like The Bronx of Zaandam. There was widespread stealing and dealing. We didn't have much money at home, so I also contributed my share of illegal activities. I mostly did it to be part of a gang, but also to make some money.

Having money was a necessity. I might have seemed destined to go off on the wrong track but I probably developed some parts of my character during that time as well. Back then, as now, it wasn't important for me to be liked by everyone. Nowadays I am fully independent, whereas before I was often tagging along with a group. I would do stupid things just to prove myself.

One time in Amsterdam, things really got out of hand. A group of about ten of us went to see a concert by Public Enemy, one of the most popular rap bands at that time. None of us had tickets because we were intending to obtain them at the concert venue. We knew there were no ticket offices there – and the concert was sold out anyway – but we thought we would just take tickets from people who did have them. When we got there we threatened some guys outside and stole their tickets so that we could gain entry to the concert. That's the kind of stuff we did. It is not something I am proud of. When you're in a gang, you do some very stupid things.

The people we had stolen the tickets from went to the police and eventually we were all arrested. I was sent to a youth detention facility called Het Poortje in Groningen in the north of Holland for three months. I was there not just for stealing the tickets, but also because they had found some stolen stuff when they had searched my home. I was always dealing in stolen goods, such as car radios or wristwatches, and it was a lucrative business. I would go out clubbing or driving with the money I stole.

I once stole a watch at a football club, but that was the first and last time I ever pulled something like that. I stopped stealing because I didn't want to do it anymore. My mother, of course, was distraught at my behaviour.

Our gang didn't have a special name. We were always together, hanging out on the streets and getting ourselves into deeper and deeper trouble. Some of those guys became drug addicts and others are now in prison facing long sentences. Several others have become drug dealers. Only my friend Oswald Snip and I never took drugs ourselves. That was partly because the two of us were always playing football and because we had a talent. If I hadn't had any talent for football, perhaps my life would have turned out completely differently. During that time, my anti-social behaviour was also at the root of my problems with my brother Carlos. It was the only period that our relationship was bad. Carlos hated the gang and the fact that I was a member, but nobody, not even Carlos, had a grip in me.

In those days I carried a knife around with me, but never a gun. I was too scared of guns. I once saw somebody get shot in his car right in the middle of the street. In hindsight the only thing that really saved me was football. Yes, I understood the difference between right and wrong, but I preferred to look the other way when I did wrong. Had I stood up and voiced my preference not to participate in certain illegal activities because I was scared, I'm sure I wouldn't have been part of the gang anymore. You're either with them or you're not.

It took a while before I could escape that world. I was very lucky that I made it out. There was always the excitement of not getting caught, but there would come a time, I knew, when it would go wrong. In hindsight it was fortunate that it happened, although I was more afraid of my mother's reaction than of the punishment by authority. I remember getting seriously beaten by my mum then, for the one and only time. I was sixteen when I had to go to prison. My mother didn't actually say much. I think she had suspected what was going on all along. She never said anything to me about always being out on the streets or about me always coming home late. I was her darling.

Fortunately, it was just a period in my life, something that is now behind me. I'm not saying that everybody should have to go through what I went through, but I am actually happy that I had a youth like that. I've seen much worse. I would never wish a youth like that on my daughter, or any other potential future children of mine. Nonetheless, it did help to mould me into the person I am right now. I've become a much stronger person because I've seen the worst.

Those three months in the detention facility did not act directly as a warning to me, but their effect certainly became clear much later on. As I left the prison doors behind me I realized that I needed a certain discipline in order to succeed at whatever I wanted to achieve, certainly as a professional footballer. I absolutely needed discipline. Afterwards I always kept in mind that if I didn't get my act together and discipline myself I would simply fall back to the life I was living in Zaandam. I now knew how I definitely did not want to live, and that thought kept me going, especially during my first years in Portugal.

My lack of discipline still showed through during my time at Telstar, where I was constantly late for training. I still had my dodgy friends back then and was doing all kinds of other things, none of which concerned football. I would be lying in bed until noon, when I could just as well have got myself a job after I left school. I really regret leaving school prematurely. I was quite good at studying but I thought it was much cooler not to try hard and not to do my homework. That way the other guys seemed to like me, and so did the girls. They let me peek at their exam papers, because I was cool. I must have been quite popular among my classmates back then.

Oswald has always remained on the right track. He never got involved with gangs the way I did. He came along once or twice with us, but he never spent time in prison. In the youth detention facility in Groningen I had to share a room with two other people. I was shocked. I was so embarrassed that I had let it get so far.

When I joined AZ Alkmaar that life was finally behind me. It was probably because Carlos played there as well and was watching over me more closely. His was a good influence. In the end I had learned my lesson. Carlos turned out to be my babysitter. At that time he was also living in the same apartment block. I had more time for football and training, and it was then that I started to reconsider my future.

Memories of my gang life were also the reason for trying to get my mother out of the apartment. I really wanted her to leave that neighbourhood. It took me a lot of energy to convince her, though. I had to buy her a house and then practically force her out of that Perim flat which, for some reason, she liked so much. Now she has adjusted to her new home and is very happy. Most of all, I am extremely grateful that in the end I was able to do something back for my mother.

I certainly owed it to her.

1 High Stilts in Surinam

I was an active child. My earliest memories are of climbing into, onto and over anything and everything in sight. No challenge was too great for me. That natural curiosity served me well later in life when it became time to travel the world.

When I was allowed to play outside, my brother Carlos, who is three years older than me, had to look after me and make sure I didn't get into trouble. Carlos and I were inseparable. The street in front of our house in Paramaribo, Surinam was a fantastic playground. We had plenty of space and the freedom to do whatever we liked. With that freedom came the irresistible urge to cause mischief and I, in particular, tested the patience of our parents, Frans Ware and Cornelli Hasselbaink. For example, when I was three, my mother sent Carlos to the neighbourhood store on the Broko Pondolaan. I was deemed to be too young to go out and was ordered to stay home. But even back then, I was strong-willed and didn't take too kindly to being ordered around. So I slipped out of the house and followed Carlos at a distance. Little did I know that this decision to disobey was to change my life forever.

I followed Carlos down the Broko Pondolaan. He didn't notice me as I moved craftily down the opposite side of the street. When he was about to enter the store, I called out to him. He was startled and waved at me, telling me to stay where I was: the road was busy with speeding traffic and it was no place for a three-year-old. I can't remember what exactly I thought at this point, but I suppose I took his gesture to mean that it was okay for me to cross. I ran out into the street and was rammed head on by a woman on a moped.

I crumpled to the ground. I was in shock and felt a sharp pain all over my body, but particularly in my right leg. I was conscious, but in a daze. I can still see the faces of the dozens of people who ran over to help me. The lady on the moped was also startled. As luck would have it she was a nurse and so she was able to provide first aid. Minutes later my mother appeared. She had hitched a ride on the back of a moped driven by a friend of Franklin, my oldest brother. I can still clearly remember her crying and screaming from the shock of seeing her child lying still in the middle of the road.

An ambulance took me to the hospital a few blocks away. My leg was broken, but it wasn't set until the following day. After a few more days of observation I was released from the hospital. It seemed as if that was it, just a lucky close call and nothing more, but, two years later, after we had moved to Holland, a doctor's check-up revealed something more sinister: my right leg had grown crooked, alarmingly so, to the point where I was effectively bow-legged. The logical explanation was that it had not been set properly back in Surinam. And yet, I'm not so sure. My mother doesn't remember exactly how it happened, but to this day she maintains that it was due to my hyper-activeness. She tells me stories about how, despite wearing splints after breaking my leg, I would run around and up and down the stairs even faster than before. Perhaps that was the real reason why my right leg started to grow crooked.

Either way, once in Holland, it was decided that I needed an operation. They re-fractured my leg and re-set it in a hard plaster cast. The doctor said everything would be all right, and he predicted I wouldn't have any more problems. I can still vividly remember running around with my friends with my leg in a big plaster cast, holding my crutches in the air. Even in that state I was much faster than all the other boys.

Like many homes in Surinam, ours was a cream-coloured wooden house with green window frames. The house was suspended on four poles with accommodation on only one floor. Underneath was a three-metre high space where you could store bicycles, garden tools and that sort of thing. Dogs would often sleep there too, as they would never be allowed inside the house. It was a typical Surinamese house: they are known as *Hoge Neuten*, or 'High Stilts'. They are built on poles to protect from vermin and floods, although, as far as I know, our house was never flooded. They weren't houses for wealthy people, they were meant for families who weren't very well off.

There was a fixed staircase of thirteen steps to reach the entrance of our home. According to my family, I used to love running up and down those stairs, even though my mother kept warning me, 'If you carry on like that, your leg won't heal.' She must have repeated it a million times. It would have been easier – and more effective – for her to tie me up.

Since our family moved to Holland in October 1978, I've been back to Surinam three times. The first time was when I was eighteen years old. I went back once more with Carlos in 2003, then again a year later. The visit with Carlos was his first, after twenty-six years away. We visited the house where we grew up, taking pictures and shooting videos. The house, which still belongs to my mother, is rented out now. The fruit trees which I remembered from the old days were still there: cherries, mango and yambo (okra). We used to climb those trees every day to pick fresh fruit but also just to play. Next to our home was a big garden where we grew vegetables and kept chickens which provided us with eggs and meat. My mother would butcher the chickens while the eldest children would pluck and clean them. There weren't many wild animals around, but there were snakes and you really had to watch out for them. Fortunately, they weren't able to crawl into the house because of the poles elevating it above ground. At least in Surinam we had lots of space, especially if you were to compare it with what we had in Zaandam and Krommenie, the towns where we lived after we moved to Holland.

I didn't have that many friends in Surinam. Whenever I played it was mostly with Carlos and my sister, Marion, who is four years older than me. Despite the age difference, I always thought of Carlos as a friend, not an older brother. Even today, we treat each other the way friends do. It has always been like that, except when he was in his adolescent years. During that time he hung out more with friends his own age. The same goes for me during my own puberty. Looking back, there was a short period in our lives when we didn't see each other at all.

Not until we had both become adults did we start to do things together again. Four of us made the trip back to Surinam in 2003: me, Carlos, and our friends Ricardo Simons and Oswald Snip. Oswald has been my friend ever since I was seven. It was a very emotional occasion for me, but it was even harder for Carlos as memories of his entire youth came flooding back to him.

I have a good relationship with my whole family but a very special bond with my mother. I was always a 'mummy's boy'. My brothers and sisters often thought it was over the top and they were right. I couldn't do without her. When my mother wasn't home, I wouldn't sleep. I would wait until she had returned, and only then would I go to bed. According to Franklin, after we moved to Holland I used to drive the whole apartment building mad by crying until my mother came home. Nothing would stop me. My mother often had to work until late at night, so you can imagine how happy my family was when she got home. When she was around, everything was good as far as I was concerned. I am still a mummy's boy now. Today, when I'm walking down the street with her, for example when we go shopping, I clamp her hand very tightly.

I'm so lucky to have the mother I do. Within the Surinamese community things can sometimes get out of hand when children start to make their own money. It can be very nasty. I don't mean because of the children's behaviour but because of the parents'. Many Surinamese parents tell their children that they have to buy them things, but my mother never asked me for anything. If it was up to her, she would still be living in the same old apartment where we were raised. If I say to her, 'Come on, Mum, we're going to buy you some new clothes, because you look terrible!' she refuses. If I try to give her 100 Euros, she won't accept it. 'Keep it for yourself,' she says.

Even today she is very thrifty. When the country switched to the Euro, people were supposed to trade in their old Dutch guilders but my mother had hidden hers away so well that she couldn't find them at first. Fortunately, when they turned up, the bank still allowed her to exchange them, even though they had already been out of circulation for several years.

Nowadays I've taken over the financial care of my mother, and I make sure that everything is in order. A few years ago I bought her a penthouse. Now I also make sure that she has enough money to get by. I'm better off than my brothers and sisters, so I've told them, 'You don't have to give her any money', but as a matter of principle they would have done the same. In absolute terms they do a lot more for my mother, because, for a start, they live close to her. Football prevents me going back to Holland as often as I would like. My brothers and sisters are always there for her. They go shopping with her, and, perhaps most important, they often arrange visits to her with the grandchildren.

I am one of six children, two girls and four boys. Renate Carmenlita was born on 24 December 1960 followed by Franklin on 22 September 1963. They both carry the last name of our father, Frans Ware. This is because he went to register their birth himself, whereas he didn't do that for the rest of the family. So that's why the youngest four children carry the name of our mother. My second brother, Iwan Delano, was born on 18 March 1965 and he was the first Hasselbaink. Marion Gwendelin was born on 2 September 1967 while Carlos was born on 13 December 1968. Then there was me, the youngest child, named 'Jerrel' and born on 27 March 1972.

My mother comes from a family of eight children, four girls and four boys. She used to have a different surname. She was called Meyerhoven, after her mother, until she was forty. Her father only allowed her to carry the name Hasselbaink when she was forty, after he recognized her as his legitimate daughter. My mother was born on 7 March 1933 and was twenty-seven years old when she gave birth to Renate. In those days that was quite late. My father Frans had three sisters. I can't really say much about my father as I can hardly remember him. The others say he was a very strict man. He died in December 2004.

Most of my family immigrated to Holland in October 1978. Only Renate and Iwan couldn't join us. Renate was already working as a nurse at that time, while Iwan was still at school. My family didn't have enough money to pay for eight tickets. However, Renate's daughter Jennifer, who was one-year-old at the time, did come with us. I remember being served fish on the plane journey, but I didn't like it at all. I'll never forget that stench, it was really disgusting. It was also strange being in an aeroplane. Everything was so small, a little scary even, because I didn't know what was awaiting me. Holland, I was told, was really far away. But what did it look like? I had no idea. When we arrived at Amsterdam's Schiphol Airport it was very cold. One of the first things I said to Carlos was, 'Hey look, Carlos, I'm smoking! Look at this! There's all this smoke coming out of my mouth.' It wasn't until later that I realized it was due to the cold.

My mother says that I kicked her a lot in her tummy when she was pregnant with me. That's how she knew she was going to have a son again. She never guessed that she would bear a professional footballer, but she did know I would be a real boy. When my mum was pregnant with me she was selling home-made sandwiches during school recess at the Cornelisschool in Paramaribo. Franklin would take her sandwiches to the nearby Willibrordusschool, where they became equally popular. When the bell rang to signal lunch, almost all the kids would head her way in order to get one of those sandwiches. My mother was short of money so she had several jobs. She also worked as a cleaning lady and acted as a hostess for the PSV (The Progressive Surinam People's Party) which at that time was chaired by Emile Wijntuin. She worked hard to earn money for us. Even now, she is sometimes recognized on the streets of Zaandam by kids who used to buy her sandwiches. My mother doesn't recognize them because they've all grown up, but she still likes to be reminded of that time.

You could say my mother raised us on her own. My father never really looked after us, particularly us younger kids. I had no bond with him at all; my oldest brother and sister knew him better. I don't remember much about him – after all, I was only five years old when we moved to Holland. He hardly came over to visit us and never called either. The only things I received from him were birthday cards. I was really angry with him when I found out that he had been boasting about the fact that I was beginning to make it as a professional footballer. He told everyone who wanted to know that I was his son Jerrel. At that time he did want to regain contact with me, but I wasn't ready anyway. I just could not find it in my heart to approach him then. In hindsight that was perhaps stupid of me. I would have liked to hear him tell me that I have done well in my life until now. I never had that affirmation, and now I will never get it.

In 1996 I became a father myself. My daughter, Ghislaine, lives with her mother in Holland. However, I do make sure that she can phone me anytime she wants. I know what it's like to be a single-parent child; I missed my father at that same age. She is nine years old now, so I'm fine with her being able to reach me whenever she needs to. I want everything to be properly taken care of for her. I'm talking about normal, not extraordinary, things. Things any normal nine-year old would need, like proper clothes, books for school and the opportunities to play sport. I'm particularly keen to arrange those sorts of things for her. In my family, money for schoolbooks was usually only available at the very last moment. Fortunately, it's much easier for me to pay for those things now.

I wish I could speak more about my father, but there aren't too many positive things to say. When he died I barely shed a tear. I didn't know what to feel. It was quite strange. Those on the outside could not understand it. I could feel them thinking, 'You're so harsh, you're so cold-hearted', but really I didn't feel a thing. I remember coming home and telling my girlfriend that my father had passed away. She was more shocked than I was. I do find it a pity, though, because I would have liked to have had a good talk with him, between father and grown-up son, but it never happened. He should have taken the initiative, but he never did. I feel quite angry about that. On my last two visits to Surinam I purposely did not visit him. Only during my visit when I was eighteen did I go to see him. How he disappointed me then.

He asked me for money, even then. At our first meeting after thirteen years, he asked me, his own flesh and blood, his eighteen-year-old son, for money. He did this even though he knew I didn't have much. Those kinds of thing stay with you. He had always had a good job and had been receiving a pension from Holland since he was fifty-five. He was trained as a tailor, but because that didn't pay well he worked for a long time at the bauxite mines of Biliton. He also bought a small pick-up truck which he used to transport wood for Bruynzeel, so he was earning money on the side. I know that during the time we still lived in Paramaribo he regularly paid for our school items and clothing.

When he was growing up, he was a very good athlete. According to my mother he used to be really good at cricket. My mother never spoke a single bad word about him. When the subject of my father came up in our conversations, she didn't want to know about it. 'Leave me alone!' she would always say, and, 'You shouldn't say or do that. After all, he is your father.' While I thought he should have contacted us, she would always cover up for him. For several months after he died I remained upset that I would never be able to ask him anything. I would have liked to have spent some time with him and learned to appreciate him. After all, he did place me in this world.

I find it especially difficult when my daughter asks me what my father was like. I'm not able to tell her. I don't know what his favourite food was, his favourite colour, which women he liked. I never had a real man-to-man talk with him. I know absolutely nothing about the man. It should have come from him, really. I couldn't continue chasing after somebody who didn't really want me, could I?

My sisters went to his funeral. They asked Carlos and I whether we would go along, but to do so would have been hypocritical. How can you go to a funeral of somebody unknown to you, somebody you don't love and never knew? My mother, his second wife, didn't go either. Before her, he had another family, a wife and children. He had several children who were born prior to my eldest sister. When we moved to Holland, he stayed with them in Surinam. I met the children from his first marriage once when I was back in Surinam the first time. I think he was living with his first wife again at that time.

In total I received twenty-six cards from him, one for every birthday, but I didn't keep them, not a single one. The only tangible signs of my father were photographs of him scattered about the house. There were a few pictures taken by him on display in our living room. There was a picture of him when he came to Holland in 1991. That was the first time he visited us. If I remember correctly, Carlos and I were both playing with AZ Alkmaar at the time. He came to watch us play but really he came over just because he wanted to see Holland with his friend. He stayed in a hotel because my mother didn't want him to stay over at our house. It was strange because I really didn't recognize him. I could have passed him on the street and not given him a second glance. He dropped by our apartment building, called the Perim, in Zaandam. He didn't stay long, and hadn't brought anything with him. He stayed in Amsterdam and spent all his time with his friend. They preferred to go out and enjoy themselves rather than spend any time with us.

Apart from my immediate family, I only have one other relative living in Holland, my niece Hortense Hasselbaink. We were raised as brother and sister. When we arrived from Surinam, we didn't have anywhere to live, so we moved in with my Auntie Wilma who, unfortunately, passed away a few years ago. We went straight from Schiphol Airport to her home in the Perim apartment building, No 168. There were nine of us living there together, in a flat with four bedrooms. Grandma Nene, who was seventy-five, lived there too. Our family spent nearly two years in Auntie Wilma's home. It was a big apartment, but after the six of us arrived, it became, of course, very cramped. Carlos, Marion and myself slept on mattresses on the floor of a small room, which was only two metres long and one-and-a-half metres wide. My eldest brother Franklin slept in Grandma Nene's room, my mother slept with Auntie Wilma in her room, while Hortense was allowed to share her big room with her boyfriend and with Jennifer, Renate's little daughter.

At that time, my mother found work in the town of Krommenie, which is why we eventually moved there. We lived at No 64 Jean Henri Dunantstraat. She was able to rent the house for 1,000 guilders per month. This was a huge amount, but since my mother didn't have a steady job, it was difficult for her to get a mortgage, which of course would have been less of a financial burden.

Franklin once told me that after we arrived in Holland he became very angry at Mr Kraakman, the man in charge of housing for the Zaandam municipality. He had visited my aunt at home and saw that nine of us were living there which was more than was permitted. Instead of finding adequate housing for us he just kept complaining. He told us that we should move back to Surinam because those who had neither proper housing nor the proper permits should return to their home country. Queen Juliana, the ruling monarch of Holland, had, however, given permission to all Surinamese citizens to move to Holland as Dutch citizens, after Surinam gained its independence in November 1975. Since we'd never been abroad we didn't have official Dutch passports. As a result, we only received our Surinamese passports just before we left for Holland. Strictly speaking, therefore, Kraakman was right but Franklin considered it outrageous, and he was right, of course. My brother could get fuming mad during those moments. Some time later, when Mr Kraakman came by once again, my mother was able to tell him that we had found a suitable house outside Zaandam, in Krommenie, for 1,000 guilders per month. According to my brother, Kraakman almost fell over in surprise.

When I was seven and Carlos ten years old, my brother started playing football at the local club, GVO ('Gestaagt Volharding Overwint' – 'Steady Perseverance Shall Conquer'). The chairman of the club, Jan de Jong, allowed me to join, despite the fact that we didn't have any money to buy football boots or even the club kit of red shirts with a black stripe. GVO was founded as a Catholic football club, which is why we would often call it 'God Voetbalt Ook' ('God Plays Football Too'). My mother didn't want me to join, partly because my right leg had been re-set just two years earlier in Zaandam. Besides, she said, playing football at a club was simply too expensive. Fortunately for me, Jan de Jong lived in the same street as we did, only a few houses from us. He had learned of our limited finances and had watched me play football with his children Hugo and Arnoud on the grassy field behind our house in the evenings. That's probably why he gave me an old shirt belonging to one of his sons, as well as some old shorts, socks and football boots.

We regularly visited the de Jong family at their house. Everything was centred on football there. I usually had to play in goal during that time because of my leg. When I joined GVO I initially played as a goalkeeper for the same reason, although later I seemed to do better as an outfield player. We spent a lot of time with the de Jong family, not just playing football but also borrowing their garden tools, as we couldn't afford those in the early days. They also had a sled, which gave me the opportunity to go tobogganing for the very first time. Obviously, I had never seen snow in Surinam. It was great, though Carlos didn't like it as much as I did because he always felt cold. Carlos also didn't like to skate, unlike me.

Yet out of all us brothers and sisters, he and I became the most Dutch in our customs and habits. The elder ones spent more of their youth in Surinam which is why they are more affected by Surinamese influences. I know where I am from and where my roots lie, but in fact I regard myself as a Dutchman. At home I was raised in the Surinamese way. I know that, I'm proud of it, and I wouldn't have missed it for the world, but I also grew up within the Dutch culture and I've integrated very well. Of course, my other siblings are well integrated too, but you can tell that Surinam is a more dominant part of them. From a young age we had Dutch friends at school as well as after school. There's one incident I'll never forget. As a young boy I returned home with two guinea pigs somebody had given me. I was told to return them immediately. There was no way I was going to be allowed to keep them. Guinea pigs stink too much, I was told. It surprised me because many of my friends owned pets, but, in Surinam, animals always stay outside the house.

I was able to settle in reasonably quickly in Holland. It was an advantage that I was only five years old when we moved there. I quickly forgot many of the daily parts of life in Surinam. For my eldest brother, however, it was very difficult. He longed to go back to Surinam, and I think he still wants to now. I didn't know any better. Being black or white wasn't an issue for me either. I have always had white friends. I went to their homes to play and I loved it. Playing at other people's houses was really fun. Often their parents were better off than we were. These friends were also allowed to play at my house, of course, but there were simply more toys to play with in their homes. We didn't have so much, so most of the time I was playing elsewhere. My brother also missed the weather in Surinam. The temperature there was always above twenty degrees Centigrade with lots of sun and very different natural surroundings. In Holland, it froze in winter, something we had never seen in Paramaribo. It was a strange notion to us that ditches could freeze over, and to go skating on top of that was even stranger. But in the end I did learn myself. Several years later I was comfortable in all forms of skating: figure skates, racing skates, hockey skates, it didn't make a difference to me. I was the only dark kid on skates so I stood out, but to me it was simply a lot of fun. Whenever I had the chance I would be on the ice. Jan de

Jong also gave me skates, those old-fashioned racing skates that were nice and fast. That man was really kind, because whenever I wanted to go fishing, he would lend me a fishing rod too.

Back then you'd have to drag me away from GVO, I was always there. On Saturday I would play myself, and on Sundays I would always go and watch the first team. Sander van der Lubbe played in midfield in that team. His brother Huub, who later became the lead vocalist of the pop band De Dijk, also played in the first team. De Dijk are now one of Holland's most successful bands. Huub could have been a very good footballer, but he turned to music very early and his game quickly deteriorated. I believe Sander was in that first team for twenty years. Later on he became a postman in Krommenie. He had excellent technique and had the ability to strike the ball with power and accuracy. Although he was slow he was a very gifted footballer. After training, if he had a little bit of time, he would stay behind and play with me. I think I learned my technique, especially the striking of the ball, from him.

Sander often took the corner kicks and he would usually try to get the ball directly into the back of the net. He was often successful at it too. I started to try that too but without success. I kept on practising, though, often with him. I really looked up to him. I liked the pace and precision of his strikes at goal and I loved the way he would play with his socks down around his ankles. For some reason or other he must have liked me, because whenever the first team had an away match, he would always invite me to travel with him in his car. On the day of the match I'd go to his house early in the morning and we would leave together for the game. He was about ten years older than me, but we got on really well. He once told me that I would reach the absolute top and become a professional footballer. I didn't believe him then, but of course it turned out that he was right.

In those days my mother left the house very early to go to work. She had to work long and hard in order to pay for our expensive house. Not only did she leave early, most of the time she wouldn't come back until six or seven in the evening. As a result, my brothers and sisters had to take turns making dinner. I wouldn't say it was a nice and homely atmosphere as my brothers and sisters were very strict with me. My mother, on the other hand, was really sweet.

Living in Krommenie was difficult for the younger children, especially me. After all, we were still attending the Pax Christi school in Zaandam. Every day we had to take the bus from Krommenie to Zaandam, which took about forty-five minutes. Marion still teases me about those bus journeys. Apparently I was always snoring like an ox in that bus, so loudly that Marion and Carlos didn't want to sit next to me. Instead, they preferred to sit as far as possible towards the rear of the bus. They were embarrassed to death by their little brother. As my older brothers and sisters were at high school or working, my aunt was the usual babysitter. As Aunt Wilma's house was just next to our school, we had lunch there. When school finished for the day, we often didn't get back home until well past 5 pm.

When my mother was home, being the youngest I wouldn't have to help so much which was nice. But when she wasn't there the older ones made me work. I had to wash the dishes, wipe them dry, vacuum clean the house, and put the rubbish outside. Everyone had their own chores to do. You had to do them, there was no getting out of it. If I hid in the toilet or bedroom, they would come after me and drag me out. I would get beaten too when that happened. I was beaten many times by my oldest brother. In Surinam it's quite common for parents to beat their children, sometimes using a belt, sometimes with a wooden spoon or a stick or something else. I deserved it, I was such a brat. For the first two years after my arrival in Holland, Aunt Wilma had problems with my behaviour. I was more than she could handle. She even had a stick that she called Jerrel. Whenever I had been bad or mischievous, and my aunt thought it was necessary to punish me, she would ask somebody else sitting at the table to get the Jerrel for her. Everyone understood at that moment that she meant the stick for beating me. They didn't remain mere threats. I received some really hard blows from my aunt with that stick. Being flat and thick like a table-tennis bat it was impossible to break. When I was beaten I had to bend over. This didn't just happen once or twice. No, it was a regular occurrence. I was really terribly mischievous in my childhood days and never wanted to listen. My mother never hit me at that time, but that was compensated for to a large extent by my aunt and my siblings. Now I can say it was nothing but deserved.

I would never hit my daughter Ghislaine though. Unfortunately, I don't see her as often as I would like, but even if I did and she misbehaved, I would never beat her. All those blows never helped me in any way. Okay, for a few minutes they might have kept me quiet, but they didn't change my behaviour. When I was a child however, it was quite normal. It's how I was raised. My mother never hit me, but she knew the others did. She never said much about it either, perhaps because we were living with our aunt those first few years. As my mother worked such long hours, my aunt really found herself with the important task of raising me. It was not something she had been planning on, I knew that, but there was no other way. I was more scared of my aunt than of my mother. Later in life I developed a very good relationship with her and she started taking me to all kinds of places. To bingo, for example. She passed away during the 1996–97 season, while I was playing in Portugal.

After having lived in Krommenie for a while we moved back to Zaandam, once again to the Perim flats, but this time to No 122. We were on the fifth floor, Aunt Wilma was on the seventh, while my friend Oswald Snip lived on the ninth. I joined ZFC, the Zaansche Football Club, which was located in sportpark Hoornseveld on the Sportlaan. I was still a real whippersnapper at that time.

My brothers and sisters worried about me. To use an understatement, I was not really timid back then. I was discovering the world and nothing would stop me. So they worried about me, which I think brought us closer together. For example, we still celebrate our birthdays now, the way we celebrated them when we were young. Almost nothing has changed. Everyone tries to come and bring a present. We still enjoy looking each other up, although that's now a bit more difficult for me. We don't really call each other that often but we do have a close bond. Of course, we have our occasional arguments, but everyone gets along with each other. And we all live close together, apart from me. Franklin lives in the Bijlmer, in south-east Amsterdam, my eldest sister lives in Assendelft, while the rest live in Zaandam.

Growing up, I was never bullied or harassed. In fact, I was actually the one bothering others. Usually I was the one acting tough. I wasn't the leader, but I would be the one doing the bullying. Of course, I would often harass my siblings, but not for too long because within no time at all, I'd get hit and, remember, I was the youngest and the smallest. I fought a lot with Marion, and she was a real scratcher, especially to my face, where she would dig her nails into my cheeks. The fights were usually my fault, because I was really very annoying. Whenever I was in trouble I would run to my mother. Marion remembers an occasion when I was trying to act brave by taking on a much bigger kid, but ended up taking a beating. Carlos, who had started karate, also couldn't take him on, but Marion could. She started hitting him in a strange way, like a windmill, driving the boy mad so that he eventually ran away with the pain from Marion's nails all over his body.

My mother always defended me. She never hit me and she always stood up for me. Her eyes would speak for her. I was also able to get her to do things for me that she wasn't prepared to do for the other kids. I was truly spoiled by her. In the beginning, when there was hardly any money, she still got me beautiful new football boots. The older children never got anything like that. And later, I frequently got boots because I was playing so much football that I regularly needed a new pair. When I started getting those presents the elder ones already had their own jobs. They earned their own money, so my mother had more money left to spend on her younger children. I think that is the advantage of being the youngest child.

As a small boy I often went to sit with my older siblings, either in order to simply hang out with them, or to spy on them and wreak havoc. I never really did what they told me, unless I was about to get hit. Whenever I could, I would play pranks. At first when we lived on the seventh floor with Aunt Wilma I regularly had to take the rubbish down and throw it in the rubbish container. I could have taken the lift, but that was too much effort. So what did I do? I threw the bag over the stair rail of the fifth floor down to the ground. As it hit the ground the bag, of course, made an enormous thud. Fortunately nobody was around. I was smart enough to check for that first. Nevertheless, a few minutes later the building manager rang the doorbell. He had found the bag after doing his regular round through the building and had seen the name Hasselbaink on several address slips. I remember getting a big scolding for that.

Strangely enough, people would often jump from our building, taking the same route as the rubbish I had thrown down. For some reason it was a popular place to commit suicide – people came from all over the country to jump off our building. Once I was playing football behind our block and thought I saw a rubbish bag falling down. That was nothing extraordinary. As I knew from my own experience, those things happened but this time it turned out to be a person. I only found out when the police arrived and a crowd of bystanders gathered round.

By the time I was fourteen, Carlos and I had drifted apart. We didn't really do a lot of things together then, unlike now. Carlos would come home late and go straight to sleep. He hardly told me anything. I had no idea what he was up to. Much later, I found out – there was no room in our house for his girl-friends!

Marion was allowed to stay out late as well. Usually I was already asleep when she went to bed. She had her own life. I think she had her first boyfriend when she was eighteen or nineteen, and she is still with the same guy. She never told us anything about him. That's a Surinamese thing. Men usually tell each other a lot of things but they never ask their sisters. We respect our sisters and do not ask about such things. It's what we learned at home. Girls ought to be protected, so they are raised in a much more sheltered environment than boys. My mother was always much stricter on my sisters. They were hardly allowed to go out. They didn't like the rules my mother made, but they understand why now. They now have children too, and they realize they were raised in a good way. I'm also happy with my upbringing. I understand now what life is about, I know its rewards and its pitfalls. I've had good training.

My relationship with my elder siblings, Renate, Franklin and Iwan, is different. Now that I am much older myself I can talk easily with them, but when I was ten and they were twenty our lives were completely different. There was little we shared then, except for the roof over our head. Now we've become really close. We used to go on daytrips together to a big amusement park called the Efteling, to the dolphinarium or to the pier in Scheveningen and the beach. My aunt would always drive us in her old green Datsun Cherry. The car had a big eagle on the bonnet. Very cool. I'll never forget that I always stepped in dog crap. I wasn't used to dogs defecating on the streets. After a while it would start smelling really bad in the car. I never noticed it myself, but it would smell like crazy. 'Hey Jerrel, check your shoes!' someone would shout. And, of course, once again I would have to get out of the car to clean the dog crap from my shoes. That happened several times. Nowadays, I always look down when I walk. It won't happen to me again anytime soon.

I was raised in a religious environment. We were part of the Evangelical Brother Community. When we lived in Holland I always had to go to church and to Sunday school. I didn't like it one bit. I think Grandma Nene made us go. She was a true believer and felt that the Church was part of a good upbringing. Whenever I am in Holland for Easter, I will go to church with my mother, because she likes that very much. I make her happy that way.

I was baptized in Alkmaar, together with my daughter, when I was twenty-three years old. When Ghislaine was born we wanted to baptize her, and because I hadn't been baptized I thought I'd better do it too. My ex-girlfriend Jane Fer is from Alkmaar. My daughter carries my name, although we were never married. Jane and I were eighteen when we first met. We were in love and all went well. You know how things go at that age. She lived with her mother, and I lived with my mother. We were already sleeping together. I was a boy, so it was all right for me. But, for my sisters it wasn't. And maybe it wasn't for Jane either.

Surinam has a multi-cultural society. You can tell by the players in the Dutch national team. For example, Aron Winter has an Indian background, but there are also many Javanese,

Creolese, Chinese, Indians, Dutch, and Indonesians, basically anything and everything. We are true Creoles. My grandfather and grandmother on my father's side first lived in Nickeri and their ancestors came from British Guyana. Although I've been back three times, I've never been to Nickeri. It's quite far from Paramaribo, much further west. My mother's family is from Coronie.

Two years ago we saw a lot of Surinam when we hired a helicopter and flew towards the Amazon. It was truly spectacular. I was there with Carlos, Ricardo Simons, Otto Gilds and another friend, Oswald Snip, as well as the pilot. We saw beautiful waterfalls and swam in them. We walked through part of the Amazon forest which was amazing. Fortunately we didn't encounter any dangerous animals as I'm quite scared when it comes to them. We could have spent the night in the forest, but that's not for me. I'm not too fond of spiders, snakes and such creatures. I would never go on holiday with a backpack and a pair of good walking boots. I prefer luxury holidays.

I have never had any desire to go camping. I once went with my high-school sweetheart, Leonie van Vooren. Leonie and I had our own little tent, and her parents had another one. We went camping in Zeeland, on the southwest coast of Holland. In the evening we went out to the nearest village. It wasn't much of a success because she was harassed about the fact that she was white and I was dark. I wasn't sure what to do but I decided we should leave. Deep inside, though, I had the urge to do something else. Afterwards, we had a long talk about this at her parents' house. Both her parents worked and Leonie even owned a horse. Sometimes I would join her when she went horse riding, and it was quite something. Horse riding, to me at least, is still a form of luxury. I myself didn't have a very good background. My mother worked and I was always in trouble. I only cared about football and often skipped class. Leonie, on the other hand, went to HAVO (a higher level of school than mine).

In the end, she broke up with me. Later I heard that it was because her father didn't think I was suitable for her. I believe her father had told her that our relationship could never succeed, so it was better if she broke up with me. Two years later, when I became a professional footballer with AZ, she wanted me back again. But for me it was over and out.

Later, when I was playing in Portugal, she tried to contact me, but I didn't respond. I hadn't forgotten. It's not like I knew immediately why she had broken up with me. I found out later. Initially we kept in contact, and we would occasionally even do things in secret. But when I found out the reason for our split I knew enough. I also started dating a girl called Dewie then. She was a very fun girl who also got along very well with my sister Marion.

So that was the first and last time I visited a campsite. It's the lack of luxury and privacy that I find hard to bear. My brothers and sisters would sometimes rent a bungalow on a campsite and take their whole family. Perhaps I would be able to do something like that for my daughter Ghislaine as well if she wanted to, though not in Surinam. That's a bit too dangerous for my taste.

Ghislaine loves camping. She experienced it last year when she went with my brother and sister, and she still talks about it.

She could play with her cousins, go swimming and do a lot of fun things. Ghislaine often plays with the children of my brother. Whenever she comes to England, she usually comes with my brother and his family. Unfortunately, I can't see her every day. Sometimes I spoil her a bit more than I would if I saw her on a daily basis. It's important to me that she has everything she needs, things I didn't have at her age. I did some bad things because my mother couldn't supply me with everything, even though she worked very hard. I did stuff that could not be tolerated and I don't want that for my daughter. Now that I have everything I need, I must be careful not to spoil her too much.

When she received very good marks on her school report, I let her know that I was proud of her and told her that I would buy her a present, since she had done her best and deserved a reward. I said this because I wanted to stimulate her to do her best again, not because I want to give her presents.

I want her to have it much easier than I did but she's not getting expensive designer-brand clothes from me. She gets good clothing but not Nikes. Even if she does, she's not getting the expensive £150 ones. Why would she be wearing expensive brands like Gucci and Dolce & Gabbana? I don't see the point, especially not for kids her age. But she knows how to play it, though, she is really smart.

For Christmas she's allowed to make a wish list which she reads to me over the phone. I usually tell her, 'You're asking Santa for a lot of stuff and I think he won't be able to bring all that with him.' So I ask her what she wants most, which is what I buy for her. For her birthday, the ritual is the same. I do regret not always being able to attend those important days. I'm hardly ever there to celebrate it with her. I'm in England while she's in Holland. My brother Carlos usually buys the present, and then takes it to her or sends it on. She knows it's from me so when she gets it she calls me up immediately. She'll unwrap it while she's talking to me, and then she thanks me. It hurts not being able to be there myself, but when I'm finished with football I'll definitely be there more often.

Being away from my daughter is hard. Ghislaine is beginning to understand that I am a professional footballer, but it's something I don't want to discuss with her. I don't want that to be important to her. I want to be important as a father, and not as Jerrel Hasselbaink, the footballer. Of course, I want other kids to like her and play with her, but not because she is the daughter of Hasselbaink. On the other hand, it is fun that with my name I can do a few special things for her. For example, she loves Destiny's Child, so I once took her to see them in concert in Rotterdam. I was able to arrange for us to go backstage and take pictures with the group. That was fun for her and something she'll never forget. She often talks about it, but, of course, such things should not become a habit.

I really can't compare her to me. Her character is completely different. For one, she is much calmer than me. She can play alone, and really keep herself busy. I always needed people around me when I was a child. The only thing I could do by myself was play with the ball outside the flat. People tell me that she looks like me, but I can't see it myself.

2 Mummy's Boy

I was quite a clever little guy, but at the same time I was too lazy to study or do my homework. In grade school I did fine. I was good at maths, but not at reading and writing, partly because I didn't like Dutch that much. It was difficult for me. Mum had wanted me to enter the Higher General Secondary Education (HAVO), for my secondary education. In Holland, you take a test at the end of your final year of grade school and, based on the results, you qualify for a certain level of secondary education. I did quite well in the exam and could have gone on to HAVO, but, upon the school's advice, I entered the MAVO (Middle General Secondary Education) which is one step lower in the Dutch secondary school system.

I didn't care so much myself. School didn't interest me anyway. I just wanted to play football, nothing less, nothing more. My mum, on the other hand, didn't want me to play at all. I had joined the grade school team and competed in the school championships of the Zaan region, which is north of Amsterdam. We won the tournament. Later, when I was playing for the Pax Christi grade school team, we became champions of the whole province of North Holland. We came close to becoming the national champions, but unfortunately things didn't work out and we ended up in sixth place. There were good players in that team, although I was the only one to make it as a professional. It's funny, I don't have any tangible mementoes of that period of my life. We had a trophy that we could keep at home for a week at a time, but I didn't keep any ribbons or things like that. I'm really bad at collecting such things because I don't attribute much value to them. Back then I played as a right winger. It would be another ten years, until I started playing with Neerlandia, before I took on the position of centre-forward.

I never repeated a year in grade school, so I was twelve years old when I went to the MAVO. In secondary school, I was held back twice, and in the end I was expelled because of fighting and other incidents. I was a real pain in the ass. I was kicked out of my first secondary school, the Cardinal de Jong MAVO, because of a fight with my best friend at the time, Brian. The argument started over something ridiculously insignificant during lunch break while we were having a game of table tennis. I don't remember what the exact cause of the argument was, but I do remember where the fight occurred. It was right in the middle of the school cafeteria!

In retrospect it was very strange because, after all, he was my best friend. We hung out together every day. I went over to his house, and he came to mine. But as our argument heated up we reached a point where we started punching each other. It didn't take long to figure out that I was stronger than him. I really beat him up. There's no two ways about it, I definitely crossed the line there. I had managed to lift him up and found myself smashing him against the wall, as hard and as often as I could, until he bled. I was expelled from school immediately, while Brian got to stay. I have never seen or spoken to him since.

Well, what can I say? I was a child and had no sense of responsibility. I was always playing pranks and making mischief. I often arrived late, didn't listen to my teachers, copied homework and exams from other kids, gave the teachers my big mouth and was involved in fights every now and then. Usually my punishment consisted of having to clean up the school yard or something similar. But not this time. This time I had definitely gone too far.

You wouldn't have seen me bawling in shame after my expulsion. Crying is not my style. But I was sorry. And then I realized I was a big jerk. Brian also came from Surinam, just like me, so our fight had nothing to do with discrimination or racism. It was the middle of the school term and I needed another school quickly. My mum enlisted me at the MAVO Zuid. The school director, Mr Morris, was also Surinamese and taught religion. He gave me another chance at his Christian school. In hindsight it was more fun than study for me. A couple of years ago I was invited to a school reunion there. Unfortunately, I wasn't able to go, otherwise I would certainly have attended. There was no fooling around with Mr Morris. All the Surinamese boys at that school got a little more personal attention from him, which was a very good thing for me.

He was very strict with us, and like many others I was really scared of the guy. He would always say something like, 'If you study hard this time, you will be all right, Jerrel.' Thinking about him now, that man was pure gold. He should get a medal. I would not go as far as to say that he was my salvation because I still pulled pranks when he wasn't looking. Despite his words of encouragement, I hardly studied and rarely completed my homework. Why should I? I had others do it for me. Either that or I copied from them. I was too lazy, and anyway, I was always on the street playing football. When we had exams, I would sit close to one of the bright girls in our class and try to copy from her. Whenever I studied, I did so at the very last moment. For the rest I mainly tried to achieve higher grades by copying from others. Unfortunately, I didn't have much luck in that. Every single teacher kept a close eye on me, which is why I had to repeat several years. During the third year, when I was seventeen, I left school. I next tried my luck at the LEAO, the Lower Economic and Administrative Education. Not much later I started playing for Telstar, and left school for good without my diploma. I regret that now but I didn't then, because in my stupidity I was convinced I didn't need any diplomas in order to play football. Talent and willpower were the necessary ingredients for that. It took a while for me to change my views. Only when I was in my twenties did I start to see things differently. Before then it was just football and street gang mischief that interested me. I even spent some time in prison and a youth penal correction facilities. It was a stroke of good fortune when I met my present manager Humphry Nijman. He became the father I never really had.

I always cared a lot about football, never much about anything else, not even music. Having said that, I do remember that the first record I bought was by Womack and Womack. I really liked music, but I was only ever really involved in it when we lived with Aunt Wilma. She had a huge record collection as well as a record player. But all I ever really wanted was to be outside playing football, or practising against the wall. You could always count on finding me behind the apartment block with a football, either alone or with other kids from the neighbourhood.

At home we didn't have the luxury of two or three televisions in the house until after everybody started working. Then we could afford a TV for my mother's bedroom and one for our own room. I watched many movies there, because I love movies. In our household it was customary that the eldest siblings could decide what we watched. Sometimes it would be *Top of the Pops*, other days *Countdown*, a music programme hosted by Erik de Zwart. On Sunday night we always watched *Studio Sport*, since it was Carlos and Franklin's favourite programme.

We only had a few posters decorating our bedrooms. I remember several posters of German Bundesliga clubs hanging in our room, such as Bayern Munich and SV Hamburg. There was also one poster of Ajax there. I was a real fan back then. Their team had the likes of Gerald Vanenburg, Wim Kieft, John van't Schip, Jesper Olsen, Marco van Basten, Frank Rijkaard, and Ronald Koeman. Johan Cruyff was the coach. They were fabulous.

When we moved to the Perim flat for the first time, space was limited so we had to share rooms. Marion, Carlos and I slept in the same relatively big room. Our room had a bunk bed, with Carlos sleeping on top while I slept below. For three people sharing however, the room was small. For example, there was not enough space for a desk. There were three closets standing in the middle of the room, and they effectively divided the room in half. The closet in the middle was turned the other way. It belonged to Marion who slept on the other side. The one next to the wall belonged to Carlos, while the closet forming part of the opening leading to Marion's bed belonged to me. Marion needed her privacy since she was already sixteen. I'm sure she didn't like it one bit having to share a room with her little brothers, but that was the way it was. It couldn't be helped. We weren't complaining, because we knew we had to make do with what we had. Back in Surinam we hadn't had much at all, in Holland we had a little bit more. That's why we were very happy regardless of our cramped circumstances, especially as we had each other. Of course, we had our confrontations, but deep down we all loved each other as we still do. I got my own room when the others left the house. By then we could afford to have a separate TV in my bedroom. You can imagine what I watched on TV and what else happened in that room afterwards!

Our home was often visited by relatives, more so than by friends. On such occasions there was always enough to eat. Birthdays were the best in that respect and involved us mostly sitting in the living room eating delicious Surinamese food with filled plates resting on our laps. That's the Surinam way. I remember the very first time I received new football boots for my birthday. I had turned eight or nine, and was given these beautiful Adidas boots with green stripes on the side. I was so happy, I'll never forget it. They were my very first football boots. The best thing about them was the replaceable studs on the bottom. At the back they were long, while the ones in front were shorter. Of course, these shoes were my very own treasure, and I often wore them inside the house as well, until my mother found out. She would make me take them off immediately because they destroyed the carpet. I would obey her most of the time, but very often she would have to warn me several times.

Birthdays in our house were fun but sober. We couldn't afford much so we spent as little as possible on decorations. At school I was allowed to go around the class and give all the kids a treat, as is customary. Usually I would hand out 'drop', the Dutch black liquorice and marshmallows. The adults often gave me money – usually about five guilders – which I would use to buy myself a present. Saving was a word absent from my vocabulary. Like any other kid, I also received toy cars and trains, but the birthday when I received my football boots is the one I remember best. I am still very grateful to my mother for that. I had – and still have – such a special relationship with her. Until I was eleven I wouldn't sleep until she returned home from work. I often sneaked into her bed or put my mattress in her room. I don't know why I always waited until she returned. Perhaps I was scared. Of course, as soon as she got home every-thing would be all right in my mind and I would fall asleep exhausted. My siblings naturally teased me about it, calling me 'Baby, baby'. They constantly made fun of me, especially when I was crying till late at night. I would get angry about it, but there was not much I could do. I was still a lot smaller than everyone else. I didn't catch up with them until much later, by which time I had stopped crying anyway.

I certainly could have obtained my MAVO or HAVO diploma, if only I had tried a bit harder. Had I done my homework, I'm sure I could have completed school successfully. But back then

I refused even to try. All I wanted was to play football and get into mischief. Only at the very last moment, when it was already too late, did I reserve time for studying. In retrospect, I often regret my behaviour and wish I had taken my studies more seriously. If I had finished high school, it would have made a world of difference. In the end, it all worked out for me, but I realize now that schooling is much more important than football. How many kids don't make it the way I did? I don't want youngsters to read this book and think 'I'm going to be just like Jimmy and become a football player.' I was lucky, really lucky. I don't know what would have become of me otherwise.

On the other hand, I think my street background actually helped me as a footballer. I think of it as an alternative – but in some ways much tougher – form of education. I have many friends who still live in the same Zaandam neighbourhood who I still bump into whenever I visit my mum. There is one big difference between them and me. They are on drugs. They sniff coke or smoke hash, they don't work and live on welfare. Whenever I see them, I can only thank God for protecting me and taking care of me, for having gone through all that trouble of keeping me on the straight path. My mother always repeated over and over to me, 'Your school, your school, do your best at school.' She didn't want me to play football for two reasons, my leg and my schooling. She thought my leg wouldn't be able to take the stress, but my right leg is actually stronger than my left leg. It's not that my leg became stronger because of the operation. I am by nature right-footed and I think because of all that shooting practice against the walls behind our flat my right leg is just more trained than my left leg.

Part of the reason I made it this far is that I am strong-willed, although 'stubborn' is probably a more apt description. It's a little less these days, but even now when I decide for myself that 'I'm going to do this', then I have to be the one to do it, and there's no chance I'll leave it to anybody else. I want to be the one who takes on the responsibility for my life, my actions and my decisions. I can't stop being like that. If I have to do something then I must do it and I will do it. Even when building my new house, I have to be the one who decides what has to be done. I'm not leaving that to anybody else, not even the building contractor or architect. Of course, I let him advise me, but the final decisions are all mine.

I think it is my street background that makes me act this way. I always had to prove myself there. Within any group of small boys I always had to be the strongest one. In order to remain on top at all times, I couldn't let my guard down. I took that with me later in life. It's a matter of not wanting to fail, not being able to fail and not letting circumstances get the better of you. It's about respect. You won't survive on the streets otherwise. You'll be rejected.

At the MAVO we had music lessons, but I couldn't have cared less about them. I liked Physical Education much better. I excelled at all ball sports and running. I loved it. If I had completed the MAVO I would probably have gone on to the CIOS, the Central Institute for Physical Education Teachers. Who knows, maybe I could have become a PE teacher. Not that I cared much for it then, but if I had done better at school there is a big chance I would have ended up doing something similar. I was especially good at baseball, and could hit the ball quite hard. Gymnastics, on the other hand, was one activity I couldn't care less about and still don't. It's for girls, and I was too much of a macho man to be interested in something like that.

After we moved from Krommenie to Zaandam I started playing at ZFC, the Zaansche Football Club. When I joined I was initially placed in the D2 team, but after several games in D2, I was quickly moved up the ranks to the first D team. It was quite an accomplishment since there were seven D teams in total. ZFC was a famous club, with many youth teams. It was the best club around Zaandam and the Saturday games were played at the highest amateur levels. The stands were always filled with supporters for first-team home matches.

My family never took me to the games. I walked every time, since it was easy to get there via the many short cuts I knew. It was my first club in Zaandam. I don't remember many players' names, since I wasn't there for very long. My brother Carlos and my friend Oswald Snip were playing at Zaanlandia, which was reason enough for me to change clubs. My brother also initially played at ZFC but then switched to Zaanlandia, I think because his friends were playing there. Oswald first played at RCZ, the Racing Club Zaandam. One year later he joined Zaanlandia.

At first I was together with Oswald in the C1 team, but because he was bigger than me he joined B1. We only really played together in our first year there. Afterwards he joined the older youth side while I stayed with C1 for one more year. My growing spurt only started when I was sixteen, and now I am 1.80 metres tall. We didn't become champions with C1. We were a good mid-table team, nothing more. During our time at

Zaanlandia both Oswald and I were selected to try out for the North Holland team. Oswald even made it into the North Holland squad. Although Oswald was selected, he had to go back to Zaanlandia because his mother couldn't afford to pay for the extra travelling expenses and training camps. There were also scouts from the bigger professional clubs, such as Ajax and Telstar. There was one player there, Mark Snijders, who went on to play for AZ Alkmaar and for Port Vale. I met him some-time later. He is not attached to any club now. He was playing in central defence at that time.

I remember going to a youth training camp in Germany towards the end of the season. Oswald and I spent a lot of time there with Edwin Huissteden, a very macho guy who was a year older than us. In Germany it was one huge battle. We really fought like madmen on the field. It started out just being feisty but quickly turned into a war zone. Edwin got himself into trouble with one of the guys from the opposing team. Within a few minutes he was fouled hard, which prompted our whole team to dive in. Knowing Edwin, I suspect he provoked it.

He also went ballistic in Marken when someone insulted his mother. Edwin and his mother were very close. His father had left them when he was very young, so he only had his mother left, and he absolutely adored her. One of the Marken guys said something about Edwin's mother being a whore. Of course, that was going too far, and Edwin exploded. He was quite good at delivering punches, and Oswald and I gladly assisted him. Fifteen years later Oswald and my brother Carlos both joined Marken. I don't think the people there remembered that inci-dent nor who exactly was involved. Still, it's a good thing that

they both left Marken after one season. Now they're both playing at Voorland.

We had a very good team, especially up front. We laughed
and had a lot of fun together, even with coach Peter Buter.
Training was twice a week, rain or shine. Skipping training was
out of the question, but I was usually late – because I'm from
Surinam. I'm not joking and it's not an excuse, it's the plain truth.
No matter if I have an important appointment at a certain time,
we Surinamese just don't know any better. I'm not lying about
that, it's just the way we are. Seriously!

I often arrived late when I played for Telstar, which was partly
why I was kicked out. The final straw came at a match in Haarlem, but it had been on the cards for some time that my stay
there was coming to an end. There was always something wrong
with me. One day I wouldn't go to training, the next day I didn't
show up because of diarrhoea. I always had some excuse. My
reasoning was that since I had a contract I must be good enough
to have earned it, but the reality was different, of course. I
thought, 'I am the man. I play professional football for Telstar,'
but it turned out that I wasn't indispensable. I was paid perhaps
1,000 guilders per month which was quite some amount at
the time. I used that money to buy a car, even though I was
only seventeen and didn't have a licence. I didn't care and drove
around anyway. Together with some guy called Reinoud van
Arnhem I bought that car from a fellow Telstar player, Radjin
de Haan.

Radjin lived in Harlem and sold us his car for 300 guilders.
It wasn't much, but it was my very first car, a red Audi 80.
There was only one problem with it, namely that the petrol

gauge was broken, so we never knew exactly when we had to fill it up. After every 100 kilometres we put twenty-five guilders worth of fuel in it, so that we could be sure of reaching our destination. I bought that car without any driving experience. But we drove – and how – and Reinoud was scared shitless. He was a little older than me, but didn't have a licence either. Tired of going by train and then by bus, we drove every day from Zaandam to Velsen. Nobody knew that we weren't legal drivers. Moreover, the car was not insured and we didn't pay car tax. The Audi was also not registered in my name, but in Reinoud's. Despite these irregularities we still drove to training every day. Then one time something happened. I had gone out with a girl and after already driving a lot that evening, I decided to drop her off at her house. I wanted to stop by our house first, but just when I reached the front of our block, the car broke down. Right on the corner there was a coffee shop, notorious for their sale of hashish and weed. The car had broken down exactly in front of that shop, and I was clueless as to what was the problem. It couldn't be the petrol because there was still enough to last a while. I found out later that it was the oil that needed replacing. Back then I didn't know that you had to fill up your car with oil too. The Audi was smoking like a chimney, right in front of that coffee shop. In Holland 'where there is smoke, there is hash', right? So you can imagine how I felt.

The car was in such a bad state that the only thing to do was to throw it out and buy a new one. I was getting very good at driving, so I bought another one for 600 guilders, a blue Honda Accord. No matter where we had to go, I drove there; Rotterdam, Amsterdam, Utrecht or The Hague. Whenever I was stopped by the police, I would just give them the name of my buddy, and tell them that I had left my driving licence at home. They made me answer a few questions, and then allowed me to drive on. That happened several times. When I turned eighteen, I immediately went for the driving test.

The theoretical exam I passed first time, because I had studied for it. I subsequently took about eighteen driving lessons in order to learn how to drive carefully and accurately. Again I passed at my first attempt. In hindsight, the illegal driving probably saved me a lot of lessons. After I got my licence, I transferred the Honda Accord to my name. Officially, that was my first car. Once, I dropped Oswald off at home. He was driving, but when he tried reversing to park, he smashed the car really hard into a parked car. I was sitting next to him in the front seat, and several people near the flat had seen and heard the crash. Fortunately it was already dark. I was frantically trying to remain as calm as possible because if the cops arrived we would be dead meat. I asked the guy near the flat if he knew who owned the car we bumped into, so that we could compensate him for the damage. The witness hurried off to fetch the owner, but when he was just out of sight we quickly drove off again. We parked the car two streets away, walked back to our flat, changed our clothes and went out to into town. We never heard anything about it ever again. It wasn't a very nice thing to do, but it was our only choice. The risk of getting the cops involved was too great. It happened more than fifteen years ago so I'm sure the statute of limitations has expired and I can tell this story today ... at least, I hope so.

I played football for about six years with Zaanlandia. I

played with more or less the same players on my team the whole time, Oswald being one of them. However, Oswald stopped playing for some time when he was fifteen because of an argument with the club. Zaanlandia played one level higher against clubs like Hollandia from Hoorn and Alkmaar. I played central midfield or right wing, while when I played at DWS (in the national youth division) I played on the left wing where I had Oswald right behind me. We regularly switched position. The reason I started playing on the left at DWS was because the trainer decided to put me there, I don't know the exact reason. I was quite comfortable in that position though, because we played 4–3–3 so I had quite a lot of space.

At one point Oswald and I joined a summer football team that played in small tournaments all over the country. In order to join you had to pay 200 guilders (about £60) up front. We would drive all the way to Rotterdam in a minivan or in two cars and participate in the tournament. I was only sixteen and the baby of the team. The prizes consisted of trophies or money, so you had the chance to win back the joining fee. We were very good and won most of our matches. Sometimes during games we would just knock the ball to each other and let our opponents chase after it. Occasionally our arrogance would do us no good and we would end up really struggling to win the game. Epi Lopez, who lived on the fourth floor of the Perim block, played for the team, along with Ciriac Gomez and Gil Rodriguez. Oswald's brother Eppie was the goalkeeper. After matches we would meet up and go to various discos in the neighbourhood.

At Zaanlandia Peter Buter became a sort of father-figure to

me. His son Roger would also always accompany us, but he didn't play in the team himself. He wasn't a very good player. Buter's young daughter was there too, and even his wife would spend time at the club. His whole family practically lived on the field. We all got on well together. He was the one who would correct us whenever we made mistakes, and when we were just fooling around. It was a lot of fun, all of us together. Back then Peter Buter was a very important man to me even though we only saw him on the field or during football camps where he would act as a counsellor of sorts.

When we arrived in Holland we didn't have much money. After some time the situation improved, especially after the older children started to work so my mother had more money to spend. After about five years I received all the kit I needed. At Zaanlandia I only had to pay for the boots myself as even the training outfits were taken care of by the sponsor. I was the top scorer in the youth team, but I didn't get any trophy or ribbon for that feat. I probably do still have some ribbons for our team results, but I wouldn't know where they are. My mother still has some mementoes.

While I was playing at DWS I met Chris Pragt. He was our team supervisor and sponsor. Advertisements for his flower business adorned our jerseys when we played. He loved hanging out with us. He had previously worked with Ruud Gullit and Frank Rijkaard at the club, but by that time Gullit had left for Haarlem while Rijkaard had gone to Ajax.

I didn't have a professional contract with Telstar, nor did I play very often there. In the end I only played four matches in the first team. I started in the winter of 1990 and left a year later. Even though I had no contract, I received about 300 guilders per week (about £100), to cover expenses. My first 'unpaid' professional game was on 27 October 1990. We played out at VVV in Venlo, where I think we lost 2–0. I was seventeen years old at the time.

Niels Overweg was the trainer there and in the end he kicked me out because I was always late. When I arrived late on the day of a match, I had tested his patience too much. He told me that I was no use to him, so I could leave immediately. I never spoke to him again. Back then I disagreed with him, but now I see he was right. My lateness was to do with my lifestyle. On the one hand I wanted to devote myself to football, but then again I also wanted to hang out on the street with my friends. I wavered between life as a footballer and life on the streets. The guys I hung out with just couldn't understand that I actually mostly wanted to play football, much less that in the end I considered football more important than them. They weren't really stimulating me to focus on my football. Thank God I learned just in time what my priorities were, and everything turned out fine.

After leaving Telstar, I was able to get myself fixed up at AZ within a month. Assistant coach Jan Fransz let me train with them, and I did enough to be offered a contract for reimbursement of expenses as well as travel costs. After the summer break I was allowed to prepare for the season with the first team. I played in the opening game of the season, and scored a goal. Three games later I found myself with my first real professional contract: 1,000 guilders per month for two seasons, excluding expenses.

The coach at that time was Henk Wullems. In my opinion,

the man had no idea about football, which was demonstrated by the fact that he didn't go on to coach a big team in Holland. Initially I played well and often. Then after some time Wullems switched to other players who were no better than me. Jan Fransz noticed it too, and he spoke up for me at the board meeting when they were discus-sing renewing my contract. Unfortunately, Wullems didn't see any point in renewal, and the board preferred to give somebody else a chance.

In those days Carlos also played for AZ, in the same team as me. I never had any problems with the other players. Sure, I was strong-willed, but I didn't act as if I was the star of the show. I had more problems with Henk Wullems because he was unable to explain things to me, or convince me of his views. He just couldn't teach me anything. Even though I've now made it, I'm sure he will never admit that he made a mistake by letting me go.

Jan Fransz had faith in me though. I was playing as a right-sided forward at the time. I played a very technical game then, although I don't think many people will believe that now. I was very good in man-to-man situations. Perhaps my biggest problem was that I knew all too clearly what I was doing. I wanted to play football and show off all my tricks. I wouldn't be surprised if the older players thought I wasn't paying them enough respect, since I was often the first to demand to take a free-kick. It was just my conviction that it was for the good of the whole team. My brother once told me I should be a bit more modest, especially since I was still young.

From the reactions of the other players, however, I don't think I was very successful in that respect. I became much more patient later. In Portugal I got fewer chances because in the Portuguese competition the emphasis lies on defence, on trying to avoid conceding a goal. This taught me when to choose the right moment to make my move. In Mediterranean countries the forward just has to score. It doesn't matter if the game as a whole was crap. If you were the forward and you scored, you did a good job. A forward is judged on his goals. So when that one chance was there I just had to score.

Scoring is largely a matter of focus. I keep calm by telling myself things like, 'Stay calm', 'It's coming', 'That chance will certainly come', 'Remain concentrated', 'Keep on waiting', etc. Concentration is the most important factor. As fatigue makes it harder to concentrate, I try to recognize when I'm tired, so that I can take some time to load myself up again. I do this by playing in a very simple manner whenever I get the ball. After a few minutes I have replenished my energy levels so that I am ready to make that one decisive move again. I play short for a little while and score when the moment is there. Choosing the moment is what I learned in Spain and Portugal.

I can keep running like an idiot but when my concentration leaves me, my shooting will never be powerful or accurate. Of course, a lot of it is experience, but mostly it's a matter of instinct. I have to play instinctively and understand the situations, knowing at which moment I can expect the ball and where.

My sisters never played football competitively although my eldest sister Renate was always a sporty type. She would jog about six kilometres every day. She often participated in the sixteen-kilometre-long Dam to Dam race, a running event from

Zaandam to the Dam Square in the centre of Amsterdam. She works as a nurse now. Marion, who works at McDonald's, is not a very sporty person. She must have thought Carlos and I were too fanatical about sports and that was enough for her. Franklin, who works in the security business, is a fanatical Ajax supporter. He will travel all over Europe to attend their games. He can't play football, and he never played at a club. Neither did my second brother Iwan. He is not sporty at all. He preferred to go out and do fun things with his friends.

When I was about eleven I played as the right-sided striker. I was more interested in juggling the ball and in showing off all kinds of tricks. Nowadays, I am much more effective and goal oriented. Back then I tried to imitate all the tricks I had seen performed on TV. I tried to imitate Gerald Vanenburg's football exercises, though there were some I simply could not do. Vanenburg had some very good technical tricks up his sleeve. I wouldn't call him my role model, but I did look up to the man. We had a video of him at home and I watched it endlessly.

I would go outside and pretend to be Gerald Vanenburg while the other kids would call themselves Marco van Basten, since Ajax players were our favourites. There was even a time when people called me Gerald instead of Jerrel. I was fine with that because Gerald was a good footballer. Unfortunately, Ajax's ground was not really near us otherwise I would have watched their training sessions. I did watch them once, when they played in Koog aan de Zaan, which was a little bit nearer. I was about thirteen years old at the time.

Ajax was absolutely my favourite club, but I never dwelled on it much. I understood, though, why Ajax never scouted me for their youth team. Until I was sixteen I was very small, so I was not the typical Ajax player; they were physically and technically perfect. However, I was very quick, especially in those days. Until I was twenty-seven I was always fast. These days I am more of a power runner. I can easily spurt off, it's in my genes. I'm quick over short distances, but I hate long-distance running. My legs are more accustomed to sprints.

I have always been able to strike the ball very hard. I took the free-kicks because I could hit the ball hard enough to score. It was my speciality. The fact I am right-footed doesn't mean that I can't strike the ball well with my left. I'm pretty powerful with my left foot as well. Thanks to all that practice when I was young, my left leg is very well developed. I also scored regularly from my left at DWS, where I came fourth in the national best youth player competition, ahead of Edgar Davids who was number five. One left-footed goal stands out. Everyone from DWS who was there and witnessed that shot still talks about that once-in-a-lifetime goal of mine against Volendam A1. The ball shot like a rocket from my own half right into the goal.

Some others tell me it was like a miracle. And yet I had shot with my under-trained left leg. I managed to strike the ball so well that it hit the top corner behind the Volendam goalie fifty-five metres away with a great curve. The ball sped past him. Of course there were defenders in front of him, but they weren't important. I first dribbled around a few opponents in the middle of the park and then shot on goal. That's how it went. I won't say it was my best goal ever, but it was an important one. It's one that I always remember very well.

After playing with ZFC I went to Zaanlandia. I regretted leaving, but Zaanlandia played in the national league. It was a much stronger team, and by playing there I faced tougher opposition, which was good for my development. I left Zaanlandia as an A-junior. I was sixteen when I told the youth coach Peter Buter that I wanted to go higher in football. Playing at the highest level was important to me. Many scouts from the professional clubs came to watch the youth games there, so who knew what chances I would get. Chris Pragt who owned a flower shop and was the club chairman later took me on amateur terms to Telstar. He was also sponsor of the youth team at DWS. Occasionally he would give me money which I used to buy football boots and pay my club fee.

With DWS we played against Ajax's A1 team where Louis van Gaal was youth coach at the time. We regularly played in the stadiums of the professional clubs such as Heerenveen and Haarlem in front of hundreds of supporters. I thought it was wonderful. Unfortunately, I left DWS under a cloud. On a Thursday night after training I stole a watch from somebody at the club and then put it on my wrist as if it were mine. I was so stupid. I was wearing the watch of a first-team player while innocently sitting at the bar in the canteen. It was a special watch with some kind of inscription.

Everyone in the club knew about that watch, except me. The guy whose watch it was had seen me wearing it. He notified the board, and I was called to explain myself. I kept on denying that I had stolen it, but I was kicked out anyway. I told the board that I had found the watch on the floor but they didn't believe me. They then asked why I hadn't handed it in. 'I should have done that, it was a mistake,' I told them, but to no avail.

I got the sack, even though I was the best player for DWS A1. It happened on the day we had to play a match. Oswald didn't know what had happened and so he kept on supporting me, since I kept denying that I had stolen the watch. Oswald told them, 'If you send him away, then you're also sending me away. You keep on saying he stole it while Jerrel says he didn't. I believe him because he is my friend.'

I told Oswald to stay there, but he was resolute in his 'no'. In the end, he left DWS soon after I had gone. Years later I told him what had really happened. He told me that deep inside he actually knew, but he didn't want to stay if I was leaving. Chris Pragt then arranged for me to train along with Telstar. He was of the opinion that my talent should not be wasted because of this one incident, and that I should be given another chance. All together I only played for three months at DWS, from September to November.

3 One More Chance

I was twenty-three years old when I headed off to Portugal, and in hindsight it was a true fairy tale. I don't know what I would be doing now had I stayed in Holland. At SC Campomaiorense I was given another chance to become a professional footballer. From small pocket money I suddenly moved up to £30,000 per season.

When I signed the contract in August, my girlfriend Jane immediately notified her employer in Holland that she would quit her job, although there was a long notice period so it still took a few months before she could actually do so.

I had been playing football in Portugal for a few weeks when she called me up from Holland to tell me that she was ten weeks pregnant. I asked her to come and join me in Portugal as soon as she could so that we could await the birth of our child together. Now I had enough money to take care of her and our baby. Everything looked fine. Just one problem. We didn't have a clue what it would actually be like to live together.

We tried, but it just didn't work. We were always arguing, always fighting. We really wanted to make it work and stay together, but it just didn't happen. Jane was often lonely while I was training or playing matches. She was pregnant and alone in a foreign country. She missed her family and the region around Alkmaar where she grew up.

The first time I saw my daughter was the day after her birth. Unfortunately I wasn't allowed to be there on the day itself, 5 April 1996. The club wouldn't allow me because I was paid to play football and Jane wanted to give birth in Holland so that she could be close to her family. I understood her feelings, but it was difficult for me. That next day I was back in Holland and we were reunited for a short time. After Campomaiorense I went to Boavista in Porto where she joined me again, but still things didn't work out.

She went back to Holland and a little while later we split up indefinitely. I tried my best to arrange as much as possible for her from Portugal, such as finding a house. Afterwards things never worked out again between us. In hindsight, you could say that everything just went way too fast – my sudden move to Portugal, and her pregnancy. It turned out to be too much for us even though I was really crazy about her, and still am. She is very special to me, the mother of my child.

After we split up our relationship was very bad for a while. You know how that goes, women aren't always the easiest to deal with. I wanted to keep seeing my daughter, as much as possible. Initially it was very difficult to have a normal relationship with Jane but when she became involved with another man things were better between us. Nowadays we call each other from time to time, which really makes me happy. We are older now, and we were too young then. It is very important for

Ghislaine that Jane and I have a good relationship.

Apart from the split the time in Portugal was a fantastic period of my life. I earned a good salary and received the recognition I felt I deserved. I have always thought that since Ghislaine's birth everything has found a way of working out. Until then really nobody had faith in me, absolutely nobody. I felt rejected. Many said I couldn't play football. Even FC Zwolle had tried to take advantage of me. Ben Hendriks was the manager there and he wanted me in his team. Together with my previous agent Sigi Lens, who was working for the VVCS, the contracted football players' union, we drove to Zwolle to negotiate my contract. I could make 1,500 guilders gross per week, but because I had to travel from Zaandam and rent a house in the region as well as buy a car for my girlfriend, that wasn't enough.

I asked the chairman, Gaston Sporre, for another 150 guilders per week as reimbursement for expenses, but the club thought that was ridiculous because it would make me one of the best-paid players there. They thought it was too much for such a young newcomer. In the end, the negotiations broke down over 600 guilders – not even £200 – a month.

Before my internship at FC Zwolle I had a week's trial at EVV Eindhoven, the second-best club behind PSV in that city, who played in the first division. The Hungarian Sandor Popovics was the manager. I trained very well there and scored in one of the practice matches, but Popovics didn't think I would be an asset to the team. I was disappointed, but these things happen.

I had less of a problem with that than what happened in Zwolle, where they tried to make a fool out of me. At least there, the technical staff thought I was good. The whole thing was all the more painful because it didn't make sense to me. At Zwolle they used the argument that I would be the best-paid player in the team. That wasn't true at all. I would have had very little money left over after paying taxes, the cost of transport and rent. In that case my girlfriend would also have had to continue working.

Sigi Lens and I had left the VVCS office in Gouda in a great mood for the drive to Zwolle. I remember exactly what I was wearing on that day; a purplish jacket with a purple shirt underneath which had a floral print on it and black trousers. I looked really smart, and I was certain that my style of clothes would leave them with a good impression of me. It's important to leave a good impression in every way, not just on the field but off it as well. Sigi called me Tavares because of that soul outfit and I felt like a true soulman.

I knew Ben Hendriks wanted to give me a contract so it was a huge anticlimax when we couldn't sort out the finances. At that moment I felt like giving up on professional football. It seemed as though I wouldn't be able to earn a living from it. Back then, had I been forced to stop playing indefinitely, I would have been in real trouble. I would have resorted to stealing and petty crime. But I had experienced that kind of life already and certainly didn't want to go back there. Of course it was still a hard decision to say no to FC Zwolle but in hindsight it was the right one. At that moment I had nothing: no money, no income, absolutely nothing. To say, 'No, I'm not taking your offer' took guts.

The drama doesn't upset me now but it did then. To think that the deal collapsed over a measly 600 guilders a month, not even £200! It really didn't make sense and it certainly wasn't fair after my excellent performance during training. I felt that my future was breaking up into tiny pieces. My future as a professional footballer had suddenly been shattered and roughly taken away from me. I felt horrible but soon I was determined to fight for another chance. I still believed that one day it would happen. Ultimately there was no other way but to make it and I was confident of my skills. After FC Zwolle I started to work out with the first-division club Haarlem in order to stay fit. I hoped that by training with a professional club I would eventually be noticed again.

I didn't play any matches in the 1993–94 season. The manager at Haarlem, Hans van Doorneveld, didn't offer me a contract. Fortunately I still lived at home so I could live frugally. I was even entitled to unemployment benefits because I had worked at AZ previously. It wasn't much, about 800 guilders (£230), a month. With AZ I had earned 12,000 guilders (£3,600) in the previous season. I was extremely happy with those 12,000 guilders because I was still living with my mother and could travel with Carlos. On top of that I received a further 200 guilders to cover travelling expenses.

Thus I lost a whole season, just training with Haarlem. After that year I had to think about giving up football completely and looking for a different job. Fortunately, in the summer of 1994, I was approached by Otto Gilds, the coach of Neerlandia, an amateur club who played their matches on Sundays. He talked with me at the Kwakoe field in the Bijlmer, in the southeastern part of Amsterdam. It's a place where the Surinamese community tend to gather. Otto Gilds told me that Neerlandia needed a centre-forward. I could play football on their sandy pitch during the summer in order to stay in shape. I could also make some extra money, he said. It turned out that it was fifty guilders for every match we won.

Bob Goeman, the Neerlandia chairman, worked at the electronic consumer goods store RAF on the Rijnstraat in Amsterdam. Back then he would give certain players some extra money from his own pocket. All together I received 7,000 guilders from him, enough to buy a car and some stereo equipment to go with it. Goeman even allowed me to buy the stereo set with a huge discount from his shop.

I loved my time at Neerlandia. I blossomed as a footballer, scoring continuously, about a goal every game. It was a fun club with a fantastic atmosphere, so I often stayed on till late at night. After training we would play card games over some beers in the canteen. Everyone at that club stayed on after training. Humphry Nijman, my present agent, spotted me playing there. He remembered seeing me at AZ, but this time he was impressed enough to ask me to call him, which I soon did.

Soon after my first call to Humphry, he asked me whether I was interested in playing abroad. My attitude was that I wanted to make it as a professional player and if I couldn't realize my aspirations in Holland then I would be happy to take my chances abroad.

I was not afraid of adventure. I didn't even see the negative aspects of moving far away. My only thoughts were, 'Yes, I'm going to do this! I, Jerrel Hasselbaink, am going to make it.' I was sure I would be able to adjust to living abroad. Within no time at all I found myself playing on an Austrian football pitch.

Humphry had been in contact with Admira Wacker who were looking for a centre-forward. I was convinced that I had made a good impression during my trial there, because in two games I scored seven times. But the situation was more complicated than I thought.

It turned out that there was an agreement that I would only be contracted if the Dutch player already on their books, Marcel Oerlemans, was sold. Unfortunately, he didn't leave, so I could forget about playing for Admira Wacker. Two weeks later Humphry called again, this time with an offer from Portugal. A minute before he called me he had received a call from someone asking him whether he knew a good forward for SC Campomaiorense of the Portuguese league.

The club had just been promoted to the top division, and would be playing Benfica, Sporting and Porto that season. Humphry asked me what I thought. I immediately replied, 'Fine, no problem,' packed my suitcase again and hopped on the plane.

After I arrived in Lisbon I waited for some time to be picked up from the airport. It was actually a funny misunderstanding. Humphry had told the club that a Dutch guy was on the plane on his way over. Expecting a tall white guy with blond hair they were surprised to see a black guy approach them. One of the people who came to collect me asked in disbelief, 'Are you really the Dutch guy?' It was funny to see the surprise on their faces.

During my trial at SC Campomaiorense I played two matches, scoring in the second one. The trainer, Manuel Fernandez, who had been a very famous Portuguese footballer, was very happy with me. He told me, 'You must stay here. You have to play here. I'll take care of it. You have to sign quickly.' I was going to make 100,000 guilders (£30,000 a year), really! I was elated, not least because I had some small debts in Holland which I could now pay off. My car insurance, fines, all kinds of things would be settled. I was finally rid of them. I was twenty-three years old and at last with some money to spend.

After my debut a Dutch football magazine called *Voetbal International* wrote that I could expect to be returning to Holland very soon. As I had already made a good impression in Portugal the article was nonsense but it proved once again that the Dutch press didn't have any faith in me. Reading the story just made me angry and even more determined to succeed.

For an unusual reason, it was awhile before I finally signed the contract in Portugal. When I arrived at Campomaiorense the club told me they wanted to delay announcing my signature. The supporters were not to know who I was or where I came from. To complete the deception, the owner of the club, Joao Manuel Goncalves Nabeiro, thought it best to give me a different name. The press was not allowed to know that I, Jerrel Hasselbaink, the former Telstar and AZ player, was now playing for Campomaiorense in Portugal. The chairman introduced himself to me and said, 'We don't want people to know who you are. Therefore, we'll just call you "Jimmy" and nothing else.'

During our first training sessions and matches there were photographers, cameramen and journalists. Of course they wanted to know who I was, but I had been told to keep my lips tightly sealed. I was so happy with the chance the club had given me I told the chairman, 'Call me whatever you like.' After a while I asked the chairman, 'Can I now be called Jerrel Hassel-baink again?' but he replied, 'No, we'll keep on calling you Jimmy.'

It was really strange. In the shops and petrol stations people would shout 'Hey Jimmy, how's it going?' But I soon got used to my new name, and reacted promptly whenever it was spoken. I became Jimmy and played with the name on the back of my shirt.

In our first competitive match, we lost 1–0 in front of 15,000 people, an enormous number considering the population of the town was only 11,000. The season went really well for me even though the team was relegated. After relegation, I was sold to Boavista for 300,000 euros even though Benfica and Sevilla had also expressed their interest in me. Boavista had just started to crawl up the ranks and had qualified for the UEFA Cup, which meant European football. I chose Boavista, reasoning that a move to Benfica would be too big a step up.

I had a great time at Campo, scoring twelve times in my season there. I proved my value to the team in the fifth league game of the campaign, a match against Gil Vicente. I missed a penalty kick but then made up for that by scoring both goals in a 2–0 victory. The captain told me that Stoilov should take the penalty. The Bulgarian was our key player but I was determined to take it. When I missed, the captain told me once more that Stoilov should have taken it. 'He never missed before, really never,' were his words. I said, 'Don't worry, man. I'll fix it. I'll score you another two today.' And that's what happened.

It was one of my best matches of the season. During half-time hardly anything was said to me, but after the game the captain approached me. He stuck out his hand and said, 'You were right, you scored twice just like you said you would.' I thought that was nice.

Carlos and Oswald Snip often admonished me for trying too hard to prove myself at a new club. I did it again at SC Campomaiorense where I started taking the free-kicks in the first minutes of my first practice match. The problem is that I would rather fail myself than be failed by others. I quickly feel responsible for the team's performance and even when I am failing myself I won't hide.

At Campo we were relegated because we lost too many home games. We had an averagely skilled team with many young and old players who had never played in the highest division before. It definitely wasn't a team which had been worked on and shaped into a coherent unit over a period of five years or so. Of the players I was with, Beto now plays with Sporting, and the keeper Ricardo came with me to Boavista.

I wanted to score as soon as I could, but the fact that it took a while didn't really matter. When I scored in the fifth match, it was a very important moment for me. From that time, things started to get moving. The Dutch press didn't immediately notice me after those two goals though, that came gradually. Sometimes there would be a phone interview with the Dutch football magazine *Voetbal International*, but not much else at first. I think they enjoyed talking with me. They viewed me as a failed Dutch footballer enjoying a Portuguese adventure but who, in the end, would probably not make it much further.

Ours wasn't a very sociable team. The big boys from Lisbon were always together, but the rest went straight home after training. After matches it was basically the same story since in Portugal and Spain they don't have a clubhouse where the players can spend time together. Everybody just went back to their own homes. However, I did hang out with the right-back from Campomaiorense. I enjoyed that, especially because his wife cooked really delicious food. He showed me around the region since he was from the same area and could speak a bit of English.

The region was slightly mountainous, and was close to the Spanish border. We often went shopping in Spain because things were cheaper there. I always got petrol in Spain, but the daily shopping was cheaper there too. We normally shopped in Badajoz although Seville was within two hours' drive. As I had been given a second-hand white Peugeot 205 by the club I was able to travel to do my shopping. The car wasn't a convertible and nor did it have air conditioning. In fact, it was a few years old but as far as I was concerned it was great and I was very happy with it.

The club wasn't very rich but the chairman was very wealthy. Joao Manuel Goncalves Nabeiro was the owner of Delta, a very big coffee producer in Portugal. He was often at the stadium in his free time, and was present for the matches.

I once had dinner at his beautiful house, a big ranch with horses. At the end of the season he hosted a big barbecue. The team and their families and the staff all gathered at his ranch. He was prepared to joke around with the players, but he soon let you know who was the boss. We respected him, especially because he paid our salaries on time at the end of every month. We players knew that that didn't occur at every club. The bad thing about Portuguese football is that the clubs pay very irregularly, and sometimes they don't pay at all. But he did. Campomaiorense was famous for paying salaries on time.

In England and Holland your salary is automatically transferred to your bank account but in Portugal I was paid by cheque. Every twenty-ninth day of the month I picked up my salary. In total I went to the bank ten times, since I was paid for ten months, not twelve. You could say I had two months of unpaid holiday. Nor did I get a thirteenth month pay nor holiday money, which is common in Holland. In Spain I got paid relatively little every month, but three times per season we received an extra big amount as a bonus.

Some of the big Portuguese clubs, such as Sporting, Vitória Guimarães and Benfica, didn't always pay on time. When I played at Boavista the salaries always arrived on time, however. Isaias, who had played with me at Boavista, had once been playing at another club when it stopped paying him his salary. He told me that one day he went to the chairman to demand his money. The chairman told him once again that this time his salary was really on its way, but Isaias's patience ran out. 'So when are you going to pay me? My children have to eat too.' It worked, because a little later the money was paid.

I know about several players who in the end never received their salaries. At Atlético Madrid there were a number of players who never got their money. I always received mine on time, though, even from Atlético Madrid. It's partly due to Humphry Nijman, because he was smart enough to ask for bank guarantees before we signed every contract. It is ninety-five per cent to his credit that I am always paid on time. Humphry is a very good businessman. He always said, 'When you are going to negotiate with a club for the first time, you should know what you want. That's what you have to agree on then. Once you have signed your contract, I don't want you having to think about it when you're on the field, because it should be perfectly arranged. As a player you shouldn't have to worry about it, that's what you've got an agent for.'

He always does his homework impeccably which is why he always demanded bank guarantees in advance. Just for that alone Humphry is worth his weight in gold. He always works with his own lawyers and with financial experts of the country where he is doing business. That's very important.

I wasn't lonely at Campo. I sometimes enjoyed having nobody around me and being able to do exactly what I wanted. I liked it when people were around me, but peace and quiet is also nice, it still is. I sometimes enjoy locking myself at home and just doing the paperwork, etc. Carlos never came by. He did come when I played at Boavista, however, as did other members of my family. Porto was easier to reach. Jane's parents came to Campo Maior once, but my mother never did. In fact, none of my family visited.

Instead I went to Holland often, about every four months. I was also able to be there at Christmas, as there is no football at that time in Portugal. My first visit was after two months abroad but I never felt homesick for Holland. Perhaps it is because I easily adapt myself to foreign locations and cultures. I picked up the Portuguese language quickly because there was no choice – my Dutch and English were of little use. It was difficult, but a lot of fun. I always engross myself in the language and cultures of the country I live in. I pick up a lot from TV, but even more by speaking to the locals. I never walk away from that. On the contrary, I enjoy it. After a few months I was able to conduct a decent conversation. Nobody spoke English in my team except for one other player and the manager. The manager was able to get across what he meant. Football language is quite universal. You try to understand as best as you can.

I lived in a terraced house that was rented by the club. Across from me lived my team-mate Stanimir Stoilov. I spent a lot of time with him as he spoke a little bit of English. I spoke to him again when he was playing at Sofia and I was at Chelsea. I enjoy going to Portugal, although I haven't been back to Campo Maior since I left.

Jane arrived about three months after I signed my contract. In the meantime I watched a lot of television at home and listened to music. I was at home a lot and very focused on my professional career. I slept early and made sure I ate well. I can cook because my mother and my siblings taught me how when I was small. My mother insisted we all learned. Now I enjoy cooking, even down to buying the ingredients in the supermarket. I don't think I'm too good to do my own shopping. It's actually harder to eat at restaurants these days because I am recognized more often. When people are coming up to talk to you or for an autograph it makes it difficult to relax. I also watched a lot of football, as I still do. I watched everything. I have always been able to watch the whole game. I focus on the strikers and the defenders, to see how they handle certain situations. Apart from my own enjoyment it is also a matter of doing my homework. It is not a hardship for me as I love staying at home. In Portugal I rented a lot of videos, but nowadays I watch the latest blockbusters on DVD. Sometimes I had access to movies that had just been released in the cinema. For example, I had already seen *Hostage* starring Bruce Willis before it was released in England.

Manuel Fernandez, my first manager at SC Campomaio-rense, was replaced by Diamantino. Fernandez was a very good manager. He had been the centre-forward for Sporting, while Diamantino had been a very good midfielder at Setúbal and Benfica. He was in his thirties when he came to Campo and had played for the Portuguese national team. Fernandez was a bit older.

While Fernandez was in charge we played with only one striker. We usually played 5–4–1 or 4–5–1. It may sound fun and prestigious to be the only striker, but in reality I didn't see much of the ball. And because we didn't have a very good team, we defended more than we attacked. Fernandez was fired halfway through November 1995 after we had lost 3–0 to FC Felgueiras, our ninth defeat in eleven games. We had only beaten Gil Vicente and drawn against Leca. It was clear something had to happen and usually the manager is the one to go. We didn't have a powerful team, so even though Diamantino did better than his predecessor, we were still relegated. This was not a disaster for me personally, although it was bad for the club and for the chairman. About three years ago, the president stopped funding the club, so they no longer play professional football.

Towards the end of the season several clubs became interested in me. It was a good feeling that other clubs wanted to sign me.

Mérida, who had just been promoted, were very interested in having me. Their chairman offered both Humphry and me a blank cheque. We could write down whatever amount we desired, but neither of us thought it would be a good idea for me to go there.

Eventually it was decided that I would go to Boavista. The first contact was made through the son of the vice-president João Loureiro. He called me up and asked if I was interested in moving to the north of Portugal. The contract was written up very quickly. Directly after signing I received the keys to a brand-new BMW 320 cabriolet. It was written in my contract that I should get one, but it surprised me nonetheless that the car was actually there. The first thing I did was to go for a drive with Humphry through the boulevards of Porto. I was so proud. A few days later I drove to Holland, for part of the trip with the roof down. That was the only time I received a car as part of my contract. I didn't want that at any of my other clubs. Once I had got my brand new car, I didn't care about it much afterwards, because what's a car, you know? Especially when you stay sober like me.

After a four-week summer break in Holland I drove to Porto, ready to start with Boavista, with Ghislaine in the back of the BMW and my girlfriend Jane next to me. It was perhaps the most beautiful moment of my life, driving the three of us back to Portugal. My own family was complete and I was moving on to a new, bigger club. I didn't think I was a success yet, but at least I was part of football. At that moment I didn't know that I would be training under three managers during the next season.

We started with Zoran Filipovic. He left after we lost 5–1 to Inter Milan in the UEFA Cup. I thought it was strange that he had to leave because we had been doing quite well. Maybe that defeat was too embarrassing for some of the club bosses. His successor, João Alves, wanted to change everything around and play with three strikers. Rui Casaca was my third manager that year. I remember the fans being furious at the keeper Alfredo, but they also attacked other players, although I was spared most of their criticism.

I only met Filipovic on the first training day of the season. He wanted to play 4–4–2 which appealed to me much more than the one-striker football of Campomaiorense. He wanted to play beautiful football, but he wasn't given enough time to prove himself. On the face of it, making the third round of the UEFA Cup wasn't exactly a bad performance, but that wasn't the issue. The club said he was fired because he took his wife with him to Italy for the match. They thought it demonstrated that he wasn't focused enough. I thought it was just an excuse, a stick with which to hit him.

We had a good team that season. Alfredo was in goal, and the right-back was Paulo Souza. Rui Bento had also played for Portugal. Tavares, our number four, played for the national team and Bobó could run like an idiot. He kicked anything and everything on the field. Even if the field was as hard as rock, he always trained with long studs on his shoes. He was a complete wacko, but away from the field he was really nice. For him it was a matter of turning that knob and off you go. Nuno Gomes was the other striker. After that season he went to Benfica for three years and then to Fiorentina. Back then he was a very good player. He was quite technical and made some impressive runs. In short, we were a team that had to be taken seriously.

Although we had good players that season wasn't too great. We finished seventh, way behind the champions Porto, winning only twelve of our thirty-four games. Fortunately, we won the Portuguese Cup which ended the season on a good note, at least. I finished second to Porto's Jardel in the scoring charts, hitting twenty goals in the competition.

In the UEFA Cup we played in the first round against OB Odense in Denmark. That was my first European match. We won 3–2 there and 2–1 at home. Yet the second round against Dynamo Tbilisi made much more of an impact on me. There were 90,000 people in that stadium – very impressive. I started on the bench and could enjoy the atmosphere. However, that swiftly ended when I came on as a substitute with twenty minutes to go. I had a chance to score with a header but in the end we lost 1–0. I didn't start the game because Filipovic didn't dare play with two strikers in that stadium.

Just before I went on the field I was full of adrenalin. I was desperate to demonstrate my skills in front of a huge audience. It had been my dream and my goal in life, so that day was one of my best, despite our defeat. I never suffered from stage-fright, not even then in Tbilisi. At home we notched an impressive 5–0 victory.

In the third round we played at Inter first. In Milan there were much fewer people in the stands. About 80,000 people fit in the Giuseppe Meazza Stadium, but it was far from sold out. However, it was one of the most beautiful stadiums I ever played in, very imposing.

At Boavista it felt more like a group of friends than when I played at Campomaiorense. I fitted in well with the group. I often went out for a snack between training sessions with Russell Latapy, Jorge Couto and Pedro Emanuel.

At Boavista we practised at 9 am in the summer, and one hour later during the winter months. The afternoon training was at 6 pm in the summer and at 5 pm in the winter. In Portugal it is normal to have a long siesta. I would usually take a nap for one-and-a-half hours after lunch, a habit I continued even after I left. We ate late at night, around 10 pm, and I would go to sleep between midnight and 1 am. When I ate at home I would, however, eat around 8 pm, especially when I was very hungry right after training.

If I had the next day off, I would sometimes stay out until about 6 or 7 am but if I had to train or play the next day I was always on time. Whenever I had a really late night, I usually woke up around noon. Then I would go to the beach or the boulevard to relax and replenish my energy. My apartment had a great view of the sea with a very wide beach right in front. My friends often stayed over because of the great location of my apartment. I had a wonderful time there. It was an old apartment, but very nice with a small balcony. Latapy sometimes stayed over, and other players lived nearby.

To begin with, Jane and Ghislaine were there as well, of course. After four months, however, the fairy tale was over and we split up. In Campo Maior our relationship was already quite rocky, but in Porto it got worse. It just hadn't worked out, and we were both sick and tired of it. In the beginning it was very difficult, because I wanted to keep on seeing my daughter. I wanted children, but perhaps it was a little too early then. I often had to go away with the club. At Campo, for home games you could sleep at home, but for away games you had to leave a day early. At Boavista it didn't matter if you played away or at home the next day. One day before the match everyone had to sleep in a hotel. As we were also playing European football I was away even more. It felt as though I was constantly flying around Europe. Jane was often left feeling alone and lonely. She tried to learn Portuguese but still didn't have any friends in Porto. She also had Ghislaine to take care of, which took up a lot of her time. I understood that she didn't want to sit at home all day, but abroad the customs are different. You have to deal with a whole different culture and with different customs. In Holland the women are more emancipated. In Portugal, Spain and Italy there are still plenty of men around with a macho attitude. I also had to find a way to deal with it. I often had to compensate for her loneliness, even though when I came home I was often tired and in need of some rest. She, on the other hand, then wanted to do something fun with me. When I wanted peace and quiet she wanted fun and social activities, which wasn't always possible. I guess back then I wasn't sympathetic enough.

In my season at Boavista I played twenty-nine games, starting nineteen of them. My first goals came in the first match of the season, against Belenenses, a club from Lisbon. We won 4–2 at their place and I scored twice. My first hat-trick in professional football was at home against Marítimo, with one goal coming from a penalty kick. That was on 2 March 1997. A little later I repeated the feat – without the penalty this time –

at home to Gil Vicente. Nuno Gomes also scored three in that match.

The fans were passionate about the rivalry between the two big clubs in the city, FC Porto and Boavista. They were hostile, but not vicious towards the opponents. I never witnessed incidents involving objects being thrown towards the opponents' supporters, which is something I often see in England. You don't see that in Portugal. At my Portuguese clubs I hardly saw any fans with my name on their jerseys. That only came for the first time when I was playing at Leeds United.

On 10 June, we played the Cup Final in Lisbon against Benfica. I was only on the bench because I had already signed for Leeds United. The trainer Rui Casaca thought I wouldn't give the full 100 per cent because I was leaving, but that was nonsense. In the end I came on for the last fifteen minutes. We had made it to the final by winning 5–0 against Estrela dos Vendos Novos, 4–0 against Oriental Lisboa, 2–0 against FC Infesca and in the quarter finals 1–0 at Estoril-Praia. In the semi-final I scored once as we beat Sporting 3–0.

We won 3–2 against Benfica and the man of the match was the Bolivian player Erwin Sanchez. He scored twice, while Nuno Gomes scored the other goal. There were about 50,000 fans in the stadium, with the Benfica fans making up eighty per cent of the crowd. Afterwards we had a big victory celebration. When we arrived back in Porto we were first treated to a dinner, but that was after the three-hour bus trip. By then everyone was already quite tanked up with different sorts of alcohol.

After dinner a large group of us went into town. The next day at least ninety per cent of the team was lost. I too was among the missing. When I woke up I had no idea where I was. I had fallen asleep under a bar somewhere. When I woke up the next morning I wasn't alone, though. There were more footballers around me. I arrived home around noon. That afternoon we had to meet the mayor at 4 pm. All the players received a gold coin from him. I still have it somewhere, it's one of the few things I still have from my time in Portugal. The previous evening we had also received a medal from the national football association as well as the competition trophy.

Fortunately, I didn't have any annoying journalists going through my private life while I was in Portugal. In England it's much more of a problem. However, I was often the alibi for Russell Latapy, the funny guy from Trinidad. He would say to me, 'Tonight, I'm hanging out with you, OK.' And I would reply, 'Oh really? You're at my place tonight?' It always went like that. He was the life and soul of the group. He would often appear at training smelling of alcohol; he was always up for a joke or two. His hangovers never put him in a bad mood.

In those days I hardly spent a penny, and saved as much as I could. The car was part of my contract while the apartment belonged to the club. It saved me a lot of money. I also didn't have to pay for flight tickets, since they were also at the club's expense. I saved because my agent insisted I did. He knew exactly how much I could save, how much I should put aside, and how I should put it aside. He brought in a financial adviser and arranged everything for me. He kept on telling me that the future is important. The money I earn now is also for the future. I wasn't difficult about it. He suggested that I should think first before I buy something big.

Nowadays I do spend a lot, but whenever I can, I save up for later. I do compare prices. Only when I go on holidays do I spend as much money as I need in order to have fun. Then I have no qualms about such spontaneous ideas as hiring a helicopter to explore Surinam.

In Portugal I learned to cook well. It was the first time I had to spend a long time by myself, although I was often found on the beach. It was wonderful, sitting on a sunny terrace when the weather was fantastic, having a nice cup of coffee, glancing at the girls. Of course, just peeking. Spoiling my eyes, so to speak. I'm human after all, and the eye needs a bit of excitement from time to time. They never approached me because they were always together with their mates and their boyfriends. Of course, sometimes they would recognize me as Boavista's Jimmy. I sometimes abused that fame but actually not that often. Latapy was the real dude.

I love women, but I never treat them badly, if you know what I mean. I have a daughter so I would feel guilty if I mistreated a woman. I wouldn't want a man coming into her life and mistreating her. He would have to deal with me then. In the past I did have some problems in that respect but not now. When I went with my friends to Surinam or Las Vegas there was absolutely no need to have any women there with us.

About two weeks before the end of the season I learned there was some interest in me from England. Humphry called to tell me that Leeds United would be coming to Portugal to watch me. He told me to remain calm, to be myself and that if I did everything would be fine. 'Keep on doing what you're good at,' he said. I was thinking, 'Wow, the English are interested.' I wasn't nervous at all for that match against Vitória Setúbal, although I felt a healthy kind of tension, a tension that said, 'OK, Let's go. Time to make your dream come true.' The game ended in a 2–2 draw and I played rather well, scoring one goal. Leeds also liked the Setúbal number ten, Bruno Ribeiro, so they took him on for the new season as well.

Apart from the Spanish league, playing in the English football league had always been a dream to me. And now there was a chance to become part of it. There were many players in the English Premiership who inspired me. I thought Ian Wright was great at Arsenal, but I also loved Glenn Helder, Dennis Bergkamp and Ruud Gullit at Chelsea. More and more good foreign players were starting to play in the Premiership.

I accepted the offer quite readily. An offer from Leeds United, a nice big club from England, is not something you turn down. They had finished in eleventh place in the Premier League. Soon after the clubs had struck their deal I had to go to Leeds for the medical check-up. That was no problem, and shortly afterwards I signed the contract. Boavista received £2 million for me. I didn't consider myself too expensive, especially not then. Others might consider it a huge amount, but that's the way it was. The more you are worth the better. Of course, it didn't mean I got those millions myself. It gave me a good feeling, though. It was strange that two years earlier nobody had wanted to give a shilling for me.

What gave me strength was that I had picked up from Dutch football circles that people were saying again that I wouldn't make it. The challenge of transforming the negative into the positive has always inspired me.

My family loved it. They have always backed me up, no matter what. Maybe they're a little more proud of me now. But even today my eldest sister wouldn't put up with it if I gave her the big mouth. She would punch me if I tried.

Of course, I can talk with my eldest brother much more easily than when I was young. I can now tell him certain things which I couldn't before, but that's mostly because the age difference doesn't matter anymore. My eldest sister Renate gets more respect from me, and the same goes for Marion. The fact that I probably show less respect to Franklin compared to my sisters has to do with the fact that he has a completely different personality.

4 Lowdown at Leeds

Leeds United gave me the opportunity to become the footballer I am now. Thanks to United I was even noticed in Holland, which resulted in me playing for 'Oranje', the Dutch national team. It was a shame about the way I left Elland Road, though.

I would have preferred a nicer farewell than the one the chairman Peter Ridsdale was willing to give me. He had a lot of power at Leeds United, but he spent money like water, money which belonged to the club. He travelled to matches on private jets, which cost the club £70,000 in one year, and spent more than £200 on tropical fish for the aquarium in his Leeds United office. That was the club's money, not his own. A few years later those stories became public but I had already left.

In the summer of 1997, when I flew to Leeds for the first time, I had no idea what to expect. I hardly owned any personal belongings, so I was travelling light. I had only brought some clothes, pictures, and kitchen utensils along with me. I didn't own much else in Portugal. In Porto, I had owned a pre-furnished house, including washing machine, television and stereo. When I arrived in England I found I had to buy everything because here things worked differently.

In Portugal the club rented the apartment for me, while here I was told that it was smarter to buy a house or apartment. One of the reasons was that in England you had to pay tax on the house provided to you by the club, since it was regarded as extra income. It is one of the reasons why footballers usually won't accept a house offered to them by a club. For me it was financially much more advantageous to buy a house myself, even though it took a lot of time. And in that first summer in England I hardly had any time. I was often on the road with the club, off to training camps and practice games. That's why I stayed for the first three months at Oulton Hall, a fantastically located hotel on the outskirts of Leeds.

I bought my first house in Chadwell, a town close to Leeds, and it cost me about £150,000. It was a detached property with four bedrooms, one big living room, a separate dining room and a big kitchen. Compared to what I was used to it was a huge house, and I had to buy a lot of new furniture. I made myself very popular with IKEA and Habitat, since almost everything in my new house came from those two stores.

I didn't have any problems adapting to life in England. Dutch people start learning English early at school. On top of that, I spent a lot of time with Bruno Ribeiro, the Portuguese player from Setúbal. I had to help him because in the beginning he didn't speak any English. I also had a lot of contact with another team-mate, David Hopkin, who was staying in the same hotel as me.

I only arrived two days before the first training session. I came straight from Holland with just a suitcase filled with clothes. Pretty soon all these clothes were dispersed over my grand room. Apart from the main room, I had a small storage room to store my belongings. It was a great five-star hotel, and initially I thought I was going to live there.

The new players were fortunate as the club arranged everything for us. It was even better than at Boavista where the players were left to themselves a lot more. At United people were assigned to help me, even for such things as buying a car. It was really top class!

In the first week I was taken to the training sessions by somebody from the club and dropped off at the hotel afterwards. In the meantime, I could get accustomed to driving on the left. It took me a while to get the hang of it. It would always be fine in the beginning, because I was concentrating, but the danger came when I started to get used to it. Once my mind started to drift off I would sometimes drive on the wrong side of the road. One time I barely managed to avoid an oncoming car. I was thinking, 'Why the hell is this guy driving straight at me? Get away, you idiot!' Fortunately I realized just in time what had happened but the incident certainly scared me.

At the first training session I was introduced to people from the club and my team-mates. The manager, George Graham, did all the talking. I didn't have much to say about myself. Graham was an authoritarian man, but that was fine by me, especially in a group made up of many egos. One of the important people at our training facilities at Thorp Arch Grange was Jack Williamson. Part of his job was to keep unwanted guests away. We used to call him 'The Rottweiler' because he was so persistent. There were many journalists who found out that there was no way past Jack. To us players he was perfect. He also washed our cars for us. It was hard to refuse such an offer, of course.

George Graham had already made his name as a football manager in England. He had worked for Arsenal from May 1986 until February 1995, before leaving after it became clear that he had illegally accepted money as part of a transfer deal. He was replaced by Bruce Rioch, who signed Dennis Bergkamp from Inter Milan in 1995. Arsenal started playing European-style football from that moment on. I have since heard many stories of managers regularly keeping part of the transfer fees in their own pockets. But those are stories. In the case of George Graham it was proven and he actually admitted it. However, in England, football managers are treated like saints and something like that rarely spells the end of their career. Footballers who cause accidents by drunk driving are also often forgiven. It happened to Tony Adams. He had to go to prison for three months and was forced to kick his alcohol habit in a clinic, yet he remained the captain of the English national team. Jermaine Pennant even played a few matches with an ankle strap containing a tracking device. The strap was the alternative to remaining in prison for driving under the influence. He was not allowed to take it off, even during matches. Lee Bowyer was caught with hashish in his bloodstream and Mark Bosnich had cocaine in his, as did Adrian Mutu.

You won't hear me saying that these things should be tolerated, but we are all human and we all make mistakes. I am the last to suggest that a player should be punished hard and never be given another chance. I have made many mistakes in my life, so I'm able to forgive others for theirs. As a player and as a human being one should learn from such situations. So long as you have learnt from your behaviour, it is acceptable to be given another chance. If players don't learn from their mistakes, then I think harsher punishments are appropriate.

There are many stories about English players in the newspapers. English journalists are always looking for the juicy details. In Holland, in contrast, a footballer is a footballer, nothing more nothing less. He may be known or even famous, but Dutch people are sober about it and don't say more than, 'Oh look! There's Dennis Bergkamp!' or 'Oh look! There goes Marco van Basten!' At most five out of ten people will ask for an autograph. In England a footballer is a superstar, and in the end almost everyone will ask for his autograph. This level of admiration makes it difficult for footballers to remain themselves, and the likelihood of them putting on airs increases dramatically. There are players who start thinking that they can get away with anything because of their fame. In Holland the TV channels don't necessarily pay you for studio interviews, while in England you can charge £1,500 per broadcast.

I met Jonathan Woodgate at Leeds United. As a teenager he was already a huge talent. He still is, but he is not the smartest cookie in the crowd. He is a fun guy, all right, a real party animal, someone who will drive at top speed on the motorway. He once told me proudly how he drove from Leeds to Middlesbrough in just over half an hour. That's fast, really fast, I can tell you.

Jonathan was an awesome player but he was always joking around. He pulled a lot of pranks and did many things forbidden by the club. One time he dyed his hair and came with his new hairdo to training. He was immediately called to Graham's office where he was told by the manager to go back to the hairdresser. Back then he was still a young reckless boy, barely eighteen years old.

Jonathan could also hit it very hard, and when I say that I don't just mean the ball. I remember one time he appeared at training as drunk as a frog. He wasn't the only one like that, though. Carlton Palmer was another who could drink all evening, but be all right for training early the next morning. Lee Sharpe could also drink like mad. One night I went out with him and I was shocked, even though what I was seeing was quite normal by English standards; filling yourself up completely and leaving it up to fate how and if you got home. This kind of drinking appears to have decreased somewhat in England over the last few years but back in my Leeds days it happened quite a lot. I like a beer myself, but I stop when I've had enough. These guys I mentioned would go on and on but I don't drink for drinking's sake.

I've never been fined for drunk driving, because whenever I drink I take a cab. I did once drive while intoxicated, but I'll never do that again. The thought of running over a child keeps me from doing that. I would never forgive myself if I did something like that. Of course, there have been times when I was tempted to play along with other guys, but thankfully I was never a real hanger-on. When I was young, I was always willing to act tough to fit in but now I won't do something just to be part of a group. If that makes me unpopular, tough!

A lot of people think I am very aggressive because of the way I am on the pitch. People have got the wrong impression about me, but perhaps that's because I don't say much about myself in interviews. I am quite private in that way, I am not one to share my life with everyone. You won't find me talking just for talking's sake. It may be out of embarrassment but I don't think so. I think it's more because I am shy. I always come across as a hard guy, but it hurts when I see people on television making fools of themselves by acting tough.

My debut in the Premiership went relatively well. I scored on my first appearance, against Arsenal, on 9 August 1997, but after the game I was in trouble with the FA. The reason was the wording on the back of my shirt. I had worn a shirt carrying the name 'Jimmy' which wasn't allowed since Jimmy wasn't my official name. The club and I each received an official letter stating that if I were to do it again I would be suspended. It was a pity because I had already scored in my first official match against Arsenal under that name. From then on I played with Hasselbaink on my back. In our second match we beat Sheffield Wednesday 3–1. Bruno Ribeiro scored one of the goals, while the other two were scored by Rod Wallace. Then we lost three times in a row, to Crystal Palace, Liverpool, and Aston Villa, before beating Blackburn Rovers 4–3. In the following match, against Bristol City in the League Cup, I scored from the penalty spot in a 3–1 win.

Yet, my productivity was not a full 100 per cent. This was because it took me longer to adapt to the English playing style than I had expected. During my first match I felt the game moved so quickly. After twenty minutes I was completely exhausted. Nowadays the game has become more continental, and is played at a slower pace. When Clyde Wijnhard joined

Leeds the following season I warned him about the different pace in England. 'Don't tire yourself out during the warm-up, or you'll be completely dead by the end of the first thirty minutes.' He shrugged it off saying, 'Ah, don't worry. I'll be fine.' He was in great shape, yet after thirty minutes he was done for. Even for Clyde the pace had been way too high. Dennis Bergkamp told me that it took him six months to adapt to the English style. Once he got used to it, though, he started to perform really well. Those first weeks were very demanding but eventually I managed to adapt successfully. It was the time when English football began to be influenced by European players. Clubs such as Arsenal, Manchester United, Chelsea and Liverpool increasingly bought players from the continent. Eventually smaller clubs started to follow suit.

George Graham demanded a great deal from his players. He was always on top of the team. He had to be because we weren't a first-rate side. I think he wanted to create an atmosphere in which we as a group wouldn't get intimidated by other, more skilled teams. We had no great players, none of us were stars. Our strength lay in our collective will. I think Graham's strategy was very successful in that respect. I thought he was excellent in his management skills. He knew how to create something with the team. He quickly picked up the qualities of every player, and, perhaps even more importantly, he understood the shortcomings of every player. He made the very most out of the players he had.

Graham had one small deficiency, in my opinion. After the 1998 World Cup I felt really tired, but just nine days after the tournament finished I had to report back to Leeds. I hadn't had enough time to rest and recuperate. That's why I started off my second season with Leeds exhausted, physically as well as mentally. I asked Graham for an extra holiday but he refused to grant it to me. In Holland, all the national players got at least three weeks off, as did most of the guys playing abroad. It wasn't a smart move by Graham, and it served neither me nor the team well.

There were other footballers at Leeds who had played for their national teams at the World Cup Finals, but they had all been eliminated at least a week before Holland were knocked out. The few days I did have off I spent in Barbados, together with my girlfriend Nellie, just lying on the beach relaxing. I gained three kilos during that time, but lost them as soon as I returned. This policy of resting players has been adopted by Arsene Wenger at Arsenal. The only difference is that he has a much better squad of players than George Graham did in 1997 at Leeds United. These are the types of manager who make players perform five to ten per cent better than their optimum. The Dutchmen Louis van Gaal and Guus Hiddink are of the same calibre.

It was clear from the outset that there was no fooling around with Graham. He always approached us very sure of his ideas. Every day he would emphasize defence over and over again. Eventually, it became our strength. Graham would rather win 1–0 than 4–1, for 1–0 meant a clean sheet. However, I still wanted the ball all the time. 'Just pass me the ball and everything will be all right,' I would say.

It didn't always turn out all right, of course. I had this boldness in me, you know. We had to create more scoring opportunities, which was part of the reason I had come from Boavista. I was convinced much more should be happening up front. I would make that clear on the pitch sometimes, which some people would not always take very well. People who didn't know me thought I was arrogant. Some people thought I was difficult because I would often express directly what I wanted. In Holland it's quite normal to express yourself like that, but the English are much more indirect. In Holland you can say, 'Do this' and 'Just do that', which is then done without much fuss. In England you have to say, 'Would you please do this?' People have to be 'pleased' more over here.

I often offered myself to receive a pass during a match, but my team-mates and I wouldn't always be on the same wave-length. George Graham saw me struggling early on, so he put me on the bench for a while until I got the hang of the system. On the other hand, he would sometimes do the reverse during training sessions and the team then had to adapt to my playing style. Really, a lot of practice went into that. A few matches on, I became used to the differences and started to score again.

On 23 November 1997 I netted twice in a 3–1 win against West Ham which took us to fourth in the Premiership. More and more supporters were coming to watch us at Elland Road and we started to attract over 30,000 people regularly. By Christmas, however, I had only scored five league goals, which wasn't satisfactory. Only after Christmas did things start to work out for me. On Boxing Day, against Aston Villa, I scored our goal in a 1–1 draw. By the end of the season I had scored twenty-six goals in all competitions, sixteen of them in the Premiership.

I often heard others say that I was a selfish player, only interested in scoring myself. However, the statistics present a different picture. I was often ranked among the top ten players for the most assists. It was unfortunate that this wasn't taken into account when people made their judgments. It must be said though that in England, the number of goals you score is so important. I could play a terrible game, but as long as I scored it didn't matter.

Gary Kelly was in that Leeds team. Gary was a real weirdo, a complete nutter, really. He would grab players from the opposing team during the match and kiss them on the mouth. Everyone would be in tears of laughter. On the last day of my first season with Leeds United Gary placed a small line of Deep Heat in my underwear. I didn't know about it nor had I seen him do it, so I just put my underwear back on. Really, it was damn hot. I went right back into the showers to take it off, but that wasn't so easy. The other guys, of course, were in stitches.

We had several more strange guys in our team. David Wetherall, in fact, really did not fit in our squad. He was the perfect gentleman, a high-society guy who spoke the Queen's English. The Norwegian Alf-Inge Haaland made his debut in the same season as I did, having come from Nottingham Forest. Haaland was a cool fellow. Gunnar Halle was the sweetest player in our group. He wouldn't even hurt a fly. He truly was one of the nicest and most considerate players I ever met. He was very polite. It is often said that polite people don't stand a chance in football, but I think he actually continued playing until he was thirty-eight. He showed me that it is possible to be civil and to be a footballer. Gunnar was the diametric opposite to that strange Irishman Gary Kelly.

Another player who seriously shocked me once during a game was David Hopkin. He joined the club at around the same time as I did. David was the most expensive acquisition of that season. Leeds United had bought him for £3.25 million from Crystal Palace. He didn't have any teeth, but I didn't know that at the time. The first time I met him he was wearing dentures. David was a great guy, really first class, nothing to complain about. Except for that one time when he shocked me out of my skin.

We were playing a pre-season match in Ireland. I was under the impression that I had got to know David quite well, as he had stayed at Oulton Hall with me. I had seen him every day at breakfast, smiling at me with his beautiful shining teeth. During the match he came up to me and tried to tell me something. I didn't understand, but he kept on mumbling. I thought, 'Are you taking the piss or what? I'm not going to fall for that. Besides, it's not the time nor the place to joke around like that.'

So I said, 'Come on, man, speak normally.'

He looked at me as if to say, 'What are you talking about?'

Then it dawned on me, and I replied in shock, 'My God, you don't have any teeth! I didn't know!'

'My teeth are still in the changing room,' he replied. 'I always leave them there. Do you want me to hold them in my hands when we play?'

After the game David put his teeth back in and everything was back to normal. You should have seen our conversation on the pitch then, it was hilarious. I had no idea, and was truly shocked when I noticed his teeth had gone missing. Needless to say, I have also had my fair share of knocks as a professional footballer, but fortunately I still have all my own teeth!

Robert Molenaar played in the centre of the defence at Leeds. He performed well there, but although Robert was strong and big he wanted to do more than just kick the ball into touch. He had good vision, but back then George Graham just wanted him to defend well and nothing more. However, Robert wanted to show that he had more skills than just a hard-tackling defender, and he was often frustrated by the manager's style. Robert and I got to know each other well and often spent time together with our girlfriends.

These days I don't see as many people from Leeds United, although I sometimes go for a drink with Lucas Radebe. David Hopkin, who lived in the house across from me, is now back in Scotland, and I occasionally speak with Bruno Ribeiro and Robert Molenaar on the phone.

George Graham had arrived at Leeds United one year before me, and he had saved the club from relegation. He had replaced Howard Wilkinson, the manager for the previous eight seasons, in September 1996. We finished fifth in our first season together, qualifying for the UEFA Cup after finishing behind champions Arsenal, Manchester United, Liverpool and Chelsea.

Leeds United are a club with a long tradition. First known as Leeds City, it was founded in 1904 when it replaced the Holbeck Club on Elland Road. In 1919 Leeds City was disbanded after it was found to have paid its footballers during the First World War, contrary to regulations. Later that year the club was reborn as Leeds United. The club has won the league title three times, most recently in 1992, the last season before the Premier League was introduced. Leeds have also won the FA

Cup (in 1972) and the League Cup and UEFA Cup (both in 1968) when Don Revie was the manager.

The biggest standard-bearers for the club have been Jack Charlton and Billy Bremner, who played twenty and seventeen seasons for United respectively. Other people always associated with the club include leading scorer Peter Lorimer, who notched 238 goals in seventeen years.

When we qualified for the UEFA Cup, I noticed that people from the club and the fans started to believe that history was going to repeat itself. They felt that fifth place was only the beginning. George Graham was responsible for this newfound belief.

Towards the end of the season we received more and more attention. We were criticized more often by the press and by the other clubs, which was actually a good sign. It meant that we were a club to be reckoned with. Graham got more publicity too. Not only that, it was finally positive publicity. After his self-inflicted problems the press now started to write stories praising him.

We played well on the counter-attack but when we had to force the game ourselves, we ran into trouble. In away games, when the opponents were under pressure to make something happen, things were a lot easier. We picked up three points at Crystal Palace where Rod Wallace and I took care of the goals in a 2–0 win. At Derby County on 15 March we even won 5–0. I scored one there. Then we beat Chelsea 3–1 at home, thanks to two goals from me and one from David Wetherall. Three weeks later I scored twice in a 3–3 home draw with Coventry City. Next, we were beaten 3–0 by Manchester United and in our last competitive match of the season we drew 1–1 at home against Wimbledon. In the FA Cup we lost 1–0 in the sixth round at home to Wolverhampton Wanderers.

In April I was chosen as footballer of the month for the third time. I had also come second and third during other club votes. In May, I was runner-up again, behind Lucas Radebe, who had been chosen an impressive four times as player of the month.

In my second season we got off to a very good start in the league, taking points in each of the first seven matches. I scored the winner in our first home match, a 1–0 win on 24 August 1998 against Blackburn Rovers. Clyde Wijnhard gave me the assist after which I scored from twenty yards with a powerful shot. We drew with Middlesbrough and Wimbledon, but then we won 3–0 against Southampton. This was followed by 0–0 draws against Everton and Aston Villa and a 3–3 draw with Tottenham Hotspur. It was Leeds United's best start to the season since the Second World War.

We also played in the UEFA Cup. In the first round against Marítimo we won 1–0 at home thanks to my goal, and away we lost by the same score. Fortunately we went through on penalties. In the second round we played against AS Roma. We lost 1–0 in Rome, having earlier played out a 0–0 draw at home so we were done with European football by 20 October.

A month earlier George Graham had suddenly quit as manager. He signed a contract with Tottenham Hotspur after the Swiss manager Christian Gross was fired on 5 September. He had wanted to go back to London as he really missed the city. On top of that, he had already got as much as he could out of the players, so his goal had been accomplished. I understood his decision, but it was a hard one to accept. I told him that I would leave if he went, in the hope of keeping him at Leeds. Unfortunately my words couldn't change his mind.

Despite the departure of George Graham our team kept on growing. After the summer several players had joined, such as Clyde Wijnhard, who strengthened us up front. Wijnhard had come from the Dutch side Willem II. Assistant manager David O'Leary was appointed by the board as Graham's successor. O'Leary did very well, because he immediately threw in some of the younger players. These young men had good technical ability, which enabled us to play a much more attractive game. It was clear that David O'Leary grew with the team, as he improved as a manager too. The strange thing was that he hardly ever led the training sessions himself. George Graham had always done so, but the new boss left it to his assistant Eddie Gray, who had been the manager of the youth team the previous season. Gray had built a good reputation as a coach and was able to develop and improve the players, and was worth double the money he received. He liked to focus on passing and holding on to the ball, which was a very European approach, similar, in fact, to David O'Leary's.

It was clear that Eddie Gray was pushing for the younger players to get more opportunities in the first team, and rightly so. Alan Smith was exceptionally talented but Ian Harte and Jonathan Woodgate were very good players as well. The same goes for Steven McPhail. After Robert Molenaar, Clyde Wijnhard and myself, another Dutch player joined the squad, Willem Korsten. Having come from Vitesse, he was a very technically gifted lad. Unfortunately, he also proved to be very susceptible to injuries.

When David O'Leary was at training sessions, he often wouldn't say anything. He was good at being the boss, though. He had watched his predecessor George Graham very closely. It felt slightly odd since not so long ago he had been the assistant. I therefore had certain reservations regarding his relationship with the players, but they proved to be unfounded. In my opinion a good assistant makes the players feel that they can trust him with anything. For some reason that didn't happen with David O'Leary, as there was always some distance between him and the rest of the group. So in that respect he was consistent when he became the manager. I had no complaints because I played in almost every match. I even finished as top scorer in the Premiership with eighteen goals, together with Michael Owen and Dwight Yorke. The club had a very good season, finishing fourth behind Manchester United, Arsenal and Chelsea, which meant we were entitled to participate in the Champions' League qualification rounds.

Some Leeds supporters felt that I abandoned them when I left the club after only two seasons. They often criticized me, saying, 'Jimmy was nobody before he joined Leeds. Nobody knew who he was, we were the ones who made him big. Now everyone knows him.' The fans expected more loyalty from me, and I understand that. But this loyalty had to come from both sides. It absolutely wasn't coming from the Leeds United board at that time. In the end, it all came down to the fact that I wanted to be treated properly. We did not part company in the proper way but I can honestly say that I never told my agent Humphry Nijman that I wanted to leave Leeds United. Even if I had been offered a bit less than I asked for, I would have stayed on. In those days my salary was not bad, but compared to others I was entitled to more.

In the second season I kept on scoring. Probably because of that the club wanted to renegotiate my contract, even though I still had two more seasons to go. The board wanted to talk, so we got round the table. Humphry made it clear that we wanted the negotiations to be concluded quickly. We weren't interested in haggling. We knew that other clubs were interested, and so did Leeds United. We told them how we would like to see the contract changed and made no exceptional demands. We also agreed to keep everything confidential.

They asked me, 'Do you want to stay at Leeds?' and I replied 'Yes, of course I do.' However, in my opinion, the financial incentives they offered me were poor. Clubs like Chelsea and Atlético Madrid were interested in signing me but Leeds United didn't even offer half of what we thought we could negotiate with Chelsea. Nonetheless talks with Leeds continued but weeks passed without an agreement being reached.

'Come on, then,' I said to the board, 'why don't you negotiate with Chelsea?'

I even had a talk with David O'Leary. I asked him, 'What is it that you want?'

'I want to keep you here. You are very important to me,' were his words.

'Then perhaps you can arrange for Leeds United to accommodate me more financially, because as the manager you probably have a large say in the matter.'

I became more and more convinced that Leeds didn't want to keep me. Their position seemed to harden with time, confirming my suspicions. The season had now finished and preparations for the following season were already well underway. Yet still we had no agreement.

Eventually we became sick of the delay, and so Humphry asked the board, 'Name an amount. How much would you like to ask for Jimmy?'

The answer was resolute. 'We are not selling Jimmy. He still has a contract for two more seasons.'

I told Humphry, 'Leeds are right. I signed for four years, so I will finish my term as it says in my contract, and then I will transfer for free.'

But that was not what Leeds had in mind. Humphry asked the club again, 'For what amount do you want to sell him?'

Again they told my agent that I wasn't allowed to leave and that if I wanted to go, I should apply for a transfer myself. But when you do something like that in this country, you don't get any signing-on money. If the club wants to sell you, however, you do get this money. Then stories started to appear in the papers about my probable departure from Leeds, even though we hadn't spoken to the press.

We became more and more upset. The atmosphere was truly awful. We knew that Atlético Madrid were prepared to pay £10 million for me. In the end that was the amount which Leeds United got for me. It was reported that it was £12 million I was sold for. The figure wasn't important to me, but it annoyed me that it made Ridsdale look better than he deserved.

Chelsea were also prepared to put a lot of money on the table, but we knew that Leeds would never sell me to an English club. In the end Ridsdale told me, 'Jimmy, you have to apply for a transfer request with the board.' Subsequently Humphry made certain written agreements with Leeds United. Among other things, it was agreed that I would get my signing-on money, despite applying for a transfer request.

I told Ridsdale, 'I will sign the transfer request, but don't inform the press, because then I will still have a chance of staying on.'

Imagine my surprise when the next morning my transfer request was all over the media. I never figured out why it was brought out in the open, but it was now clear that Leeds United wanted to get rid of me and I was the one to be blamed. Ridsdale told Humphry that Leeds wanted to sign Emile Heskey from Leicester City to replace me and only then would I be able to leave without any problems. The only problem was that Heskey couldn't reach an agreement with Leeds, so Ridsdale suddenly revoked his permission for me to speak with Atlético Madrid.

A big conflict arose. Humphry took advice from some of the best lawyers in England. Then he called Peter Ridsdale and told him that he had four hours to give us permission to resume talks with Atlético Madrid or else he would call a press conference in London the next day, and would invite two major nationwide television channels. Within half an hour Ridsdale had backed down.

Leeds had bought me for £2 million and I think they just wanted to cash in. They would sell me for £12 million, it was announced, and that money would be used to invest in new players. I had quickly made a name in England, so I could be sold at a vast profit.

The Leeds United chairman appeared as if he had done something good. In fact, the opposite was true. He had planted a knife in my back. He knew exactly how our negotiations had proceeded and what I had said. I told him several times that I didn't want to leave, that I only wanted an increase in salary. I knew what I was worth, and how my salary compared with the other players. I repeatedly told him, 'Let's just settle it.' It should have remained a man-to-man, word-for-word agreement with everything staying between us, but the next day he had told his side of the story to the papers. When I read his version of events, I was speechless.

Peter Ridsdale loved publicity. I have never seen a chairman who was more in the news than his players. He ended up buying one centre-forward after another: Mark Viduka joined for £6 million, Robbie Keane for £12 million, then Robbie Fowler for £11 million. They also paid £18 million for defender Rio Ferdinand. They were throwing around money as if it was sand, even though the club's youth set-up was superb. Great young players like Alan Smith, Ian Harte and Jonathan Woodgate were all about to come through the ranks. The problem for the club was that they were thinking too big. Everything began to go wrong within a year of my transfer. Qualification for the Champions' League had led to vastly improved television and sponsorship contracts but they then spent so much money they could no longer afford not to finish in the top four. Even now they are still paying money owed to several of their players. Of course, clubs in the First Division can't afford to pay as much as those in the Premiership, while the players, of course, demand the salaries written in their contracts.

I still appeared in the Leeds United team photograph ahead of the 1999/2000 season. I was told to appear in the photo so I did, even though everyone knew by then that I was likely to be leaving.

I had a wonderful time at Leeds United. I try to watch their matches when they are playing on television, but I don't have time to visit. Perhaps, subconsciously, I don't make the time for it. In the end I didn't leave with very good feelings. A lot of players return to their old clubs but I don't see myself returning to Leeds. It's a different matter with Chelsea. In London I left with very good feelings. Recently Ken Bates, my chairman at Chelsea, has become chairman of Leeds United. Life is full of surprises, isn't it! I've always got along very well with him and with his wife Suzannah.

The manner in which I left the club rankled with me, because I would never have become the player I am now without Leeds United. George Graham took a gamble on me, and it worked out so I am actually very grateful to them, and when I played there the fans were extremely good to me. It is, of course, nice when you're loved, but when I left I experienced the other side of the coin. The fans didn't know the whole story, and it was unfortunate that I could not say anything in my defence at that time. Now that I can speak my mind and describe how in my view the chairman destroyed the club, it feels like a weight off my shoulders.

I think that the Dutch people are regarded in England as being very open. We are a very direct bunch of people who know where they want to go. The British also know what they want, but they are much less open about it. I find that British courtesy superficial. The British appear very open minded, but then they get very uptight when it comes to sex.

In England you don't often see naked women on television. Even in a soft-porn movie, you actually don't see very much. Should you want to, in Holland you can often see people having sex on television if you stay up late enough. It's very normal there. I think the British employ double standards. For example, in Holland you will not find any newspaper showing a naked girl on page three. I think the Dutch type of openness is better.

The number of teenage pregnancies is much higher in England than it is in the Netherlands. Perhaps that's because it's extremely rare for people to talk about sex openly here. But behind closed doors the British are more naughty than we Dutchmen.

In England people also need to be 'pleased' more. If you ask someone 'Can you do this?' they will reply with a curt 'What?' Only if you add 'please' will they do what you asked. Of course, it is courtesy. I find it good when a child speaks like that, but when adults start fussing about it, it's too much for my taste.

Another thing I noticed when I arrived here was that people eat chips with vinegar. It's disgusting! I can't understand how people can lick their lips about that. The way I learned to eat chips, dipped in mayonnaise and ketchup, on the other hand, seems to be unheard of here. I love Yorkshire puddings on the other hand. Sometimes I have dinner over at the house of my friend Karim Amrouch. His wife Lesley will almost always cook me a wonderful dinner. They are really down-to-earth people who will tell me, 'Come on, Jimmy, get normal!' whenever I go too far. Their interest in me is genuine. With some other people I am often surprised, and that's the polite way to put it.

As more games are played in England than in Portugal there is less training. In Portugal, training usually took place twice a day. At Leeds we also trained twice, but the second session was often quite light. On Tuesdays we usually had an extra half hour of endurance training. I have never felt that training day-in day-out would make a difference. Sometimes if you do too much you can become more susceptible to injury.

I had to have an operation for the first time two years ago when I was playing for Chelsea. One of my veins had narrowed and had to be replaced. As a footballer there is not much you can do about that. The doctors replaced the vein in my knee.

I must admit I prefer to be treated by my own physiotherapist, Guido Couwenberg. If I have to I will have him flown over from the Netherlands, especially if I've torn a muscle or need to be completely loosened up. I have him take care of my muscle cramps once a month. He will come over for two or three days from his practice in Amsterdam. I've used him for more than eight years as I first got to know him during my time at Neerlandia when he was doing his internship. Whenever I have a muscle problem I only want to be treated by him.

Of course, all the clubs I have played for have had their own physiotherapists. And whenever I had torn a muscle, like I did at Leeds or Atlético, then they have treated me as well, but if I were to finish treatment at, say, 12 noon, I would have Guido give me some more attention at home. The torn muscle healed much faster that way. The clubs knew about his existence but they didn't have any problems with that.

On 3 May 2005 Lucas Radebe had his testimonial at Leeds United, and I played for the old Leeds team. In Holland testimonial matches are fairly rare but in England it is common to have one after you've played for a long time with one club. Loyalty is duly credited here. I had expected to get harassed by the Leeds fans, but it didn't happen. I even received applause from the Leeds supporters, which was very nice. The club has some of the best followers in England. The fans are just really passionate about their team. The stadium was almost completely full for Lucas, which is very rare for a testimonial. The fact that they turn up in large numbers even when the club is not playing at the top level says something about their loyalty. For one moment on that night, the memories of those two wonderful years filled with fun and crazy footballers came flashing back to me. Despite everything that had happened, it was once again a great pleasure to play for Leeds United.

5 Oranje

The first time I was called up to play for the Dutch national team was at the end of the 1997–98 season. I had scored eighteen goals in my first season in the Premiership and that accomplishment hadn't slipped the watchful eye of the national manager. Guus Hiddink came to watch our second-to-last home game of the season, against Coventry City, and I scored twice in a 3–3 draw. One week earlier Ronald Spelbos, a former player for Oranje, AZ and Ajax, had come to watch me play against Bolton Wanderers where I had scored in a 3–2 victory.

I only found out afterwards that Guus Hiddink had come to watch me play when George Graham told me about it. The next day Hiddink called me to say that I had been selected for the national squad. I was one of two surprise inclusions in the squad, along with Edgar Davids. Davids had at last been forgiven for an incident at Euro 96 when he had insulted both Hiddink and the team captain Danny Blind. I was exhilarated and millions of thoughts raced through my mind. I had been selected for the Dutch national squad and was probably going to participate in the World Cup Finals of 1998 in France.

Michael Mols had been on Hiddink's list of prospective players, but apparently he had not impressed the manager enough. Another option, Youri Mulder, had suffered a long-term knee injury. Hiddink kept a spot open for him until the very last moment, but unfortunately his injury still needed more time to heal. Other players to miss out on selection included Johan de Kock, Jean-Paul van Gastel, Peter Hoekstra, Andre Ooijer and Ferdy Vierklau.

After the decision had been made public my phone didn't stop ringing. My eldest brother, Franklin, asked me if I could arrange Dennis Bergkamp's autograph for him, and whether I could get him tickets for every World Cup match. At the very least he wanted to see all the Oranje games, and wanted to follow me around France. And that's exactly what the idiot did! But at that time I was still rather wary. I had no idea what to make of the rest of the guys in the squad. Fortunately, I hadn't booked any holidays so my selection didn't create any scheduling problems for me.

The first time I had to report for duty at Huis ter Duin in Noordwijk was on 21 May 1998. I didn't know any of the players socially. I had encountered Dennis Bergkamp at Arsenal and Ed de Goey at Chelsea once or twice, but we had hardly exchanged any words. I had never even spoken to most of the players. I knew who Patrick Kluivert was, of course. I had seen him around in Amsterdam nightclubs but even that didn't amount to much more than a brief hello and a nod of the head. It was as if I had just arrived in a new country, with a new squad where everyone was still finding their way. I was quite nervous because I really had no idea what to think nor what to expect.

The first person to speak to me was Aron Winter. He told me, 'You shouldn't think you are less than the others. You have to deal with things that way.' I thought, 'Wow! Here is the famous Aron Winter giving me advice!' The fact that Winter was looking after me made me feel very special.

I initially thought that some players were to be eliminated from the World Cup party and was expecting to have to prove myself, but to my surprise I was already part of the final squad. That's why when I first arrived there I didn't dare to be truly cheerful. After all, I hadn't even played one minute with them, and had not had a chance to prove myself.

That opportunity came a little later at our training camp in Nyon, in Switzerland. We played against Lausanne Sport and beat them 4–1. I played the first 45 minutes, and it went rather well, particularly as I scored. Wearing the national jersey of the Netherlands was a special feeling, even though it wasn't an official international match. It was still a big step up for me. Initially I played without thinking much but later on I was able to consider positioning and strategy. There was no time for failure, because we would soon be playing at the World Cup Finals for real. It had to be perfect from the start.

It wasn't easy. Most of the other guys already knew each other since they had played together before. They knew each other's games. I felt a little like a foreigner. Perhaps you can compare it to an Australian who goes to England, and who despite speaking the same language, feels like a stranger. Of course, previously I had been new to both Portugal as well as England, but at least then I had had some time to adjust to the situation. This time we had to be a team after a mere three to four weeks.

After our training camp in Nyon we returned to Holland and settled down in the Veluwe, a Dutch nature reserve, staying at the Residence Victoria hotel in Hoenderloo. From there we travelled to the various stadiums for our warm-up matches.

My first official match playing for Oranje was against Cameroon in the Gelredome stadium in Arnhem, on 27 May 1998. I found out later that I had become the 629th Dutch international football player. The game ended in a 0–0 draw, and we didn't really play well, partly because several players were struggling with some minor injuries. Dennis Bergkamp, for example, was not completely fit.

Our second practice match, against Paraguay in Eindhoven on 1 June, was much better. I scored once in a 5–1 victory. A few days later we played another friendly, our send-off for the World Cup in front of our own fans, in Amsterdam against Nigeria. I scored again, and once more we won 5–1.

The atmosphere was pleasant as we left for France feeling confident. Although I had contributed during the preparations I was told that I would not be starting the first match. I had expected that it would be very difficult to get into the team, as we had so many great forwards, with Patrick Kluivert, Dennis Bergkamp and Pierre van Hooijdonk in the middle and Boudewijn Zenden and Marc Overmars on the flanks. Scoring two goals out of ten was not a bad effort, but not quite remarkable enough. It was a very exciting time though. Until the beginning of the World Cup preparations I had never played for Oranje, so every minute I played was good.

For the World Cup, my brother Carlos and friend Oswald Snip travelled back and forth from Holland to France, while my other brother Franklin stayed in towns close to where the Dutch squad was billeted. In order to get enough time off from work, he had called in sick with his employer, which almost got him fired when they found out. I don't think he would have minded that at all, though. He was crazy about football, and was always there for our training sessions and matches. There was nothing he wouldn't have done in order to be there.

My sisters also came to watch the first game in Paris. We played our first World Cup match on 13 June against Belgium in the sold-out new French national stadium, the Stade de France. Fortunately, it was easy to get tickets for the whole family. My agent, Humphry Nijman, was also very proud. He had always told me to keep working hard because then I would be noticed. He was right.

As one or two players weren't fully fit I ended up starting the match, together with Edwin van der Sar, Aron Winter, Jaap Stam, Frank de Boer, Arthur Numan, Ronald de Boer, Philip Cocu, Marc Overmars, Clarence Seedorf, and Patrick Kluivert. I wasn't doing too badly, but I missed an opportunity. It wasn't an easy chance, but also not too difficult. In hindsight I really should have scored. Normally, I would score eight out of ten times in a similar situation. Had I scored, it would have been the winning goal as the game finished 0–0, and I would probably have stayed on the field much longer. Perhaps I would have kept my starting position for longer as well.

Dennis Bergkamp was returning to fitness, and he and Patrick Kluivert had already made a name with Oranje and at their own clubs. Dennis replaced me after about two-thirds of the game. He was a world-class player back then and had been named the best player in the Premier League that season. He had been injured just before the FA Cup Final and had only had a month to recover.

Patrick Kluivert left the field with a red card in that match after the Belgian defender Lorenzo Staelens provoked him. Little Pat lost control, and elbowed the Belgian who, in turn, was a little too eager to fall to the ground. Since Kluivert was now suspended for two matches, against South Korea and Mexico, I thought I would regain my starting position, alongside Dennis Bergkamp, who was getting back into shape. However, I was on the bench at the start against South Korea and didn't leave it for the rest of the match.

Guus Hiddink completely changed round the team, leaving me dejected on the bench. Cocu played in my position, next to Dennis Bergkamp and Marc Overmars against South Korea as we won easily, 5–0. Pierre van Hooijdonk was the one to come on for Bergkamp. In our third group match against Mexico Guus Hiddink started with Cocu, Bergkamp and Overmars again. This time, however, I replaced Bergkamp twelve minutes from time. The game ended 2–2 and we had qualified for the next stage as winners of group E.

During the first match I had been replaced by Bergkamp, while in the third match I replaced him. Unfortunately I wasn't able to play with him. It's not that I have preferences about whom I play with up front, but Bergkamp is a very special footballer, and I would have loved to have played with him. I think I formed a very good partnership with Patrick Kluivert. He suited me best. I believe that, apart from Dennis Bergkamp of course, I also suited Kluivert best.

I shared my hotel room with Giovanni van Bronckhorst. The senior players had their own rooms, which was fine by me. Giovanni and I have been very good friends ever since. Our girlfriends also liked each other very much. Our contact has faded a little bit though since he moved to Barcelona and I broke up with my girlfriend, Nellie.

I also spent a lot of time with Aron Winter and Patrick Kluivert, and to a lesser extent with our captain, Frank de Boer. He kept a bit more to himself. His twin brother, Ronald, was always the joker. He is a really funny guy. Jaap Stam was also very quiet, and he always stuck with Philip Cocu and the other PSV players Boudewijn Zenden and Wim Jonk.

There was some tension between Edgar Davids and myself. Our characters are diametric opposites. Sometimes we got along fine, other times we couldn't. Perhaps it was because we are both very stubborn, although I must say that he was much more stubborn than I was. You never knew quite where you were with him – he could change his mood 180 degrees in no time. I never had any real big issues with him, but he was not somebody you could always rely on. When we went out at night, he was fun and sociable, but the next day he could completely close himself off and not tolerate any kind of interruption.

With the others at least I knew what to expect. Clarence Seedorf was very talkative – he would chatter like an old lady and never shut up. I don't mean it in an unkind way, but he is also extremely stubborn. He always had to know better than you did, no matter what the subject was. For example, if you said something was blue, Seedorf would insist it was green, despite that fact that I don't think he is colour blind. It really drove me up the wall sometimes. On the other hand, he is a very sociable guy, and very group-oriented.

Patrick Kluivert was always the little boy of the group. Even though he would do the strangest or most unacceptable things within or outside the group, you just couldn't stay angry with him for long. He was usually the first to be up for adventure during the training camp.

Aron Winter was the heart and soul of the group. I often saw him light a huge cigar and stick it in his mouth. It was a ridiculous sight, but he smoked cigars like a chimney. Dennis Bergkamp usually remained in the hotel, together with Wim Jonk and Ed de Goey, who was one of the substitute goalies. I hardly saw those players in town, while the others would go out. I had a great time then, although at the end of the World Cup I just wanted to go home.

I enjoyed working with Guus Hiddink, but the training sessions run by Ronald Koeman, Johan Neeskens and Frank Rijkaard were also a fantastic experience. Those were foot-ballers who had won European Cups. It was especially exciting to work with Frank Rijkaard, who had always been my idol. After the second group game against South Korea he came to talk to me. I told him that I felt a little stiff in my legs. It was apparent that he didn't consider that very professional of me because he asked what would have happened if I had been asked to go on as a substitute. Not awaiting my answer, he immediately called the physiotherapist and had me massaged.

After coming on for Dennis Bergkamp against Mexico I never got another opportunity to play in France. I can't say whether that was the right decision. I didn't think I had screwed up but, then again, I hadn't shown everything I was capable of, in particular as I hadn't scored. Frank Rijkaard's criticism hit me hard. Later on however, I was happy that he had criticized me that way, because it gave me something to work on. At least I had played two matches in the World Cup and nobody would be able to take that away from me. Playing for Oranje didn't make me arrogant. There wasn't really any reason to act the big celebrity since I wasn't one of the stars of the Dutch team. The people on the street would look first to Dennis Bergkamp or Patrick Kluivert. It's different in England. A few months ago Michael Reiziger mentioned that he had noticed how often I was stopped here, whereas in Holland I remained largely anonymous, probably because I never played for a big club like Ajax, Feyenoord or PSV.

My biggest disappointment of the 1998 World Cup is that I didn't score. It's also too bad that we didn't win the trophy. We were better than Brazil in our semi-final on 7 July but we had no luck. Moments into the second half we went behind 1–0 thanks to a goal by Ronaldo. Then, just before the final whistle Patrick Kluivert equalized to make it 1–1. There were no further goals, so penalties would decide the match. We missed two, the first by Philip Cocu and the second by Ronald de Boer, and so lost the shootout. My God, how Frank de Boer was angry with his twin brother! They had lost the opportunity of playing in the World Cup Final, and Frank was cursing his brother to hell, right in front of everyone. I was a little shocked to see that. But I suppose you can always say a little bit more to your brother than to other people, even on the pitch.

After the match we were physically broken and mentally drained. A few days later we had to play the third-place play-off against Croatia but it soon became apparent that the squad had lost all its motivation. We finished in fourth place, when we felt that we should have been playing in the final. We had grown throughout the tournament as a group and it had a positive effect on the quality of our game. According to many, we were playing the best football of the tournament.

I talked about it sometime later with Marcel Desailly, who played together with me at Chelsea for a few seasons. He told me that he was so happy that Brazil had beaten us. He had been so scared of Holland and told me, 'If we had had to play against you guys, our team would have lost.' That was a great compliment from a great champion. Of course, it makes no difference. France became the world champions while we remained empty-handed.

During the tournament we read Dutch newspapers in our hotel and watched Dutch television, so we knew what the mood was like back in Holland. I gave a few television interviews with Henk Spaan, which I think went all right. He was a really nice man, who asked me several good questions. It was a good opportunity for me, because I hadn't given many interviews in Holland before then. The British press approached us at a much later stage, after their own national team had been eliminated. Most of the English press were interested in Dennis Bergkamp, although I was also interviewed several times. We were careful to tread cautiously because of all the media attention.

A few weeks before the World Cup in France the Dutch paper *Het Algemene Dagblad* had come out with a World Cup special filled with features on all the Dutch players. I was not featured because I only made the squad at the very last moment. The players received something like 9,000 euros per person for the interviews. In Holland that was new, although in England such things had been around for a while. They're much more advanced here in that respect. For example, if you've played for England the English PFA might call to ask whether you could be present at an official opening in your local area. If you do go, you can get paid really well. In Holland, such things work differently. Former footballers are less likely to be called up to attend such events. In England they really love ex-footballers and treat them like celebrities.

After the World Cup in France I immediately went on holiday, since there were only nine days off before I had to go back to Leeds United. During that holiday I just rested and slept. I was exhausted. Meanwhile Hiddink's assistant Frank Rijkaard was appointed as the new national manager even though he had no previous experience as a coach. I was initially happy with his appointment but I became quickly disillusioned. It took more than one season before I was called up by him. I was finally picked on 18 August 1999 for a friendly match against Denmark. It was when I had just signed with Atlético Madrid.

We started the match with Patrick Kluivert, Ruud van Nistelrooy and I all up front but it didn't work at all. Rijkaard replaced me ten minutes before the end with Clarence Seedorf but it didn't make much difference as the game ended in a 0–0 draw. I felt that the new Dutch national coach didn't have much faith in me and that certainly didn't help me to perform with Oranje. Rijkaard was continuously experimenting with the team. He could afford to do so since Holland was the co-host of Euro 2000, together with Belgium. Rijkaard made us practise and practise and work through his different schemes. His rotation policy with the forwards didn't work, so I was sacrificed. For a while I wasn't part of the team, although I was selected when the others were not available, but then I often ended up sitting in the stands anyway. Six months after the Denmark game I played for ten minutes against Germany.

It was an annoying period. I was unable to turn down the offer to play for Oranje because I didn't think it was appropriate to snub the national team. However, I felt unwanted most of the time, even though I was convinced I was good enough. I was never given a real opportunity under Frank Rijkaard – if I played, it was usually for the last fifteen minutes which is not enough to show your full potential. Even when I did play there were six or seven other players who also felt they had to prove themselves on the field, so there was never a comfortable settled team on the pitch in which my role was clearly defined.

Most of the matches ended in draws, so I can't say that we had a very strong team under Rijkaard. At the European Championship itself, Holland didn't play very well. The 6–1 win in the quarter-finals against Yugoslavia was their best performance, but in the opening match against the Czech Republic Oranje had trouble beating them 1–0, and could only do so thanks to a lucky penalty. Frank de Boer took that chance one minute before the end. In the third group match Holland played a second-string French team since France had already qualified for the quarter-finals. Oranje won 3–2, after going 2–1 down.

Until right before Euro 2000 I was part of the twenty-five player national squad. After the training camp in Switzerland three players were to drop out. These proved to be André Ooijer, Winston Bogarde and myself. Winston Bogarde was injured, so that made sense. André Ooijer was pretty mad, and so was I, especially because I wasn't told by Rijkaard himself but by the captain, Frank de Boer. I didn't even hear it directly from him, but picked it up via other people who knew about an interview he had given after our last practice match in Lausanne.

I had half-expected that I wouldn't be going to Euro 2000, even though Ruud van Nistelrooy was injured. Dennis Bergkamp, Roy Makaay, Patrick Kluivert and Pierre van Hooijdonk were selected as the strikers. I thought it was a ridiculous selection. Peter van Vossen, who was at Ajax with Rijkaard in the mid-nineties, was also included. The whole thing just didn't add up. For two years I hadn't been given a proper chance even though I had proven myself in the Spanish as well as the English league. Apparently that didn't count.

After the European Cup I met Rijkaard in Sardinia. He said that if he were managing a club he would love to have me as a player, but I thought that was plain bullshit. Roy Makaay also never got a real chance for the sole reason that he never gave the manager a hard time. He was the same as me with Oranje. We are not the type to slam our fists on the table when we want something. I would do so at my club, but the national team is a different matter, that's more of an honour.

Frank Rijkaard really disappointed me, especially since he had played at the highest level himself. Maybe because of his background I expected something more from him, since he should have known exactly how the game is played. I think he just wanted to avoid any problems, especially with the press. I occasionally had the feeling that he was afraid to favour the coloured players because he was coloured himself. I'm not saying that was actually the case, it was just my feeling. For example, Clarence Seedorf was often put on the bench while lesser players were in the team.

Maybe my expectations of him were just too high. Since he had been my idol, I probably expected a little more from him. I didn't care about the fact that I was disappointed, but I did care about how I had been let down. He didn't give me a chance. In contrast, Guus Hiddink always made things very simple. That was his strength. He kept things short and clear. 'Boys, this is it, and that's the way we'll do it,' he would say. Guus Hiddink wasn't a very great footballer himself, but he was able to understand the players. Frank Rijkaard did win everything there is to win as a player, but as a coach he couldn't analyse your mind. I'm not the only one to have noticed that.

I couldn't bear to stay in Holland during Euro 2000 so I went to Jamaica and followed the tournament from there. I didn't think Holland played very well. I talked to my brother Franklin often by phone and he was even more annoyed about my non-selection than I was. He said that he wished Holland would lose all its matches because I hadn't been allowed to participate. Under normal circumstances he is Oranje's most loyal supporter, but not that time.

Rijkaard was lucky that he didn't have to go through the qualifying rounds. In total he only won four games, drew eleven and lost twice. It was hopeless, really. We even lost against Morocco, 2–1 in Arnhem. It was terrible. He selected thirty-five different players in seventeen matches. Doesn't that mean he never really knew what he was doing? The fact that Oranje played in the semi-finals was purely down to the quality of the players.

The most embarrassing moment was the replacement of Boudewijn Zenden against Italy. At the very last moment Peter van Vossen was selected to play. If you really needed a player who could score you should have put Pierre van Hooijdonk on the pitch. He is somebody who can make a difference in such situations. But he didn't play for a single minute. Why take him along then? I can't imagine that Rijkaard thought that van Vossen would be able to slice through the Italian defence and score. How old was van Vossen then? Thirty-two?

I returned to the squad when Louis van Gaal was appointed manager and we were trying to qualify for the 2002 World Cup. He said something very strange to me after he had announced the line-up for the match against Spain.

He extended his hand to me and said, 'Are you going to do it for me?'

I thought, 'What does he mean "are you going to do it for me?" What a strange question!'

Again he asked, 'Are you going to do it for me?'

'What do you mean?' I asked him.

'Are you going to do it for me?'

'No, I'm going to do it for myself,' upon which he replied 'OK,' and walked away.

I already knew van Gaal from Spain, where I had played with Atlético Madrid against his Barcelona team. I scored in our 2–1 victory against Spain in Seville, but was sent off after a clash with Fernando Hierro who also had to leave the pitch. Hierro had annoyed me throughout the whole game by constantly talking, making comments, using his elbows and basically trying to be a smart arse. I felt like getting my own back. Just after I scored and with about fifteen minutes to go, I stepped on his toe. Perhaps it wasn't totally by accident, but I just wanted to get him off my back. He then head-butted me, and I went down. It probably looked really bad. After that we continued wrestling for a little bit and we both got a red card. I was really upset about that.

As we both walked towards the side of the pitch I shouted to Hierro, 'You better start running because I'm coming after you!'

He sprinted towards his changing room with me about to chase after him. Edgar Davids shouted to Clarence Seedorf, 'Stop him! He's going to beat him up! He's really going to kill him!' So Seedorf grabbed hold of me and said, 'Jim, calm down. Just calm down.' A little later I was brought to the changing rooms by one of our physios. Philip Cocu was there. He had witnessed everything on television, and thought it was ridiculous what had happened.

After the match there was an interview with Spanish television, but I was still raving mad. Normally, after a game you can go out and have a beer together, forgive and forget, but not this time. I was still seething. I told the journalist, 'Normally I consider Fernando Hierro a very good footballer, but tonight he was a disaster. It's a disgrace that somebody like that can be captain of the Spanish national football team.' Under normal circumstances I would never say something like that after a match. Really, any clashes on the pitch are best left there and immediately forgotten. I was suspended for one match, so I was not able to play in the friendly against Turkey.

A few months later I was again part of the Dutch team, to play against Andorra in Barcelona on 24 March 2001. We won that World Cup qualifying match 5–0 and I scored the first goal. Patrick Kluivert scored the second before he was substituted by Pierre van Hooijdonk who scored another two goals. Pierre had been out of the team for a while so he was eager to show that he could still score. Mark van Bommel scored the final goal.

When we flew to Portugal we knew that victory would make us hot favourites to qualify for the World Cup. We played brilliantly until about ten minutes before the end, even leading 2–0 at one point but the game finished in a 2–2 draw. The home fans were deathly quiet, and it was not because of the rain. I was replaced by van Hooijdonk. I didn't understand why I wasn't replaced by a defensive midfielder, especially since Roy Makaay was playing on the right flank. Makaay could have played as a striker after I had left the field. That way we could have kept up the pressure on the Portuguese defence.

During the team meeting prior to the Portugal match, Louis van Gaal had placed the team formation on a white board with perfectly aligned little signs and pictures. He then started talking about penalties. 'So, who is going to take them?' he asked, and looked around. Nobody volunteered so he wrote my name on the board without asking me. When he had finished writing my name down, he said, '…or didn't you want to take them?' Van Gaal loved to put you on the spot. I liked that. I had to laugh and said, 'No, why shouldn't I? I'll take it.'

And of course a penalty was awarded, after only eighteen minutes. I was fouled, and we usually have the unofficial rule that if you are tackled you don't take the penalty yourself. But then Patrick Kluivert picked up the ball and handed it to me. I thought, 'If I miss this penalty, my career with Holland is over.' At that moment I didn't feel very confident, yet I didn't have the balls to tell Kluivert to take it himself. Happily the shot went in, giving us a 1–0 advantage. Afterwards I kissed the ground over and over again.

When I am taking a penalty I only place the ball on the spot at the last moment. Before that I pick it up and roll it in front of me. As the ball is not yet on the spot I don't have to think about how I will shoot. I postpone that thought as much as possible. The less time I have to think about it, the better it is for me. If you put the ball down immediately you often have to wait for some time before you are able to take the penalty, especially if the keeper is not ready. Ninety per cent of keepers have a side to which they prefer to dive. I know that because I always watch them. It is recorded somewhere on the hard disc inside my head. I often end up choosing the same corner as the keeper but the most important thing is that I always strike the ball with a lot of power.

People always say you should score from a penalty but taking a penalty is not a simple task. A lot of courage is needed. I always think that you show more courage by saying 'I'm not going to take the penalty' rather than by taking it. If you stand in front of 100 players and ask them to take a penalty, eighty of them would say yes. At least half of those eighty say yes because they don't want to look like a coward in front of the others. The other twenty say 'No, I'm not good at taking penalties, so I don't want to take them.' With penalties you can transform yourself from a national hero into a national joke in an instant. See what happened to David Beckham or Clarence Seedorf. You should only take a penalty when you're really not scared. I never refuse to take penalties myself because I am not afraid. The coach should know who his mentally strongest players are, and those are the ones who should take the penalties.

At Chelsea I took about thirteen or fourteen penalties. At Leeds I took six penalties and missed three, at Atlético Madrid I took one and in Portugal I took one as well. From about eighty penalties I missed perhaps ten per cent. Of course you have to consider the goalkeeper. The Dutch national keeper Edwin van der Sar knows how I take them, because we have often practised together. I have to think deeply about how he will expect me to take them. It's a big psychological game. Those are the hardest penalties for me, because I start thinking about how he is expecting me to shoot. I could try to place the ball in the corner with a powerful kick, but Edwin is so tall that I would probably have to put it in the inside of the side netting.

Not so long ago Chelsea were awarded a penalty in the last minute of a match against Fulham when we were 1–0 down. I had to think about what I should do as it was a really impor- tant opportunity and I was the player who had been brought down. In the end I gave the ball to Bolo Zenden and fortunately he beat Edwin. It wouldn't have been wise to take it myself.

I haven't spoken to Louis van Gaal for a long time but if we were to chat it would be in a very good atmosphere. I think he is a very honest man, and I like that. He is straight to the point so you know immediately what your role is. He was not a bully like many people have said. I've heard people say that with van Gaal as manager we had to train so hard, but it actually wasn't that much harder than under Dick Advocaat or Frank Rijkaard. The worst thing was that we often had running and fitness training. That was horrible. I wanted to play football, not just run. I think he was rightly criticized for that, because sometimes there was too much emphasis on the running.

He also had a problem with Ruud van Nistelrooy who didn't like him. I saw that for myself. Once during a training session they got into an argument. Jaap Stam told van Nistelrooy, 'Keep that goddamn ball with you for a change, will you?' to which Ruud replied, 'Get lost!' Louis van Gaal overheard them and was angry with van Nistelrooy. The manager, inches away from his face, said to him, 'So you think you know better, eh?' Ruud then mumbled something and Van Gaal exploded. 'What did you say? What did you say?' Ruud said, 'Nothing,' but you knew there was something between them.

In those days there was talk that Louis van Gaal would go to Manchester United to replace Alex Ferguson as manager, but van Nistelrooy told the powers-that-be at Old Trafford that if van Gaal came to the club, he would leave. I heard him say so myself.

Even though they didn't get along, van Gaal did select van

Nistelrooy when we played another crucial qualifier, against the Republic of Ireland in Dublin. I admired that in van Gaal. I think van Nistelrooy must have appreciated that too. After the match, which we lost 1–0, van Gaal shouted at us for quite some time. He told us that he was very disappointed in us, although he didn't mention any specific names. It was mostly about a handful of players who he felt had turned their backs on him. I think he was talking about a few players from Barcelona, but van Nistelrooy thought he was talking about him. The atmosphere then in that changing room was very tense, very charged. Everybody realized that we had screwed up. Losing an away game is acceptable, but we shouldn't have allowed ourselves to drop points to both Portugal and Ireland, and now our 2002 World Cup hopes were in ruins.

Five days later, on 5 September 2001 we played Estonia in the PSV stadium, after having been already eliminated from the World Cup Finals. The atmosphere in the stadium started off okay, but it became increasingly unpleasant. Patrick Kluivert received a huge whistling when his name was read out prior to the game. Mario Melchiot and Clarence Seedorf also got their own whistling concerts and I received mine when I came on as a substitute. I hadn't even played the whole game in Dublin, yet I was targeted by the boo boys in Eindhoven. Even *Voetbal International* wrote that it was strange that I was criticized. In the words of journalist Ted van Leeuwen, 'The spectators acted disgracefully, not our boys.'

The current Dutch national coach, Marco van Basten, has never selected either Clarence Seedorf, Edgar Davids, Patrick Kluivert or me for any of his squads. People have said and written things about the Surinamese players in the Dutch team who, in the past, would allegedly segregate themselves from the rest of the squad. However, that really never was an issue. In my time with Holland under Dick Advocaat, Louis van Gaal, Frank Rijkaard and Guus Hiddink, we had three big dining tables at which we always ate. The boys who were playing at PSV usually sat together. Sometimes we mixed and I would join them. I definitely never had any problems with any of the other Dutch players.

After a friendly match against Denmark on 10 November 2001, there was an incident in our hotel in Copenhagen that made the headlines. I didn't witness it, but I heard that a Danish friend of Patrick Kluivert had invited a group of models to a party in the hotel. Louis van Gaal saw these models going upstairs to the floor where the players were staying and lost his rag. He got security to check all the players' rooms, it was complete chaos, and the story made a big splash back in Denmark, where the national newspaper *Berlinske Tidende* wrote that the Danish pornstar Kira Eggers was one of the models involved.

Another time there was a problem at the team's hotel at Schipol airport. Van Gaal saw a pretty girl walking into the hotel and thought she had come to see one of the players. He was so angry that he called a team meeting, warning us that if he found out who was involved, that player's career would be over – and, what's more, he would inform the player's wife!

Fernando Ricksen was left out of the team by manager Dick Advocaat after misbehaving in the hotel and at the airport. You never hear anybody talk about that. On the other hand, if he had punished Ruud van Nistelrooy more sternly after he kicked everything down in the dugout after being taken off the whole country would have gone crazy. That incident marked the end for Dick Advocaat as national coach as he had clearly lost his grasp on the team. I think Willem van Hanegem could have done better as Advocaat's assistant by making more use of his standing but instead he was always laughing.

I sometimes feel that a lot of journalists just didn't want to see coloured footballers playing for Oranje. I felt that we coloured guys were not treated in the same way as the others. We always had to prove ourselves 200 per cent, time and time again. If something happened it was always one of the coloured players who was responsible. Once there was a small conflict between Edgar Davids and Mark van Bommel during a match in Eindhoven. Everything went wrong in the first half, but van Bommel didn't seem to want to know. The second half went much better and then van Bommel suddenly started barking orders, even to Edgar Davids who had been trying to give directions to the team in the first half. After the game Davids told van Bommel, 'You have to command when things are not going well, not when we are ahead by a wide margin. That's when we don't need it anymore. When things are going bad, that's when you should open your mouth.' Davids said it in that typical fierce manner of his.

There was another clash with van Nistelrooy during a team meeting. Ruud told Davids, 'You're always so fierce, man. Calm down a bit.' Edgar disagreed and told him so. Ruud then said something to the effect of, 'I have the feeling that you don't want to pass me the ball.' That really surprised Davids so he burst out, 'What the hell does that mean? I just want to win. And if you are in a good position, I'll play you the ball. And if you score I'm elated.' I thought the worst part was that van Nistelrooy actually thought that Davids wasn't passing the ball to him on purpose. This is the sort of thing that went on between the Dutch players. Of course, there is always somebody who you don't get along with as much, but in the end you are all team-mates and you play in a team in order to win. You don't have to be best friends, but you should be able to respect each other.

The problem with that Dutch team was that the players didn't want to play for each other. Every one thought he was the key player in the team. It wasn't that we had no leader, but the fact that everybody wanted to be in charge. Nobody would say, 'Why don't you go ahead and shine while I do the dirty work down here', which was how things had gone in 1998.

During Euro 2004 in Portugal it became a management problem. Everybody in the world could see that things weren't well between Patrick Kluivert and Ruud van Nistelrooy, so Kluivert sat on the bench for the whole tournament while van Nistelrooy played. How can you not have someone in your team who always performed in matches when it mattered and who had a fantastic goal average? Everybody knew that it was a ridiculous situation. Dick Advocaat needed to win, but Kluivert wasn't going on, not even as a substitute. I don't understand why he didn't get a start, because it was not as if the others were playing that well.

Suddenly, we had Rafaël van der Vaart playing behind the strikers. Very nice for him, but that guy hasn't done anything substantial yet. Van der Vaart has never ever pulled the team together. But all the journalists were parroting to each other that he should play instead of Kluivert, so that's what happened. I also didn't understand why Roy Makaay played so little. Roy is not the kind of guy with a big mouth. Apparently, having a big mouth is a necessity in order to play football. I never understood that. It's my opinion that the manager has to decide objectively who gets to play and who doesn't. He should completely disregard what others are whispering into his ear.

The line-ups for matches started appearing in the morning papers. The players themselves were passing the information on to the journalists. There were guys who would send text messages to their favourite journalists; I know who they were. It was stupid. It was just handing an advantage to the opposition. The only reason to do it was to stop journalists writing bad stories about you. Being friends with the press was oh so important. The atmosphere within the squad was totally ruined.

In Euro 2004 I will admit that Holland played well against the Czech Republic in the beginning, but everything fell apart after Arjen Robben was replaced. There were many other factors involved in team selection, not just the quality of the player. Edgar Davids didn't play at Inter last season, but can you name me a better midfielder than Davids? Clarence Seedorf was very stubborn when it came to obeying orders, but Marco van Basten and Johan Cruyff were also quite stubborn when they were playing. Somebody who dictates a game needs to be a little stubborn, I think.

When Dick Advocaat took charge, he gave me a chance immediately. On 21 August 2002 I came on as a substitute against Norway. It wasn't a very good game, although we won 1–0. After the game, Advocaat took me aside and told me that he wasn't very happy with my performance. He told me if I didn't play better I would lose my place in the squad. Of course, I wasn't happy with that threat, but at least I knew what was expected of me, and what to do next. I played against Belarus in the next game, scoring once. I stayed on the bench for the game against Austria and came on against Germany on 20 November 2002 when the score was 1–1. I scored to make it 2–1 and a little later van Nistelrooy made it 3–1. This proved to be my last international appearance as Advocaat didn't select me again. I have no idea why. Humphry Nijman phoned to tell him that it was strange that I didn't get to play anymore without telling me before he called what he was going to do. I didn't know anything about their conversation until Dick Advocaat called me up sounding very angry. He told me that I should tell him myself if I had any problems with the selection procedure. After that I never got another minute of playing time.

In April 2005 Advocaat resigned from his position at Borussia Mönchengladbach. In my opinion, he's not as good a coach as people think. He is very insecure, always reacting to what the media says instead of doing things in his own way. He is a good assistant, though. I think his main problem is his defensive approach. When you play very defensively, there is more pressure to score on the counter-attack. If you play an attack-minded game, on the other hand, it becomes easier for the defenders to remain strong, but Dick Advocaat never understood that. He ended up trying to use attacking players as defenders for Oranje.

Considering my age and the lack of interest shown by present coach Marco van Basten, my role with Holland is finished. I am not part of his game plan. The same goes for Patrick Kluivert and Clarence Seedorf. I can understand that Patrick Kluivert is not part of the team since he recently finished a poor season with Newcastle United, but Clarence Seedorf is doing really well at AC Milan. I don't understand why Seedorf isn't part of the team but I guess that is the vision of the present manager.

I always behaved differently with the Dutch team than at my own club. It was because I constantly felt that I needed to prove myself. I didn't have to do that at my own club, since there my ability was trusted. Admittedly, Louis van Gaal showed a lot of faith in me right from the start and during his time as manager I played my best football for the Dutch national team. Only in an away game against the Republic of Ireland did he fail to give me his trust. I started on the bench before going on to play on the right flank. If you were to ask van Gaal now I think he would admit that he made a mistake and that I should have played more centrally.

You are selected for the national team because you're playing well at your club but then you have to prove yourself every time you play because there are so many good forwards competing for a place. I think it would be better if you were guaranteed five matches in a row. Then, if you screwed up you would have to go to the end of the line for the time being. On the other hand, it is good to know that you have to remain sharp, because somebody else is breathing down your neck ready to take your place. It only makes you better. That kind of competition is only healthy, and in the end you win more matches that way.

Holland always has the best players and the best team on paper. It was said and written many, many times. Yet the team never won an international trophy, and why? It's because so many players thought that the others had to do the work for them because they were the star. I experienced this myself and it was such a waste. You don't win because all eleven players want to be the man of the match. That's how you end up winning nothing. If the left-back doesn't want to take the extra step for the left or central midfielder, then you just won't make it as a team. I always thought that was our biggest shortcoming.

I don't have much contact with the former managers. I would love it, though, if Guus Hiddink or Louis van Gaal started coaching in England. In that case I would love to become their assistant trainer. I would really talk to them a lot about the job and try to learn from them. I would want to know what they think about all kinds of game situations. I would want to know what goes on inside their head when they are taking a training session, how they put a team together, or why they put somebody on the left or on the right.

Guus Hiddink actually wanted to take me to Eindhoven last season, to play for PSV. Part of me would have liked to have gone as I would have liked to play for him. If he had been appointed coach in England I wouldn't have cared which team it was he was managing. If he wanted me, I would go immediately. But not in Holland. I think I will never be better treated than I am in England. In Holland I can't win. If it went well, it would just go well. But if it went badly, they would be saying, 'I told you so.'

It's not that I am avoiding that challenge, of course. I'm

convinced that if I played with one of the top three clubs in Holland I would score at least thirty goals per season. Look at Mateja Kezman. He did that at PSV. And then look at him at Chelsea. Scoring thirty goals in the Dutch Mickey Mouse competition is quite a different story from playing football in the Premier League.

6 Little Madrid

It was a strange summer in 1999. I had been convinced that I would remain with Leeds United for another two years, never thinking I would be moving to Spain, even though I was aware of Atlético Madrid's interest in me. I was enjoying myself in Yorkshire, and had just finished as joint-top scorer in the English league.

Nellie and I went to Mauritius, an island in the Indian Ocean, for a holiday. It was wonderful to be able to relax and recover from a successful season, without the burden of having to think about football or anything else. At last my girlfriend and I were able to spend a good length of time together, just enjoying each other's company.

Upon my return to Chadwell from Mauritius, negotiations with Peter Ridsdale began. As it started to become apparent that there would be no deal I started to view Atlético Madrid as my next club. Humphry Nijman had told me they were interested but I didn't think it would be a serious option and hadn't yet spoken to anybody from the club. However, it wasn't an unattractive option as it meant playing in the Primera Liga with at least 50,000 people in the stands for every home game.

In early August I flew to Madrid for the medical check-up and to sign my new four-year contract. Nellie, Humphry, and his lawyer joined me on the flight from Gatwick to Madrid, and we were also joined by a Spanish journalist.

I was still living in Chadwell with Nellie but I wasn't safe there anymore. Increasingly, people appeared at my doorstep shouting at me and generally harassing me. The press never left my side either. Everywhere I went they would appear, asking me for an exclusive reaction to my upcoming transfer and why I was leaving Leeds.

Arriving at the airport in Madrid was an amazing experience. I had thought that we would drive straight to the club without any fuss but instead there were hundreds of people waiting to greet me. Maybe even 1,000 people, just for me. They all wanted to touch me, while many of them took pictures and asked for my autograph.

From the airport we drove straight to the Estadio Vicente Calderón. The car had to take a special route so that the fans were unable to follow us, and we drove to a car park underneath the stadium. I felt so special. Thoughts like 'Wow, this really is all for me' were flying through my head, giving me goose bumps. I could hardly digest what was happening to me. That only happened later, when I finally got some rest in the hotel room. Even then I was pinching my arm to see if I was dreaming.

It was for real.

After the medical check-up I took a good look around. It was a beautiful stadium. Besides the car park underneath the pitch and the medical clinic, it even featured a dental practice. The dentist wasn't there regularly for the matches, but it was possible to make an appointment with him. There was even a gynaecologist for the players' wives.

I heard almost immediately that the results of the medical were in order. The tests showed that my body didn't have any physical deficiencies. It was what I had expected but you can never be sure. People have been declared unfit even when they've been convinced they're in fine physical shape. A few hours later I was introduced to the press and the public. That was another very special moment. Microphones were thrust in front of my nose, while everybody wanted an exclusive story for their radio and television channels. I was dead tired at the end of the day, which we finished off with a nice cosy dinner. The next day I went back to Leeds to pack my belongings. If I had had more time I would have been able to take some more personal belongings along with me. The remaining part of our relocation had to be arranged by Nellie.

All the contract preparation had been done by the general director, Miguel Angel Gil. He had done it well, because the signatures were on paper very quickly. I formed a favourable impression of the chairman's son when I met him. Miguel Angel turned out to be a bright businessman who spoke English very well. It was clear that he understood his business. I didn't meet chairman Jesús Gil y Gil until much later. I was a little intimidated by all the stories about him and didn't know what to think about 'Papa Gil'. I had heard stories about him having spent time in jail and had watched him punch someone on television. He had status but his name did not always have positive connotations in the press. I heard a lot from Dutch journalists about what he had said about coloured Ajax players but I can only say that he treated me impeccably. He was always helpful and genuinely nice to me.

After my season with Atlético I went on holiday to Marbella, the southern coastal city where he was mayor. When he found out that I was staying in one of the city's hotels, I was approached by his chauffeur. He told me that 'Papa Gil' wanted me to call him if I needed anything. The chauffeur had been instructed by Gil y Gil to honour and arrange all my requests. Before he left me he gave me the keys to a fast car that was waiting outside. I had been given the keys to a Ferrari! During my stay in Marbella I was allowed to drive that car. It was amazing. I took on his offer with pleasure, and before I left I returned the keys to Gil's chauffeur.

The rivalry between Atlético and Real Madrid was less fierce than the one between Barcelona and Real. I was able to show up in practically all of Madrid, although there were a few Real areas in which it was better not to set foot. There were special restaurants frequented only by Madrid players, and others where only footballers from Atlético could eat, although the players did mix from time to time.

Whenever you went out for dinner in Madrid you never had to pay. As a famous footballer you could even get free drinks in the bars. There were always so many fans around. It was special. Atlético was, of course, the inferior little brother of Real Madrid, despite us beating them in their own Santiago Bernabeu stadium that season. It had been ten years since Atlético Madrid had beaten Real there. That miracle happened on 30 October 1999 and was cause for a spontaneous party in the stands. We won 3–1 and I scored twice before being substituted by the manager Claudio Ranieri, so that I could receive a standing ovation from the supporters. I won't forget that in a hurry. Even the Real Madrid supporters applauded as I left the field.

Ranieri liked his players to be in top physical condition. Every six weeks we had to undergo blood tests, so that the iron level in our blood could be checked. We were given many tests during short sprint routines and other demanding running exercises. Ranieri had just come from Valencia and life wasn't easy for him. Spanish players don't like to strain themselves too much. They just want to play and practise with the ball but Ranieri was an extremely demanding manager.

It had been tough going from Boavista to Leeds because of the huge change in tempo but this time it was the change in temperature which was difficult. Living in Madrid was like living in a frying pan. Forty degrees in midsummer was normal out there. The tempo of the game therefore was much slower. In contrast to England, football in Spain involves a lot of moving the ball and passing it around quickly. The ball has to do most of the work. In England it is mostly kicking and running. In the Premier League there were many teams, such as Wimbledon, Leicester City, Crystal Palace and Aston Villa who played 'kick and rush'.

I had a great time in Madrid. Many chances were created for me, so as the striker there was a lot more for me to do. In every match there would be a real opportunity for me, and often it was more than just a single chance so I was able to score more goals. It was perfect. However, it took three weeks before I scored my first goal, which I found rather disappointing.

Our first home game was against Rayo Vallecano, another Madrid team. We lost that derby in our own stadium, 2–0. The thing I remember most from that match was the heat. It was boiling hot and because Madrid is located on one of the Spanish high plains the air is thin there at the best of times. I felt incredibly sick after that match. The whole evening I was throwing up and unable to sleep. I was awake the whole time despite being exhausted. I think I finally fell asleep at around five in the morning. It was wrong that there was no water-drinking break during the game, and that we were not allowed to accept filled water bottles during the match. I hadn't been warned about the heat so I had no idea what was lying in store for me. It wasn't the reason why we lost the match, though, since the Rayo Vallecano players were suffering just as much as we were.

We lost our second match, at Real Sociedad, 4–1 after taking the lead. We played very well in the first half, but made careless mistakes in defence in the second. In our third game we lost at home to Celta Vigo. They scored in the last minute to make it 1–2. Finally, in our fourth match we won our first point in a 1–1 draw with Real Zaragoza. I scored my first goal in Zaragoza, but I also scored in the following three matches, so that my tally became four from seven. It was striking that after eleven matches Rayo Vallecano were on top of the Primera Liga, followed by Real Zaragoza, Deportivo la Coruña and Celta Vigo. It turned out that we had played four of the stronger teams that season in our first matches. We didn't have to worry yet about being relegated; that came later.

Clarence Seedorf was playing for Real Madrid at the time. He had also been born in Surinam and was now an important player for the Dutch national team. I spoke with him from time to time, but not regularly as he was always busy. I could always call him for advice, but since Clarence was playing in the Champions' League that season he was on the road a lot.

The club arranged a house for me to rent in Madrid. Atlético employed all kinds of people to take care of the players. There were two young sisters who often helped me; they spoke English very well so it was easy to communicate with them. They took care of flight tickets for the family and of accommodation for visitors. If there were problems with the house, for example, if I needed a plumber, then they would take care of that too. We didn't have players from the youth teams cleaning our boots. Atlético, like most Spanish clubs, instead had a man in charge of the kit. We called him 'El Gitano', the gypsy. He worked there with his younger brother and part of their job was to take care of our boots.

Relegation at the end of the season came as a big surprise. You would have struck it rich if you had placed a bet on that before the league got underway. Part of the reason lay with the club management. Some players hadn't received their salary for a very long time and because they weren't getting paid they lost their motivation, which was very understandable. I myself had made tight arrangements with the management, so I received my salary on time at the end of every month. But in the dressing room I heard many stories from players who hadn't been paid for months on end.

I shared a room with Veljko Paunovic who was one of those

who hadn't been paid. The club was in deep financial difficulties and was being investigated by the fiscal court as well as by the tax office. When enough evidence had been dug up, Jesús Gil y Gil was forced to resign the chairmanship.

Apart from that, life in Madrid was excellent. The siesta was a positive aspect of life as far as I was concerned. Even now, I still take a one-hour nap in the afternoon, as I started to do when I played in Portugal. The Spanish lifestyle suited me perfectly.

People from southern European countries don't like sitting at home. They all go into the streets at night, or meet each other in restaurants or bars. I certainly enjoyed going out there. I could do all sorts of things. It was, after all, a very cosmopolitan city.

The day before an away match we would usually gather in the players' hotel and fly to wherever we had to play the next day. There were some long flights as well, such as when we had to play in Mallorca or Tenerife. We usually took a regular flight, although sometimes we would charter a plane. The procedure for an away game was as follows: a training session in the morning, rest in the afternoon, and then meeting up together again later on. For home games we trained a day earlier and were then allowed to go home. Then, in the evening we had to go to the hotel for a shared meal and a stay over. In the summer months in Spain many matches are played at 9 pm because of the heat, but after away games we still flew home immediately so that we could sleep in our own beds.

We had a decent team at Atlético, but certainly not top notch. There were no stars, although we had some very good players such as Kiko, Juan Carlos Valéron, Rubén Baraja and

José Mari. We hadn't invented a nickname for Ranieri yet. It wasn't until Chelsea that he became known as the Tinkerman. The Italian, who was born on 20 October 1951 had won the Copa del Rey with Valencia the previous season. That was during his third season there. Before that he had won the Italian Cup with Fiorentina in 1996. He had also won the Italian equivalent of the Charity Shield, the Supercoppa.

The nice thing about Atlético was that the Estadio Vicente Calderón was usually sold out. The city derby against Real was a very special occasion, as was the away game against Barcelona. There, in the fanatically Catalan Nou Camp we lost 2–1. I scored our only goal, and Bolo Zenden scored a beautiful goal for the other side.

By then I knew the other players from the Dutch national squad, but I wouldn't go out of my way to say hello to them before the match. In those days, and even now, I usually remained in the dressing room. Afterwards I would speak with some of the opposition players or sometimes I would say something to them as we entered the field. It has always been enjoyable to share a joke or two in this way.

Playing in enormous stadiums was the best thing about my time in Spain. The Nou Camp and the Bernabeu could hold around 100,000 people. Sevilla and Valencia also had big stadiums. The only time a stadium was not completely full was when we played in Barcelona. It was towards the end of the season and the Catalan public didn't consider us an important opponent anymore. The city derby against Real, on the other hand, had the Bernabeu at capacity.

It took me a while to learn how to play in front of a big

crowd. You have to be able to handle it mentally. There were many players who couldn't deal with it but fortunately I never really had a problem with it. Some players also struggled with the amount of travel. For away games, you had to leave one day prior to the match, and kill time playing cards, making telephone calls or watching a movie.

Spain is very obviously a Catholic country. There are many holidays celebrating certain saints. For example, San Isidoro is the patron saint of Madrid. The whole week around his festival day, 15 May, is filled with singing and dancing events. There was even a small chapel in our stadium so you could say a prayer before the match. We weren't expected to pray before meals, however. We just tucked straight into those typical Spanish salads, often served with tuna. There was usually a pleasant atmosphere at the table. Perhaps some of us became extra cheerful because of the wine that was served. In England at Leeds United it wasn't very common to have wine for dinner, but under Claudio Ranieri it was allowed. It was part of the south European culture.

Unfortunately, the season ended in a terrible way. Our ambition at the start had been to qualify for the Champions' League but things went horribly awry. I think that the club's financial problems were the most important reason for our relegation. More and more players started to complain and became increasingly demotivated because they were not receiving their salary.

Jésus Gil y Gil was, of course, quite a character, although I was never able to gauge him exactly. I was actually very much impressed by him at one point. I was in no position to judge him on things he had done in the past, since I hadn't been there. He was absolutely 'The King' at the club. The atmosphere always changed suddenly when he was around. Whatever he ordered was immediately done without any questioning or discussion. It wasn't nasty, but it was a kind of dictatorship. I'm sure he was a true football lover as he was always there for the matches, although I never saw him at training sessions. Perhaps that was because he had to be present at Marbella town hall during the week, since he was the mayor there.

Claudio Ranieri quit in the spring of 2000. You would imagine that he was fired because of the bad results, but in fact what happened was that the auditor told him that if he didn't win the next game he would be fired. But instead of trying to encourage the man by putting him under pressure, the threat had the opposite effect. Ranieri's response was, 'If that's your opinion then I might as well quit now. So I announce my resignation. You can find yourself a new manager.' I personally thought Ranieri had shown great courage by not yielding to the pressures of a banker, somebody who knew about money but had no understanding of football.

Radomir Antic succeeded Ranieri soon afterwards. The auditor didn't know the history of the club and asked Antic back, even though he had left several years before in the midst of a big conflict. Nobody liked Antic, least of all the players. A month later we got another manager, a Spaniard, but he was not much of a success either.

On 13 May we played our last home game. It was already clear that we wouldn't survive. The fans were angry with us and made their frustrations clear by throwing hundreds of eggs onto the pitch during the match. The game could not be finished because the broken eggshells might have caused nasty cuts. That was quite comical, but the unsatisfied fans often caused problems. On one occasion our cars got badly scratched. I had mine fixed immediately, but after that I hitched a ride with another player or had Nellie drop me off.

We ended our season with a 2–1 win against Mallorca. It didn't make any difference as we had already been relegated. It was such a shame, but fortunately I didn't have to play in the Second Division. Although I had signed for four years, there was a clause in my contract saying that I could leave in the event of relegation. That this clause had been inserted was fully to the credit of Humphry Nijman. The positive consequence for the club was that they could make very good use of the money they earned by selling me, as they were in deep financial difficulties.

It was strange that I had finished the season with twenty-four goals and was joint second-top scorer in the Primera Liga and yet we were relegated. The top scorer was Salva Ballesta of Santander who had scored twenty-seven goals, eleven of which were penalties. I had only scored three penalties, so I had mixed feelings about that second place and was not too overjoyed about that shared silver boot. In fact, I never went to pick it up.

We did however manage to reach the final of the Copa del Rey, where we lost to Espanyol after penalties. It was a big disappointment, as we had focused on the match for weeks, after relegation had become a fact. It was a hard blow for all of us. Our poor season could have been compensated for somewhat by winning the Copa del Rey. Instead we lost to Espanyol, for crying out loud! It was the first time I ever cried after a match.

I was a broken man and all the emotions of that troublesome season finally came pouring out.

The day after we lost the match, I left the club and have never returned. Before the final I already knew that I would be moving to a different club. However, it wasn't until I went on holiday that I found out exactly which clubs had made serious approaches. I got a call from Humphry Nijman. He said that Colin Hutchinson from Chelsea had told him that the clubs had reached an agreement about my transfer fee. A year earlier it hadn't worked out, but this time it did. It couldn't have been better, even though in the Primera Liga I had played against such fantastic players as Hierro, Raul, Kluivert, Figo, Seedorf and Rivaldo. It was time for a fresh beginning again.

7 Battles at the Bridge

The fact that Chelsea were still interested in me was absolutely fantastic. One year earlier, before my departure for Atlético Madrid, their manager Gianluca Vialli had expressed his eagerness to have me on board. However, since they had just signed Chris Sutton, I expected that their interest in me had now waned. Fortunately, this didn't turn out to be the case. Looking back now, I can say that I had the best time of my life at Chelsea. As it turned out, Chris Sutton's arrival at Stamford Bridge had no effect on my acquisition. Sutton had arrived from Blackburn Rovers in July 1999 for £10 million, a record amount for Chelsea at the time. Gianluca Vialli was still looking for a centre-forward for his team, and since, to everyone's surprise, Atlético Madrid had been relegated, I was able to return to the Premier League sooner than I had imagined.

Vialli called me up just before the Spanish Cup Final between Atlético Madrid and Espanyol. He reached me on my mobile phone when I was on the bus with the team heading towards the hotel in Valencia for the match. He started off by asking me how long my holiday was that summer. I wasn't exactly sure since I was scheduled to head off to the Euro 2000 training camp in Switzerland with the Dutch squad. Vialli said he wanted me with him as soon as possible, and so I promised him that I would join. I ended up not being chosen for the Dutch Euro 2000 final squad by manager Frank Rijkaard, so I was able to go on holiday earlier than I had anticipated and still have three weeks off.

I spent that holiday in Mexico with Nellie and Carlos, his girlfriend Saskia and their son, but it rained for days on end. After four days in the wet, we left for New York. On the way, during a stopover, I noticed that my agent Humphry Nijman had left a message on my phone saying that Atlético Madrid and Chelsea had reached an agreement on my transfer. Colin Hutchinson had called him about it, and Humphry wanted to hear from me personally about what my thoughts were. 'Of course I want to go there,' I told him. 'There is nothing I'd rather do. Vialli wants me to be there, and I want to go too. Please quickly arrange everything with Chelsea because this is my big opportunity. It's truly fantastic!'

A few days earlier Glasgow Rangers had also enquired about me. Their manager Dick Advocaat spoke to Humphry about me on the phone. Advocaat said that he was very keen to take me to Scotland. I never spoke to the former Dutch national manager myself about it. In any case, I wasn't interested in going to Glasgow. It wasn't a big enough challenge for me. There are only two clubs who really compete for the national title, Rangers and Celtic. There were also two top Spanish clubs who wanted to sign me, but it would have been a lot more difficult to move from Atlético Madrid to Real Madrid or

Above At home with Iwan, Carlos and Marion (front), with Renate, carrying me, and Franklin.

Above My brother Carlos and I outside our house in Surinam.

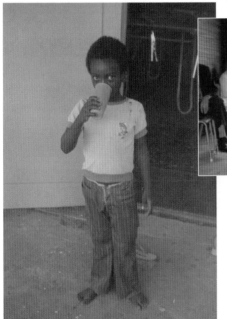

Above Cooling off, as a five-year-old.

Right My sister Marion, with my niece Jennifer, and little me with the ball.

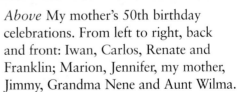

Above My mother's 50th birthday celebrations. From left to right, back and front: Iwan, Carlos, Renate and Franklin; Marion, Jennifer, my mother, Jimmy, Grandma Nene and Aunt Wilma.

Right Enjoying the skating in Krommenie.

Above The Hasselbaink clan relax in the sun outside the family home in Surinam.

Right At the bar with Arshi and my best friend Oswald Snip (centre).

Above Attending Zaandam school for my MAVO. Aged 15, I'm in the second row.

Right My beautiful daughter, Ghislaine, who was born in 1996.

Left My first real professional contract, when playing for AZ Alkmaar in 1991, was worth just 1,000 guilders (£270) per month for two seasons.

Above An AZ team photo from the 1992–93 season. I'm in the front row, far left.

Left Brothers United. Carlos and I didn't get on with Henk Wullems, as this AZ dressing room photo shows.

Right George
Graham demanded
a great deal from
his Leeds players.
He was always on
top of the team.
But I respected
him for that.

Right My trademark
cartwheel celebration
after scoring for Leeds.

Far right I scored on my
debut for Leeds, at home
to Arsenal, in August
1997. After spells with
Campomaiorense and
Boavista in Portugal, it
was good to test myself
in the Premiership.

Heading in to make it 3-1 against West Ham in front of the Elland Rd faithful.

Above I made my international debut for Holland in a 0-0 draw with Belgium at the 1998 World Cup Finals – and I should have scored!

Left Exchanging frank words with Clarence Seedorf. There were some strong personalities in the Dutch team, and perhaps we should have done better in the major tournaments.

I was proud to gain 23 caps for my country Holland and to score 9 goals.

Left After a season with Atlético Madrid, signing for Chelsea in the summer of 2000 was a very special moment for me.

Above No better place than Wembley stadium to net my debut goal for Chelsea, against Manchester United in the 2000 Charity Shield.

Left Claudio Ranieri's training methods at Chelsea were very strange. We complained to him and fitness trainer Roberto Sassi – but nothing changed.

Above Dennis Wise was the best captain I ever played under.

Left Best of friends. Eidur Gudjohnsen and I hit it off straight away, both on and off the field.

Above Chelsea v Coventry, Stamford Bridge, October 2000 and I was on the score-sheet four times for the Blues.

Above World class. Marcel Desailly was the one of the best footballers I ever played with.

Above Arriving in Israel for our controversial UEFA Cup tie against Hapoel Tel Aviv, a little over a month after the 9/11 attacks. Doesn't John Terry look young?

Above Saluting the Chelsea fans. My special bond with Stamford Bridge lasts to this day.

Right Celebrating my winning goal for Chelsea against Liverpool in the opening Premiership match of 2003/04 at Anfield. Geremi is obviously happy for me!

Above My agent Humphry Nijman, without whom I never would have made it as a professional footballer, and Frank Rijkaard congratulate me on my 1997/98 Golden Boot award.

Below Enjoying a spot of DJ-ing. I've loved music since I was a young boy.

Above I scored in Holland's 2-1 win over Spain in the 2002 World Cup qualifier in Seville, but was then sent off for wrestling with Fernando Hierro.

Above I liked playing for Guus Hiddink. His strength when managing Holland was that he kept things simple.

Left I was delighted to sign for Middlesbrough in the summer of 2004, after four years with Chelsea.

Above North-east derbies were always hard-fought matches. I'm challenging Newcastle's Shay Given for the ball in my first match for Middlesbrough, 14 August 2004.

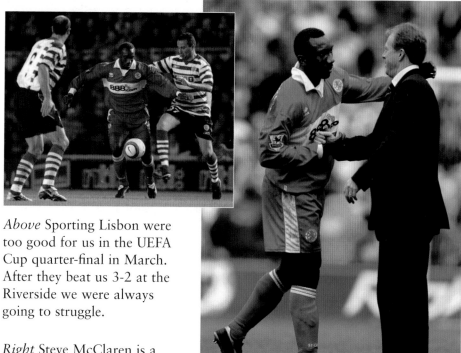

Above Sporting Lisbon were too good for us in the UEFA Cup quarter-final in March. After they beat us 3-2 at the Riverside we were always going to struggle.

Right Steve McClaren is a top-class manager. I'm lucky to be playing for him at Boro.

Above We're in Europe again! Robbie Fowler's penalty is saved by Mark Schwarzer, which meant Boro qualified for the 2005/06 UEFA Cup at the expense of Manchester City.

Left 'You know you'll get this back sometime, eh?' I jokingly warned John Terry after our clash at the Riverside in September 2004. He's a great player.

Above We will miss Bolo Zenden, who moved to Liverpool in the 2005 close season. He scored some crucial goals for us in his final year at the Riverside.

Above I went back to visit my old club Zaanlandia with Ghislaine.

Above Returning to Chelsea's old training ground at Harlington, which brought back many fond memories.

Above Mario Melchiot and I went our separate ways after playing together at Chelsea. He's now at Birmingham, but we still keep in touch.

I hope to continue scoring goals for Middlesbrough this season.

Valencia. Real Madrid first had to get rid of Nicolas Anelka so they asked me if I could wait for that to happen. It wasn't really what I wanted to do, moreover I needed more security than that. If I waited too long, then I probably would have been made to play Segundo División football. It was also too expensive for Atlético to pay me to play in the second tier. That's why, when Humphry called, I told him immediately that I wanted to go to London and play for Chelsea. Once I had given him the go ahead, matters were rapidly sorted out.

When I reported for my first week of training at Chelsea, the Norwegian footballer Tore André Flo was still at the club. He later left for Glasgow Rangers for £12 million. I assumed he was the second choice of Rangers, in case I refused to go. Chelsea must have been delighted with the money they got for him, since my transfer had cost them £15 million. It was a record amount in those days, not only for a Dutch footballer, but also for Chelsea. The fact that Tore André left was mostly due to the fact that he wasn't very happy at the club. He was on the bench most of the time, and Vialli and his successor Ranieri usually employed him on the right flank. As he had been bought cheaply, Chelsea were naturally interested in cashing in on him big time. The club made a fortune since they had originally paid only about £200,000 when they bought him from the Norwegian club SK Brann.

My brother Carlos was also very excited. He often came to watch me play in Madrid, but I think he always preferred England. I think it was because he liked the English people better. He felt more at home with them. I had been to London with Carlos before. For example, he came over when Leeds United played against Tottenham Hotspur at White Hart Lane. After the match we went out and explored the London night scene. At Leeds we were allowed to stay on after an away game – they were never very difficult about it. In Holland something like that would not be permitted. There you leave together and return together.

Eventually London became 'my town'. When I started with Chelsea I hardly knew anything about it. During Euro 96 I drove past the British capital, having only heard things about it before. At that time I was playing for Boavista, and together with Bob Goeman, my brother Carlos, Randy and two other friends we passed London on our way to Birmingham. We had come over in order to watch Holland play against Switzerland as well as a few other games. Back then I would never have dared to imagine that two years later I would find myself playing in the World Cup in France.

In my youth I never really had one particular favourite English club. When Ruud Gullit started playing for Chelsea, however, I started to follow them a little more closely. I also knew from my nights out during my time with Leeds that the club was located in the most fun area of London. However, on the pitch Chelsea had not been successful for many years. Their most recent championship title had been in 1955. It took them another fifty years to obtain their second one. In Europe Chelsea had won the Cup-Winners' Cup in 1971 after winning the FA Cup the previous year.

The club was founded in 1905. They were therefore able to celebrate their centenary with their second-ever championship title. The Mears brothers, who developed Stamford Bridge

Athletic Ground into a real football stadium, had also drawn up grand plans for the nearby Fulham club at one time, but they never got off the ground. They had wanted to name the club Kensington or London, but in the end they settled for Chelsea. The club was impoverished in the 1980s but has attracted more and more money since then. It has played in the highest division continuously since 1989. Chairman Ken Bates pumped massive sums of money in the club with the help of others such as Matthew Harding. The stadium was completely renovated, increasing the capacity to 41,000 and luxury box seats and restaurants were introduced. The record number of spectators, 82,905 for the match against Arsenal on 12 October 1935, will never be beaten. Of course, in those days most people stood.

Ken Bates also had big plans for hotels and conference halls on the site. He was very ambitious, which was also visible on the pitch as more and more great footballers from abroad came to play for the club. For example, Gianluca Vialli, Ruud Gullit, Gianfranco Zola, Roberto di Matteo, Frank Leboeuf and goalie Ed de Goey all signed for Chelsea. When Ruud Gullit won the FA Cup in 1997 as player-manager he became the first foreigner to accomplish the feat. It was clear then that Ken Bates's heavy investment in players was beginning to bear fruit. A year later Chelsea won the UEFA Cup in Stockholm, although by then Vialli had succeeded Gullit as manager. The team beat VFB Stuttgart 1–0 in the final thanks to a goal from Zola.

In my last season at Leeds United Ruud Gullit had wanted to take me to Newcastle where he was then manager. It was very flattering to have somebody like Gullit express an interest in me. So, when Vialli first wanted to sign me, I also had Gullit's offer to consider. They had both been great footballers who were now trying to prove themselves as managers. At Chelsea however I would be playing football with exceptionally good players – footballers as talented as Gianfranco Zola for example – and that was a great incentive for me. It meant that my own game was sure to improve. Another important reason for choosing Chelsea was the type of football they played. The club had started to play a more continental type of football, a revolution for the English game. At that time only Manchester United were playing a more continental style although Chelsea, Arsenal and Liverpool were starting to experiment with it as well.

All these thoughts rushed through my head when Gianluca called me up on the coach to Valencia. That's why it didn't take me very long to decide – maybe about two seconds! It just felt right. Vialli told me, 'With you on board, we'll become champions.' That was nice and made me feel especially good. Playing football with the aim of becoming champions felt wonderful. I was sold on the idea immediately.

I heard that the deal was done while I was on a plane heading for New York, so I asked for a small glass of champagne. I didn't hear about the £15 million – a record amount – until much later. I liked the idea that I was worth that much, although I always treated it with a certain nonchalance. Even so, I enjoyed the pressure of having to deliver my worth. I thought, 'Fifteen million? Chelsea must have a lot of faith in me.' It made me feel even sharper and determined to do well for them. On the other hand, too much faith in a person can be a dangerous thing.

I arrived at Chelsea as a hero, but I was still regarded as a troublemaker by the rest of England. I was the one who had left Leeds under a cloud, with accusations of greed thrown at me. Most people thought that I had chosen money ahead of football when I left Elland Road. At that time I received a universally bad press. Papers regularly wrote stories basically saying that I was a bad apple who didn't fit in with the group. It wasn't easy to deal with that external pressure as every move I made was scrutinized by the press, and most of their stories were about me being difficult.

I must admit that I didn't make too much of an effort to become loved, and I hardly gave any interviews. Perhaps I didn't help myself but I have never been keen on revealing too much of myself to strangers. The press never got a lot from me. Of course I am much more emotional on the pitch but there I'm a completely different person. I don't try to suppress my feelings. I complain a lot on the pitch, but that is typical for a Dutch footballer. I always want to win and I am willing to do a lot to make that happen.

When I joined Chelsea I rejoined the English league with a bad stain on my reputation. I needed to conquer it, and I knew people were watching my every move. On top of that I had come for £15 million, so I had a lot to prove. Moreover, Chelsea wanted to become champions. They had bought me for my goals, not for my looks or my personality. It was crystal clear what was expected of me. In the beginning things didn't go so well at the club but the problems had nothing to do with me. The squad suffered because of some very screwed-up internal relations. Gianluca Vialli, however, was not aware of what was causing the unhappiness.

Like Ruud Gullit, Vialli had first been a player at Chelsea before taking over as manager. While he was still just one of the players and didn't have much say in how the club was run he got along fine with everyone – he was always joking around with the rest of the squad. Things changed, however, when he became manager and started picking the team. It was easy for me to understand how this could create some tension but I had never played with him, so I thought of him only as my manager. Some of the other players, however, still regarded him as their friend and they expected him to keep on treating them in the way that he always had done. Vialli wasn't able to solve this problem, however, and that led to the emergence of two factions within the team, one set of players supporting him and one set opposing him.

Gianfranco Zola was one of the great players in the team, and like Vialli he was an Italian who had made it big both in England and in his native Italy. Zola was professional enough to be able to work under Vialli, but their previously close relationship was over. They had been very good friends before, but something happened between them. Something snapped, but I can't tell you exactly what it was. It was obvious though that their friendship was finished.

Something similar happened with Roberto di Matteo. He and Vialli had been together every day, and suddenly Vialli was his boss. The change was too much and led to the break-up of their friendship. There was sure to be conflict when one of these guys was left out of the team. In fact, it wasn't always tolerated, although I don't think that these two were the biggest problem. They were professional enough to separate their personal feelings from their work. Frank Leboeuf, however, wasn't able to do so. The Frenchman hated the new manager so much that Vialli eventually decided to replace him with a new central defender. There was some contact with Gareth Southgate, but Aston Villa didn't want to let him go.

With two conflicting groups in the team, it was not surprising that things didn't go smoothly. Players like Leboeuf bypassed the manager and took their complaints to the chairman, but I'm sure that Zola and Di Matteo never went that far. After a few weeks it was decided that the club could not carry on this way and the manager was sacked. I was shocked since Vialli had brought me to Chelsea only a few months earlier.

It had been a difficult time for Vialli. Zola wanted to play in every match, but Gianluca had different ideas. He knew that if they were to play against, say, Leeds United, Zola would be in for a gruelling match. That was reason enough for Vialli to leave Zola out of the team so he would be fresh for the following game. Vialli did not want Zola getting injured and having to miss important matches. However, as with every footballer, Zola wanted to play in every game.

During my very first training sessions I was able to observe the nature of some of the relationships within the squad. It was clear that Zola was sorry that he couldn't hang out with Vialli anymore. Vialli had decided not to take part in any kind of after-work socializing with his former friends in the team because he was afraid pictures would appear in the press giving the impression that he was favouring certain players. He felt that he had to separate his work from his play. It was very understandable, in my opinion, but it was clearly a downside of becoming manager.

At that time Dennis Wise was Chelsea's captain. He had played for the team for ten seasons after joining from Wimbledon for £1.6 million in July 1990. He was the best captain I ever worked under. Dennis tried to hold the two rival groups together. The captain was good friends with both Zola and Vialli. He was truly neutral and dedicated to the captaincy. I didn't speak with him about the tedious situation. I think Dennis didn't like me at first but that was because he didn't really know me. We became good friends later and eventually started doing fun things outside of football together. Although Dennis had played ten seasons for Chelsea and I was only in my first, I was already prepared to speak my mind. I would sometimes complain about the mess I had joined. I always speak out when I see that things are about to go wrong. It's in my nature. I think it's partly due to my directness and outspokenness that Dennis Wise initially considered me a rather stubborn team-mate – not just stubborn, but also one with a big mouth.

When he got to know me better he came to regard me differently. We are still in regular contact today. We got on much better as soon as he realized that I meant well. The fact that he was able to change his opinion about me for the good was important to me. Part of his change of heart was down to me delivering on the pitch. After all, that's how things work in football. If you want to be loved, you have to score and play well. At the same time it doesn't mean that you can get away with more. If you have a good team surrounding you it doesn't matter, but things can go badly wrong if you're constantly praised to the skies. I never went there with the idea that everybody had to like me. If that had been what I was aiming for then I would probably never have opened my mouth on the pitch.

Sometimes you get into an argument with your opponent because he is kicking you or hassling one of your team-mates, but once that final whistle blows and you come off the pitch all of that should be left behind. You have to be able to separate your emotions on and off the pitch, or else you will get into trouble.

Martin Keown of Arsenal was continuously kicking people and whacking his arms around. In my opinion, that was part of his job, so I had absolutely no problem with it. After the game I could easily go out for a drink with him and talk about the game. Fights with those kinds of defenders are always sharp and good to watch. As an attacker, it's my job to make the defender fail in his task. It's a nice confrontation. However, it's important that once the game is over, the confrontation stops.

I've played against some great defenders during my time in the Premiership. I think Marcel Desailly and Gareth Southgate were two of the best. Rio Ferdinand caused me the most problems though. I never played well against him. I don't think I've ever scored a goal against the Manchester United defender. Really, never. Not in my time at Leeds, not with Chelsea and not even later at Boro. It always bugs me when I think about that, I don't know how that's possible. I've played against Sol Campbell, he's a nuisance too, but at least I've scored against him. When I first joined Chelsea, John Terry was a youngster who had yet to break into the first team but even in those days he was a difficult opponent.

Talking of young players, I think it's a pity that most youth team players no longer have to carry out the menial jobs at football clubs that help define their character. For example, they don't clean the boots of the senior players anymore. In the past, one or two young players accompanied the squad to away games, where they would have to carry the bags and help the kit man with his things. They would also have to do things like make cups of tea for the pros. I've always believed that is a good way to learn your trade.

Nowadays it's a rare thing. I saw it happen during my time at Leeds, but not at Chelsea and never when I later joined Boro. Now only the kit man helps out. The youngsters are earning more money and many seem to have big mouths with it. Don't get be wrong, I don't begrudge them the money, but I think some up-and-coming stars could be better managed by their family or by their own manager and club. If I could give any piece of advice to a young player, it would be to always be yourself. That's very important. And listen to the friends you already know when you first become a pro. This doesn't mean that young players have to stick together all the time, in their own little group, but you should keep an eye out for each other. Many people will want to be your best friend, but when it's over they are gone. That's why I stay true to myself.

I wasn't the first Dutchman in the Chelsea team when I arrived. Ed de Goey was there already as a goalie, and Mario Melchiot had been there for one season. He had come from Ajax on a free transfer, although that was practically forgotten by everyone because of a serious injury that had kept him out for a long time. Two other Dutchmen joined later, Winston

Bogarde and Boudewijn Zenden. Winston was taken on by Vialli only one week before he was fired.

In the beginning I hung out a lot with Mario, although I hadn't known him from before, despite the fact he'd been raised in Amsterdam. I spent less time with Ed de Goey, partly because he was always very calm and quiet. Ed was usually quite introverted. He did things his own way, and I respected him for that. Ed de Goey remained true to himself. Many football players will behave out of character in order to attract interest from the outside world. I guess they want to distinguish themselves from the rest of the squad and look for ways to ensure they receive all the attention. Occasionally, they behave like prima donnas. Ed de Goey, on the other hand, never cared about what he looked like. He was neither concerned with his looks nor his image. He just didn't consider it important. At one point we noticed he was wearing the exact same tracksuit each and every day. He probably had several of the same tracksuits since the one he wore was never dirty. The guys on the team were getting so sick of seeing him wear the same clothes every day that they cut one of his tracksuits to shreds. They did the same to his boots. He ended up going home in a Chelsea training shirt and in a bad mood. It didn't have much effect, though, since the following day Ed came back wearing the same old tracksuit. I suppose he had enough of them at home!

The Chelsea player who I really regarded as world class was Marcel Desailly. I thought he was very intelligent, not just as a footballer, but also as a person. He was a true champion. Although he was born in Ghana, he had become a world champion in 1998 and subsequently a European champion in 2000 with France. He was one of the best footballers I ever played with. Gustavo Poyet was also very intelligent. He wasn't the quickest player around but he was always there in time to put the ball in the net. There was another side to him as well. He could be just as mean and dirty as Dennis Wise. He would do anything to win, really anything. Dennis called Gustavo 'the radio' because he kept on talking. He blabbered about everything, it was terrible. Whenever we played against Manchester United, he was always squabbling with Roy Keane. The fights between those two were unbelievable.

My very first match for Chelsea was against Manchester United. They had become the English champions while we had won the FA Cup the previous season, so we played at Wembley for the Charity Shield. We won 2–0. Roy Keane received a red card for a very bad tackle on Poyet. Our radioman from Montevideo should have been grateful to the Lord that he didn't break anything. Poyet was somebody who would always warn the opponent to take it easy if his next game was an important one, especially if it was some kind of final. Poyet would say, 'I'm sure you want to play in that important match next week, don't you? Well, then, it's probably better to take it a little easy today. You know, it would really be a shame if you couldn't participate next week because you got injured today. Lucky for you, that it is up to you to decide.' However, if Poyet noticed that his warnings were having little effect on his opponent, he would take action and start playing a little rougher. He often went in for those kinds of tricks. Only smart players like him could get away with it.

Things immediately clicked between me and Eidur Gudjohnsen. We started at Chelsea in the same year. His father had been a legend at the Belgian club Anderlecht, and in his youth he himself had played in the PSV youth team. He was from Iceland, but because of his background he spoke very good Dutch. He was to become one of my best mates. Since I started playing for Middlesbrough it's been difficult to stay in close contact with him, but there was a time during our Chelsea days that we were together every day. We still talk to each other every now and then. In Harrogate, where I live now, I don't see too many former team-mates. It's the normal way of life in football. When you leave, it's over. Footballers are strange that way, because they play together, they have fun together, but when they leave it's over. I actually don't have many friends who are professional footballers. By 'friends' I mean people I talk to every week. Mario Melchiot I speak to often. The same goes for Geremi, Lucas Radebe and Juan Manuel Lopez from Spain. That's about it.

I don't remember much about my introduction at Chelsea. I do remember having to choose my number. That was nice. I chose number nine. Nine has always been my lucky number. Some multiple of nine is also good, like the number twenty-seven I had at Atlético Madrid. At AZ and Telstar I didn't have a regular number. The first-team players were simply handed out the numbers one to eleven. It was not until later that Dutch clubs issued players their own personal number. In Holland I was never allowed to choose. That didn't happen until I went to Portugal. At Leeds United I had number nine, at Atlético number twenty-seven and at Boavista it was again nine. At Chelsea I also had a shirt with number nine and now at Middlesbrough I have eighteen.

It's the same with houses. Coincidentally, I now live in a house whose number is sixty-three, and used to live in a number six, which, of course, is an upside-down nine. I bought a piece of land close to London, where I'm building a house that will also be number nine. It's partly because of the number that I want to live there. Of course, it's not the only thing that matters, but it definitely is an asset. I just think it's a great number and I would happily get a tattoo with the number nine.

I have that with everything. If I look at a house and the house number is thirty-six, sixty-three or nine then I usually like it. But that's about it. I won't go as far as to say that my ninth game is always the most important. However, it's funny that if you keep on noticing the pattern, it somehow acquires some magical quality.

I'm not the sort of person to freely divulge how much I get paid in football. It's not something I want to share with everyone. All I will say is that when journalists write that I earn about £20,000 per week, they are not far off. When the Brazilian striker Romario was at PSV, he earned much more than some of his team-mates. He once said something to the extent of, 'There are workhorses and there are racing horses. That's what makes the difference.' I wouldn't put it that way myself, but there will always be a difference. It doesn't bother me. When I put my signature at the bottom of a contract it means I am satisfied with my salary. If then somebody comes along who earns more, I don't care. I'll say to him 'Congratulations, very good job!' I've always been satisfied with the agreements I've made, so there has never been any reason to complain afterwards. It's very straightforward for me. During my periods with English clubs, there have been no differences when it comes to bonuses for the players. It wouldn't be fair if there was. Everybody should get the same amount, since it is based on a team effort.

My start at Wembley was memorable. We put on a great performance, completely destroying the 2000 champions. I scored the first goal and Mario made it 2–0. This victory gave me my very first trophy in England. It wasn't the most important prize in English football, but it was important to me. It was a fantastic way to put down my marker in England again. After that match, all of us at Chelsea were convinced we would become Premiership champions that season.

To be driven into Wembley stadium in the team coach was a very special experience. We passed thousands of fans who were cheering us on, before being dropped off right in front of our dressing room. I made sure I soaked up the atmosphere and enjoyed every bit of it. This was the top-level football I had practised and trained for all these years. All those years in front of the Perim flat in Zaandam had not been for nothing.

All the ingredients for a special match were in place, and we outplayed United from the start. Jaap Stam had taken part in Euro 2000 with the Dutch team and because of his holiday he had hardly had a chance to train. In fact, he wasn't supposed to play at all, but United brought him off the bench after only fifteen minutes because we were giving their defence such a hard time. That early substitution was a big compliment to us.

Despite Stam's introduction, I scored six minutes later. I skipped past Ronny Johnsen, and my shot was deflected off the extended leg of Jaap Stam and the fingertips of goalie Fabien Barthez.

The great thing was that Mario Melchiot scored the other goal. He had been injured for the whole of the previous season. It was liberating for him to be able to show the public that he could still play football and even score a goal.

After the match, I had to give several press interviews. It felt good to be in the spotlight of the English media again, especially in a positive way. One week later we played our first league game of the season, at Stamford Bridge against West Ham United on 19 August 2000. I scored from a penalty kick, with a shot right down the middle of the goal. West Ham's keeper, David James, could do nothing but watch the ball hit the net despite his despairing dive.

I was pleased that I was trusted to take the penalties in our very first league match. Dennis Wise handed me the ball, saying, 'Come on, Jimmy. Do it for us.' He made me feel so important to the team. It was a special moment for me. It was also an important goal, because I was determined to make a good start at my new club.

In the same game Mario Stanic scored an amazing goal. Direct from a corner kick he killed the ball's momentum with his chest, dropped it on his thigh, then volleyed it with his right foot. *Boom!!* Just like that. It was such an unbelievable strike. On the back of that we achieved our first victory of the 2000–01 season, winning 4–2.

The next match was our first away game, against Bradford, where we lost 2–0. I pulled my hamstring early on and indicated to the physio in the dugout what had happened. He, in turn, informed Gianluca Vialli. I didn't tell him myself because I was afraid I would be substituted. I didn't want to be replaced because we were losing 1–0 and I had only just started playing for the Blues. There was no way I could ask to be taken off in only my third game for the club. However, after about an hour I was substituted. I didn't like it, but I understood the manager's decision. I was a bit upset so I slammed the roof of the dugout with my fists. It was all over the papers the next day where it was claimed that I was angry with Vialli, but that wasn't the reason for me letting off steam in the dugout. I understood why he had replaced me, I was just frustrated about my injury. Of course, everyone said that I was being difficult again, but there was not the slightest bit of trouble between Vialli and me.

I had already experienced how the press can sometimes blow up stories from my time at Leeds United. There is nothing you can do to prevent it happening. The only thing you can do is to explain yourself afterwards. Vialli understood, and he explained what had gone through my mind at the press conference after-wards. It wasn't really important. I don't mind so much if people write about me. I can only be myself.

In Birmingham we played out a 1–1 draw against Aston Villa, while on 6 September Arsenal came to visit us. This Lon-don derby ended in a 2–2 draw after I had scored the first goal of the game. We were ahead 2–0 with only ten minutes to go but Arsenal made good the deficit. We were all quite shaken up after the match. As one of the championship contenders we needed to win our home games against the other favourites.

Vialli did not lose his job immediately after that match against the Gunners, that happened on 9 September 2000 after a 0–0 draw with Newcastle United. I was dismayed when it was announced. He had brought me to Chelsea and I couldn't understand it – I only found out the reasons for his sacking later. Graham Rix, who had been second in command, became Vialli's temporary successor for the match against Leicester City. Claudio Ranieri came to watch us on 17 September, and a week later my former Atlético Madrid manager was sitting in the dugout as our manager for the Manchester United–Chelsea game. It was rather strange to meet him again in England, not least because he didn't speak any English. I had worked with him for seven months so I knew what was in store for Chelsea. However, the atmosphere in the squad didn't change immediately after he started working with us.

Ranieri wanted to impose his own training style right from the start, which consisted of a lot of running exercises and fitness tests, as well as blood tests every six weeks. The Tinkerman seemed more concerned with the physical aspect of football rather than with the game itself. I think that was his mistake. Whenever we didn't focus on our physical condition but instead practised football-related exercises, the team performed much better.

Sometimes work at our Harlington training ground was very demanding, especially on Tuesdays and Wednesdays. On those days we had to do a lot of running and were generally given a hard time. On Fridays we had a quick warm-up and played a short match, while on Saturday we had the real game. Match days were quite tough because you were still exhausted from the week's training.

Ranieri often followed the advice of his fitness trainer, Roberto Sassi. After a while, Sassi came to be hated by all the players because he was the one who made us practise so hard. It was abnormal. We often complained to him, but he always thought that our attacks were just personal, which was not the case at all. Sassi was an Italian who had somehow become more important than the manager. The players weren't very happy about this so we started giving him a hard time. He was really bullied by us. Sometimes we would hit or kick him. If there was snow, we would smear it all over him, or throw compacted snowballs at him. If there was a big puddle of water, you'd be sure that old Roberto would be thrown in there.

At one stage it got so bad that he practically begged to be left alone. This happened after he demonstrated a new training idea of his, in which he played the part of the ball. Sassi had all the players stand in their respective positions while he walked from one side of the pitch to the other. As a player, you had to follow the ball, i.e. him. The routine also required that you took your proper defensive position very carefully. After a while we all got tired of it and said, 'And now it's time to score!' Then we ran up to Sassi, picked him up and threw him into the goal.

Once when there was a lot of snow, we chased after him planning to rub it all over his face. However, in the tackle by Mario Melchiot to stop him escaping, he broke a rib. For an instant, we all stopped and shut up. We were shocked. We had gone too far this time. For the next few weeks we were good boys again, but after he recovered we went back to our old ways. Really, nobody liked the guy. He just made us run, run and run some more. When he had nothing to do he became very moody as well and started complaining to the manager.

Ranieri believed that we would play better football if we

were in better shape. Ironically, when we had to play a game on Saturdays we were just plain tired. Ranieri constantly had our blood checked. That was another idea of Roberto Sassi's. We often asked for the reason for the blood check-ups, but we never got a straightforward answer. I also never heard him toy with the idea of us not training for two days so that we could recuperate a little bit. There were never any extra rest days. Football in England is so physically demanding that when you don't have to play a match on a weekday you usually get Wednesdays and Sundays off. At Chelsea we often had to train on Wednesdays as well, so that Sunday was our only day off. Taking rests was apparently not very important to Ranieri.

I once got into a fight with Sassi. I was fooling around with him. He had a huge bruise and I gave it a little pat with my hand, which he understandably didn't like very much. He gave me a hard punch. I told him, 'Sassi, what are you doing? Stop it!' I couldn't believe he was taking it so seriously. These things happen all the time on the training ground. I probably should have given him a few slaps on the face to put an end to it.

Ranieri didn't speak any English, so Gianfranco Zola often had to translate for him. Sometimes Marcel Desailly or Gustavo Poyet would also lend their linguistic skills, so Ranieri was not short of interpreters. However, just the fact that certain players had to interpret for him caused problems. Eventually these players didn't want to translate for him anymore. Poyet once got into an argument with the manager because he was fed up with being in and out of the starting eleven. It drove Gustavo crazy. During a team meeting it was his turn to translate, but he had previously told the other players, 'If I don't get to play, I won't translate either.' Gustavo didn't want to back down in front of the others so he told the manager that he didn't want to translate this time. He said, 'Boss, please leave me out of it. I don't want to translate anymore.' This went down badly with Ranieri. The two of them never resolved their differences and in the end Gustavo was sold to Tottenham Hotspur. I don't know exactly how the manager felt about it, but it was clear that he didn't tolerate insubordination.

When you needed him, however, the manager could be a genuinely nice man. He was often sympathetic if you were struggling with something. But if he was against you, he could be extremely stubborn and difficult. His fellow countryman Christian Panucci got into such a row with him that he never played for Chelsea again. Never. I think Panucci only played eight matches for Chelsea in total. The same goes for Winston Bogarde. However, I could never do what Winston did. At one point he was even told to train with the youth team, and that is what Winston did. He kept it up for almost four years. I wouldn't have been able to do that. I would have asked for a transfer. If I had had such problems with the manager, I would at least have made sure that I was able to play football again as soon as possible. I don't know exactly what issues lay at the root of their conflict. All I know is that their's was an unreconcilable situation.

Winston was a player who always tackled hard and played tough during training. He was very fair but also fierce. During a match against Ipswich Town on Boxing Day 2000 we were leading 2–0 when Winston came on. Soon afterwards the score became 2–1. The game ended in a 2–2 draw. Ranieri was very angry after the game and told Bogarde, 'During training you kick everybody off the pitch, but in a match you show nothing, absolutely nothing.'

In effect, he had placed all the blame for the 2–2 draw on Winston. I know they had more confrontations after that incident. Things never improved between them afterwards. On 3 February 2001 Winston played in the match against Leicester City, but that was his final league game for Chelsea. He did play once in the League Cup, and he also had a knee injury that prevented him from playing for four months. After that he trained for another three-and-a-half years with Chelsea and subsequently a little bit with AZ, but he wasn't playing first-team football.

He told me himself, 'I am very stubborn, I'm staying on for as long as I have a contract with them.' He carried on until the very last day. Marcel Desailly asked him once, 'What are you doing, Winston? Are you sure you know what you are doing? Wouldn't you rather play football?' In the end he wasn't even given a shirt number. I used to speak to him about it, but he was so determined – 'If they start hassling me, I will hassle them right back' he would say. In the end he only hurt himself. In trying to drive home his point he left football with a bad reputation. People always remember the last thing you did, and for him that last thing is what happened at Chelsea. Even though he was a very good footballer the general public don't remember that he also won a Champions' League medal, or that he played for Barcelona and the Dutch national team. They only remember the difficult Winston Bogarde, and that, I think, is a real shame.

On the one hand I could understand his pride, but I thought it was stupid pride. There were plenty of clubs who wanted to sign him in those three-and-a-half years but he didn't want to go anywhere else. Eventually he got so overweight it would have taken at least three months and a lot of hard work to get him back into shape. It was too bad because he was such a good footballer.

That season turned out to be a difficult one for us. It was largely because of the manager being replaced. For me personally it was a season I will not forget easily. In thirty-five competitive matches I scored twenty-three goals, making me the top scorer of the FA Premier League for the second time. On 21 October 2000 I even scored four times in a game, in a 6–1 victory over Coventry City. In hindsight I had the chance to break Andy Cole's record of five goals in one Premier League match (for Manchester United against Ipswich Town). However, Coventry's Chris Kirkland made several good saves from me. Of course, I was also Chelsea's top scorer as well, although I still had a long way to go if I was to break Jimmy Greaves' record of forty-one goals in the 1960–61 season.

One of my four goals against Coventry came from a penalty kick. I was taken down by Kirkland, who was given a red card. In England it is traditional that if you score three goals in a game you get to keep the match ball. I have a few of these balls at home now, with a lot of signatures and small messages on them. Dennis Wise wrote, 'What a wonderful four goals by a great striker.' Claudio Ranieri wrote, 'Well done,' while somebody else wrote 'Sniff for the goal.' Those are nice messages. I am proud to have such memories.

Yet we were a disappointment that 2000–01 season. It took until 7 March 2001 for us to win an away game. Finally we beat West Ham United 2–0 at Upton Park with me contributing one of the goals. Exactly one month later, we won away for the second time. Again I got one of the goals as we beat Derby County 4–0. I don't know why it took so long for us to win an away game. Perhaps it was to do with the newly implemented rotation system by Ranieri. The manager used substitutes very often, and in my opinion too much. He clearly wanted to place his own mark on the squad. He wanted to play 3–4–3, so he preferred players who suited that system. However, he usually found himself playing 3–6–1 due to the type of players he had. He often switched back and forth between the two systems, far too often in my opinion. The latter system took a lot of energy out of the players, which was perhaps the reason for the over-emphasis on our physical condition. We often told him about our concerns, but he viewed our complaints as votes of no confidence. He should have been a little better at accepting criticism. As a boss he was unwilling to tolerate any interference from the players over his style of playing. He always felt somehow attacked by us, and was unable to accept that criticism from the players might be constructive and positive. Instead, he viewed any kind of criticism as an undermining of his authority.

It was also a disappointing season in Europe. We were soon eliminated from the UEFA Cup by St Gallen of Switzerland. On 14 September we won 1–0 at home but then we lost 2–0 away. Our European adventure had reached its end on 28 September 2000. It was shameful considering the quality of the players in our team.

Personally, it was great for me to finish as top scorer in the Premier League in my first season with Chelsea. Second that season was Marcus Stewart from Ipswich Town with nineteen goals and in shared third place were Thierry Henry of Arsenal and Mark Viduka of Leeds United with seventeen goals each. If Chelsea had become champions that season with me as top scorer it would, of course, have been even better.

Instead, our season was a near miss. On the other hand, for me it was a personal triumph because I had dealt effectively with pressures from the press. I had needed to prove myself that season and show them who I really was. And I had done just that. I had been taken on for a lot of money, which had made the expectations all the more demanding. Fortunately I was given a lot of scoring opportunities and was able to convert many of them.

Of course, I became upset whenever I missed chances, but I had to get over them very quickly and forget about them. The more chances you get during a match the more likely it is that you will score. When you only get a few chances, scoring becomes much more difficult. In those situations I usually become a little nervous, although that never lasts for very long. You have to dare to fail. You either have that drive or you don't. It's a matter of always trying to remain confident and calm. Sometimes I'm seething inside, while I still need to remain as calm as possible. It's part of my character: keep on going, always try to reach the limit, and don't give up easily.

If I possessed a better technique I suppose I would have gone much further in the game, although this is easily said with the benefit of hindsight. It all started in my youth, when I kicked that ball day in day out against the wall in the Perim flat.

I am reasonably calm whenever I have a one-on-one with the goalkeeper. It is difficult to say what I'm thinking during those moments. It is different every time, since every situation is unique. Sometimes I think of nothing, other times I think of the goalie in front of me. What is he going to do? Sometimes I think about the defender right behind me. Some defenders are quicker than I am, so I always try to make myself as wide as possible and cut them off so that they have to find a way around me. It costs them time that way.

I am usually able to sense when they are going to make a sliding tackle or when they are about to kick me. Perhaps that is why I don't get injured very often. I also think that my pain threshold is perhaps a little higher than the average player. Last season, when Johan Cruyff was talking about the injured Arjen Robben he said that 'not getting injured is an additional football quality of a player'. He said it in such a way that it appeared as if he had never been injured himself. It's amazing, everybody in Holland parrots what he says. The whole country listens to the man as if he is some kind of prophet handing down absolute truths. Who knows, Johan Cruyff might soon explain to everyone the right way to make love to a woman, you know what I'm saying?

As a matter of interest, I never received my golden boot. I never went to pick it up, and it was never sent to me. I have no idea what happened to that top-scorer trophy. I never found out, because I went on holiday as soon the season finished. I do know that the club made several attempts to retrieve it for me, but all to no avail. The next season I again scored twenty-three goals but that was only good enough for joint second place, together with Alan Shearer of Newcastle United and Ruud van Nistelrooy of Manchester United. Thierry Henry was top scorer of the 2001–2 season with twenty-four goals.

8 Money, Money, Money

I was never really conscious about the fact that there were five Dutchmen playing at Chelsea. As players from similar backgrounds we mixed a lot, but my best buddy was actually Eidur Gudjohnsen. One of the reasons Eidur and I spent so much time together had to do with the fact that we roomed together. Moreover, our girlfriends got along very well too. It's funny to think that I was born in tropical Surinam while he hailed from Iceland, which is close to the North Pole. Despite our difference in origin, we were actually very similar. We could talk about everything and anything. We were able to trust each other with things that were going on in our private lives as well, and we grew very close.

When we were both at Chelsea we often went to the casino for some fun. At one period we could be found in the casino every day. We weren't there only to gamble, but also to relax and to have a drink or a bite to eat. Eidur was once confronted by a journalist who had done some research into his gambling habits and who had noticed that we were spending serious amounts of money. In the newspaper it was written that he had spent about £400,000 on gambling, and that he had a gambling addiction. I think at some point he must indeed have been addicted. We were both acting a little strangely back then.

The papers also claimed that I had spent a lot of money gambling. That was true, although the amount of money I had allegedly spent was wrong. The article claimed that I had gambled £1.1 million and had lost £169,400 over two years. The gambling habits of footballers such as Jesper Gronkjaer, Paul Gascoigne and Kieron Dyer were also discussed. The fact remains that the £1.1 million figure attributed to me was truly ridiculous. The true amount was much less. I hadn't told the journalist anything, so he had come up with an estimate by himself. He probably based it on the assumption that I earned more than Eidur, and could therefore gamble more money away. Eidur, on the other hand, had told the journalist everything, so the figures about him were correct. There was even a story in the papers that I had been gambling in Liverpool the day before we had to play a match there. That was not true, and so I took that specific newspaper to court. They ended up having to pay me a huge amount in compensation. I donated the money to a hospital in London that takes care of children with AIDS.

I was actually at the casino so much because I was having trouble at home with my girlfriend Nellie. I think Eidur was there for very similar reasons. Sometimes we would go to the casino not to gamble but just to spend our money on alcohol. When we did gamble the stakes would occasionally be high. I must have lost over £100,000. I just didn't want to be at home at that time. I basically drank and gambled away my time.

I think Eidur has overcome his gambling habit now. I still go to the casino occasionally. Seeing those stories in the papers did give me a wake-up call however. I had several sleepless nights about it, because £100,000 is a lot of money to me. I know that most people don't earn that kind of money in a year. Some people don't even earn that in ten years. I understand the value of money and should have used it much more carefully. The fact that I earn that kind of money in a relatively short time doesn't mean I can just throw it overboard. People will think that I can easily do without the money. I can, but it is up to me if I choose to miss it or not.

On the other hand, if I did gamble away £10 million, it would be my choice. It's my money, I earned it. The press can write whatever they want, it is still up to me to decide what to do with my money. If I went bankrupt and had to go to the social services office and ask for welfare benefit I would be entitled to it since I've paid my taxes. In fact, I pay much more tax than most other taxpayers. I know very well that I make a lot of money, and that most professional footballers make much less. There are some who make more than me, but I can't do anything about that. I am very happy about what I earn. In fact, I am extremely happy. That's why I never look at the income of others.

The flipside of the coin is that many people expect you to pay for everything, particularly when you go out. Often people just expect me to foot the bill. Of course, I will pay the bill most of the time, but I think the basic idea behind it is wrong. If I suspect I'm just there to pay for things I won't remain friends with those people for very long. I do realize that I can afford more than most people. On the other hand, only hanging out with the filthy rich is not my cup of tea.

We started the 2001–02 season with a home game against Newcastle United on 19 August 2001. The rebuilding of Stamford Bridge had been completed so more than 40,000 people had a good view of the action. The game ended 1–1 which was a mediocre result for us. Newcomer Boudewijn Zenden immediately left a good impression by scoring our goal in his first-ever Premier League game. It was a good debut for him. He also fitted in well with the other players. It was unfortunate, however, that Ed de Goey was beaten after a blunder on his part. It would have been better for us to have won, of course, but we didn't achieve our first victory until our first away game of the season. We won 2–0 at Southampton where I scored my first goal of the campaign. Getting our first victory was important, since the previous year it had taken us much longer before we claimed three points from a game.

On 8 September 2001 we played at home against Arsenal. Again it finished 1–1. I scored our goal but was then sent off. My red card was later overturned by the FA. One week later, on 16 September, we played at White Hart Lane where we beat Spurs 3–2 and Frank Lampard was sent off. In that same week Lampard, Jody Morris, Eidur Gudjohnsen and John Terry were fined two weeks' wages for going on a drunken rampage in a Heathrow hotel bar packed with grieving Americans, just a few hours after the 9/11 terrorist attacks.

I was pleased that new players had joined the squad. It kept the team fresh and sharp. Apart from 'Bolo' Zenden we were also strengthened by the arrival of Emmanuel Petit from

Barcelona, £11 million signing Frank Lampard from West Ham, and the Frenchman William Gallas who had played for Olympique Marseille the previous season. Chelsea bought those four players for a total of £32 million.

Everyone thought that £11 million for Frank Lampard was a huge amount, since when he came he wasn't nearly as good as he is now. He has learned so much in recent years and has improved enormously. He is someone who has grown tremendously as a footballer. It's not for nothing that he was chosen as Footballer of the Year in 2005. In his first year at Chelsea he was still a few kilos overweight, but now he doesn't carry any excess baggage.

I also had to deal with weight problems that season – my holiday had been a little too comfortable. After six weeks of doing nothing I arrived at our training camp in Roccaporena much too heavy. We did a lot of running there, and when I arrived I was at least eight kilos overweight. As expected with our manager, there were many fitness tests. For one of them you had to run faster than the previous lap. But after two laps, everybody had overtaken me. Everyone was laughing at me uncontrollably. They made so much fun of me, while I was feeling bad and aching everywhere. I could neither run nor walk. I was determined never to go through this sort of misery again, but it turned out to become one of my best seasons ever.

Roccaporena itself was awful. It is a place of pilgrimage and consists of a chapel on top of a mountain. We stayed in a small hotel nearby without any air conditioning or cable television. There were about 200 people living in that village, while the village itself marked the end of the road leading into the area.

We only got to drink water, while our Spartan diet consisted of a small slice of meat and a little bit of pasta. It was like a prison camp. We were stuck in that dump for sixteen days. There was really nothing to do, no bars, nothing. The only thing you could do after training in the evening was buy yourself an ice cream.

There was this one young but not very attractive woman working at the hotel reception. But after six days she started looking beautiful in our eyes. Another three days passed and the guys were thinking, 'Wow, She's actually pretty hot,' while after ten days they were fighting over her and making moves on her. We ended up going there for three summers. Every time there was the same young girl, and every time the guys' eyes became bigger with time.

That season turned out to be the last one at the club for captain Dennis Wise. After spending eleven seasons in southwest London he moved to Leicester City. Eidur Gudjohnsen and I formed a perfect attacking duo. Between us we were responsible for thirty-seven goals that season, fourteen of which were his. Apart from that he also gave nine assists, while I contributed ten. Chelsea scored sixty-six times that season, with the two of us scoring more than half of those goals. That season I was also nominated as one of the six best footballers of the year. It was a great achievement for me. Ruud van Nistelrooy was elected the PFA Player of the Year for 2002. Freddie Ljungberg of Arsenal became Barclaycard Player of the Year, while his teammate Robert Pires was chosen by the football writers as their Footballer of the Year. Arsene Wenger was chosen as best manager. We were very disappointed to finish in only sixth place, behind Leeds United, but in front of West Ham.

We didn't fare much better in the UEFA Cup. In the first round we played against Levski Sofia. We beat them 2–0 in Bulgaria on 27 September 2001 after winning 3–0 the previous week at Stamford Bridge. After that result our manager felt that we would do well in the competition. However, things took an unexpected turn because of the 9/11 attacks. In the second round we had to play against Hapoel Tel Aviv. Generally, they're not an opponent to give you many headaches, but this time it signified the halt of our international ambitions that year.

Our home game on 1 November ended in a draw, which wasn't enough since we had lost 2–0 in Israel. That defeat had an unusual cause, though. The match was played in Israel a little over a month after the terror attacks in the United States. There was still a lot of tension in the air. Everyone was badly shaken by the collapse of the twin towers and at that time the world didn't look like a very fun place to live, to put it mildly.

We had wanted to alter the venue of the match, but UEFA refused permission. Chelsea told UEFA that the club didn't want to fly to the Middle East because many players were afraid of their safety. In the meantime the state of Israel guaranteed that nothing would happen to us footballers and we would be given excellent security. Despite the Israeli promises, however, the club allowed the players to decide whether they would travel or not. Some, like Graeme Le Saux, did indeed remain at home. Emmanuel Petit was also unwilling to travel. I had trouble understanding their decision as the Israelis had guaranteed us twenty-four-hour security. In the end it turned out that everything was indeed as safe as they had promised.

We lost 2–0 because many key players stayed at home and their places were taken by youth-team players. Unfortunately, we couldn't make up the deficit during our home game, so that season our European campaign was once again a farce. John Terry came with us to Israel and he showed no fear. I myself was also not afraid. I knew that we had never been safer, what with security planes in the air and much more besides. I also never felt any fear inside the stadium.

The season turned out to be all right for me personally. In total I scored twenty-nine goals, twenty-three in the league, three in the FA Cup and three in the League Cup. We reached the League Cup semi-finals by beating Coventry City, Leeds United and Newcastle United. In the semi-finals we beat Spurs 2–1 at home, but in the return match we lost 5–1. I was sent off during the game at White Hart Lane after a fracas in the penalty area. Mike Riley had seen a dark hand reach for the head of Teddy Sheringham, drew his own conclusion, and showed me the red card. 'Ref, it wasn't me!' I told him, and pointed to Mario Melchiot, whereupon even Mario admitted, 'It was me. I did it.' But Riley had made his mind up to send me off and nothing would change that. After the match, he apologized to me, but it was no use by then. It was a huge disappointment that we lost the second game, and especially annoying after we beat Spurs 4–0 a few weeks later, on 13 March. In the end it was Blackburn Rovers who took the trophy home as they beat Tottenham 2–1 in the final at Cardiff.

We didn't do too badly in the FA Cup where we knocked out Norwich City, West Ham United and Preston North End. In the quarter-finals we were drawn against Tottenham Hotspur but this time we got our act together and beat them 4–0 at Stamford Bridge, the same scoreline as in our league match three days later when I scored a hat-trick. In the semi-finals we beat Fulham at Villa Park. John Terry scored the only goal of the game, but it was enough to get us into the final. As Wembley was being renovated, the FA Cup Final was held at the Millennium Stadium instead. Our opponents were to be Arsenal who had beaten Middlesbrough 2–0 in the other semi-final.

Unfortunately I got injured in the final, which we lost 2–0 after goals from Ray Parlour and Freddie Ljungberg. As Arsenal had already won the league they had therefore achieved the double. To make the end of our season even more disappointing, it became clear that Roberto di Matteo would have to retire from football because of a badly broken leg.

A few weeks before the final I received an injury that, it turned out, was allowing only twenty-five per cent of my blood to flow through an artery in my right leg. The artery was basically blocked. Perhaps I had been bruised during a match or training, but the exact cause has never been found. In fact, I almost lost my leg. The problem wasn't diagnosed initially so I didn't know that I was taking a big risk by continuing to play. It only came to light after I felt an enormous cramp in my leg when walking down the street one day. I panicked because I had never felt something like that before. I even had Guido Couwenberg fly over from Holland to give me extra physiotherapy. However, even after his intensive massages the injury still bothered me. A few days later, on 27 April 2002, we were due to play against Middlesbrough. During the warm-up at the Riverside I kept on feeling pain and told the manager that I couldn't play as my calf was hurting badly. I then flew to Holland for a few days for more intensive treatment. Afterwards I went to a specialist in England but he also couldn't find the cause. He placed me on some kind of machine and told me to walk it off, thinking that the problem would get rid of itself that way.

This treatment felt effective so I started the Cup Final feeling much more at ease. However, I didn't last for much longer than an hour. I really didn't feel well and couldn't play at all. Since it was a final, I was willing to take a big risk. I wasn't fit, but like any footballer, I just didn't want to miss such a big day. If I had known the real extent of the problem, I would never have walked on the pitch that day. The following week I couldn't train at all because of the pain, and the problems with my calf merely continued.

One week later, on 11 May 2002, we played our last league match of the season against Aston Villa which we lost 1–0. The Thursday before the match I saw a specialist in a hospital. He couldn't feel any pulse in my foot. The doctor became visibly nervous and suddenly left the room. He was very worried but didn't tell me anything. A little later he asked me to come back on the Saturday for the result of his tests. But that day was our final game of the season. He said to me, 'Jim, that match is not important, forget about it. We are going to the hospital to have you checked up completely.' We then went to a vascular expert and he made a cut in my groin. He injected a blue liquid into me. Using his special equipment he could see where the liquid was flowing in my arteries and where it wasn't. This is how he found out that only twenty-five per cent of my blood was flowing through my right foot. Something was wrong, very wrong, and I had to be operated on immediately. It took three months before I could play football again, but because it was summer I didn't miss many games.

The blockage had come about because something had grown in my artery, cutting off the circulation in my leg. Until this day I do not know what it was and the doctors never saw it either. It could well be that it happened as a result of me being kicked there. I am just incredibly happy that I recovered. It was a real relief that the problem was finally diagnosed. I should never have played in that final. The doctor told me that I had been extremely lucky. I wasn't allowed to do anything that summer of 2002. I wasn't even allowed to fly, so I stayed at home in London for six weeks. After that period, I was at last fully recovered.

I entertained myself that summer by watching the World Cup. I even worked for ITV for a short while, which proved a nice diversion. For two weeks I was picked up every day and taken to the studio where I commentated on the various games that were taking place in Japan and South Korea. Many people were surprised by my spontaneity. It was good to hear positive comments about me for a change. I heard people say that I wasn't such a scary guy after all. It meant a lot to me. Perhaps now England had finally got to see the true Jimmy. I think they realized that there was another side to me, a side that they had never encountered before. They had never discovered that part of me during my first years in England.

It was partly thanks to the television crew who really helped me feel at ease. The television hostess Gabby Yorath was very nice to work with. I was there with Andy Townsend, Terry Venables and Robbie Earle. They asked me to talk about various international strikers, as well as discuss two to three matches per day, usually together with two or three other people.

The other host was Bob Wilson. He was the goalkeeping coach at Arsenal where he had also been a player. He was very nice, and we talked a lot together. I had not realized that he'd had a great career with Arsenal behind him.

'Oh, you were a footballer before?'

I thought he was only well known because he was a television personality.

He looked at me strangely, as if to say, 'Are you kidding me?'

I then made things worse for myself by saying, 'Get out of here! Are you really a goalkeeping coach?'

He replied, 'I've been the goalkeeping coach at Arsenal for years. I even stood in goal there myself.'

Again, I said, 'No way. Stop it!' Only afterwards did I find out that he was actually an Arsenal legend. I was so ashamed, I had to apologise to him. Fortunately, he was able to laugh about it. That year he stopped working at ITV after having been there for a short spell following more than twenty years at the BBC.

I had a difficult start to my third season at Chelsea. For the second time we went to our favourite Italian hangout, Roccaporena, led by our manager Claudio Ranieri. This time it was even harder on me because I had to get back in shape after recovering from the injury. Yet I was fit in time to participate in the opening game of the season for Chelsea. I was allowed to start slowly in the preparation phase and had a separate coach who just worked with me. Even though I played in the opening match of the 2002–03 season, I certainly didn't play for ninety minutes in many games throughout the campaign. The Tinkerman had been pondering all summer about the coming season's strategy and had come up with a new system that was not to my advantage.

We opened the season on 17 August 2002 with an away game against Charlton Athletic which we won 3–2. It was a good start, considering that Ranieri had just introduced his infamous rotation system. He had decided that he would build the team around Gianfranco Zola that season. Zola would become the key figure and play up front with everyone else rotating around him. Now, I don't want to say anything bad about Gianfranco, because he was a fantastic player, but I didn't think the system functioned very well. The previous year Eidur Gudjohnsen and I had played together up front and done well. With this new system, on the other hand, we hardly ever played together anymore. I often didn't feature in the starting line-up. However, for games we definitely had to win I was always on from the start. I thought that was strange, and I told the manager so.

Part of the problem was that I kept on getting minor injuries, not serious ones, but enough to interfere with my football. It turned out to be a very frustrating season for me. Yet I was keen to play all the time, and I felt as if I could. Gianfranco played well and he deserved to start, but why wasn't he playing in the hole behind Eidur and me? I think that would have been the perfect setup. I didn't understand why we didn't play that way. It had nothing to do with the fact that Zola was getting older and needed someone close to him, because he was still as fresh as a daisy. In that case I would have understood.

It turned out to be my most disappointing year since leaving Portugal. The Chelsea fans didn't understand the situation very well. They demanded the same amount of goals from me as in previous seasons even though I was playing less well after my injury. It took a lot of energy for me to return to full strength after the injury and that was why it took eight matches before I scored my first goal. Finally, on 28 September I got one of the goals as we beat West Ham 3–0. I had failed to score against Charlton Athletic, Manchester United, Southampton, Arsenal, Blackburn Rovers, Newcastle United and Fulham. I had seriously started to worry in the meantime. That goal against West Ham could not have come any later. I was already worrying more and more about when I would show the fans that I really hadn't lost my touch. In my defence, in those days I was often on the bench and if I played it wasn't for much more than fifteen minutes, so I didn't have a lot of time to prove myself.

On the face of it, it wasn't a bad season for the club but for me it was disastrous. We ended in fourth place, qualifying for the preliminary rounds of the Champions' League. Manchester United were champions with Ruud van Nistelrooy finishing as the Premier League's top scorer with twenty-five goals. Arsenal came second while Newcastle ended third.

Halfway through the season I was almost transferred to Barcelona. Louis van Gaal had become manager there for the second time in May 2002. He was keen for me to join him, and in January 2003 the clubs reached an agreement. However, at the very last moment it was called off. On 18 January we played at Manchester United where we lost 2–1. Claudio Ranieri came to me on the morning of the match and asked me whether I could play that day. I said that I could but halfway through the game I was kicked on the ankle by Phil Neville. I had to leave the pitch because my ankle was starting to swell and I was worried about having to go to the Catalan capital two days later. If I couldn't travel I would have to leave it to Humphry Nijman to sort everything out. The clubs had agreed that the transfer fee would be in the region of £8 million.

Barcelona weren't playing very well that season. Van Gaal's return there as manager had not fulfilled the club's expectations. That weekend Barcelona lost at home to Valencia, and for the Catalans that was the final straw. The white handkerchiefs in the Nou Camp were signalling his departure. On the Monday, the day I was supposed to put my signature on the contract, van Gaal was fired. My bag had been packed and I had been ready to go. I felt bad about it since I was looking forward to playing with Patrick Kluivert again. From my time with Oranje I knew that we formed a good strike pairing. Moreover, Barcelona was of course a great club, as well as a fantastic and beautiful city. They also had a history of employing Dutch players, which was important to me. But most of all, I had really been looking forward to working with van Gaal again. That was the most painful part of all. If van Gaal had been fired one week later I would have joined the club. I hadn't actually spoken to him directly since all the dealings had gone through Humphry. Fortunately, nobody outside the club knew how serious the transfer had been, so I was able to easily switch my mind back to where I was, and wasn't constantly reminded by everyone about it.

Chelsea had wanted to sell me because they were in some financial trouble and could really have done with the £8 million. I knew they were having financial difficulties by looking at the bonus system they employed for the European campaign that season. As FA Cup finalists the previous season we had qualified for the UEFA Cup because the Cup winners Arsenal had also won the league and were therefore playing in the Champions' League. We were supposed to get about £20,000 per player for qualifying for the UEFA Cup, but we didn't receive that money as we hadn't qualified through our league position or by winning the Cup. We argued it was a ridiculous twisting of the agreement. It wasn't a coincidence that a new financial manager had just been appointed at Chelsea whose sole task was to bring the club back from the red.

After our last match, I didn't feel glad that the season was over. Nellie had still been with me during my third Chelsea season, but not much later we split up. It is still difficult for me to talk about it but I will at least try to explain. After having spent a few years together it just wasn't working anymore. The love was finished on my part. I felt more and more that Nellie was living with Jerrel Hasselbaink the footballer, instead of Jerrel the person. You get to know your friends in bad times, not in good times. I got to know her in bad times and I was shocked. I finished the relationship, and perhaps that was the reason why she was so upset. I haven't talked to her very often since then, just a few times on the phone, but usually it has ended in us arguing. We split up in a bad way after being together for five years. It's too bad that it had to end the way it did because it wasn't a trivial relationship.

Things got so bad that if I were to see her on the street now, I would walk straight past her. It's really such a shame, because it didn't have to end so acrimoniously. Where there are two fighting, there are two to blame. I also carry the blame for the failure of our relationship. I had trouble dealing with it for a very long time. It made it very difficult for me to trust people, even now when I meet new girlfriends. I haven't had another serious relationship since Nellie. I am seeing someone else now, but our relationship is only in its early stages. You know, many people still only see the footballer Hasselbaink in front of them, and it takes time and energy to really get to know a person, and I often don't know if that's what they want. I have a daughter, and I could easily have had more children, but it is very important to find the right person if you are going to do that.

What I went through with my other ex, the mother of my daughter, was not fun, since it meant that I wasn't able to be there for my daughter Ghislaine. Fortunately, I have a good relationship with Ghislaine's mother now. If I had only known what I know now, I might have been able to continue that relationship. I should have given it a little bit more effort back then. But I was young and thought that I wouldn't be able to make her happy in Portugal. I felt then that I was giving as much as I could, even though it wasn't true. I learned from it though. Ninety per cent of what I learn, I learn the hard way. I have to hit my head first. That's my true character, and it is the same where football is concerned. First you have to learn to take things seriously and then realize that you have to grab every opportunity. Usually you don't get a second chance but fortunately, I was given a second chance as a footballer.

9 Down the Roman Road

Although 2002–03 had proved to be a good season for the club, the following summer turned out to be one of turmoil. There was more and more speculation that Chelsea was to be sold. The club was in financial trouble and chairman Ken Bates had been approached by a Russian oil tycoon, Roman Abramovich, to take over the club. Chelsea was about £75 million in the red at the time on account of the construction of Chelsea Village. There was not enough money left over to invest in players. The squad was therefore due for some substantial reduction. However, Roman Abramovich didn't only want to take care of the debt, he also wanted to invest, so he pumped a lot of money into the club.

There were also many rumours going around that our manager Claudio Ranieri was to be dismissed. The Tinkerman was to go and make way for the Swedish coach of the English national team, Sven-Goran Eriksson. There was something about it in the papers every day. Abramovich and Eriksson were friends and our new chairman regularly went to the Swede to ask for advice. They saw each other frequently, which merely fed the speculation. Personally, I think Eriksson probably would have become our new manager if the FA had let him go. Ranieri would have been bought off, and since Roman Abramovich had several billion to play with, that wouldn't have been a problem. A year later, on 1 July 2004, the Italian was in fact replaced by Jose Mourinho from Portugal.

The speculation wasn't only about a new manager however, but also about new players. There were rumours that Christian Vieri, Patrick Vieira, Francesco Totti and Wayne Rooney would sign for Chelsea. In the end none of these players came. On the other hand, Wayne Bridge came from Southampton, Juan Sebastian Veron from Manchester United, Claude Makelele from Real Madrid, Adrian Mutu from Parma, Geremi from Real Madrid and Damien Duff from Blackburn Rovers. For Winston Bogarde the season ended in silence. He wasn't even assigned a number anymore, even though he had a contract for one more season.

In the 2003–04 season several important players left. Graeme Le Saux went back to Southampton, and after their relegation in 2004–05 he retired completely. Gianfranco Zola returned to Italy, having been the best player Chelsea had ever had. More-over, he was very popular with the fans. On 7 July 2003 he said farewell at a press conference. The irony is that if the club had been taken over a few days earlier he could have stayed on. The offer on the table on 2 July was much better than the offer from 1 July, which asked him to be satisfied with a lower salary. However, he had agreed to join Cagliari on that day. Cagliari were playing in Serie B at that time. Zola was still very fit and had promised his Italian fans and the club that he would be heading home. Ed de Goey, Albert Ferrer and Jody Morris also left that summer. Jody was a boy who always had a lot of problems, mainly to do with drink. I remember an away trip to Rome, on our final evening in the city, when I went with Jody, Mario Melchiot and a few of the English lads to a hotel with a roof-garden. They got very drunk and started urinating down onto the street, and throwing beer at anyone who was passing by. I left them to it. I wasn't used to that. It's a shame for Jody, he could have been such a big player for Chelsea.

On Thursday 3 July we had our blood checked once again. The training started at 8.30 am and we were made to do a lot of sprints. A few days later we were back in Italy for a few days at our training camp in Roccaporena. A week later we flew to Malaysia for the Asian Cup. It was a long flight to Kuala Lumpur, and when we arrived at the airport we were overwhelmed by the heat and the humidity. On 25 July we played a match against a Malaysian team, which we won 4–1. I didn't start the game but came on later as a substitute for Joe Cole. Two days later we played out a 0–0 draw in the final against Newcastle United before winning 5–4 on penalties. On Sunday 29 July we returned to England with the second cup we had won during my time at Chelsea.

Following all the acquisitions it was clear that several more players would be leaving. Boudewijn Zenden was loaned to Middlesbrough. There was a lot of speculation about me as well, but I was allowed to stay.

Roman Abramovich visited us for the first time at our training facility at Imperial College's sports ground at Harlington. Of course, we each had our own thoughts about him, but he behaved very normally. He was wearing jeans and a jacket and appeared at ease. He had a small goatee beard back then. He shook us all by the hand, and told us that he was the new owner. I thought he was very relaxed. In previous years Ken Bates had been our chairman. I think that man deserves a statue for getting the club to the top of the tree after years of struggle. He brought the big names to Chelsea, and it was under him that Chelsea won the UEFA Cup.

Along with the chairman a lot of players found their new home at Chelsea. Initially the reinforcements seemed fine to me, but eventually it started to appear as if the manager no longer had any confidence in the players who were already there. We had so many new faces that the manager was practically able to put out a team without using any of the players from the previous season. It looked like he felt we weren't good enough. I didn't think every acquisition was a real asset to the team either.

Despite all the reinforcements Ranieri didn't seem to expect us to win any of the competitions. I thought that strange, since with the quality he now had under his command he would have been entitled to demand it. Jose Mourinho, on the other hand, stated immediately after his arrival that Chelsea should become champions. Ranieri just wasn't clear enough about what he expected. Moreover, there was a completely different team on the pitch every time we played. Even if you played well in one match, it was no guarantee that you would start the next game.

He brought in Juan Sebastian Veron from Manchester United, but why? If Veron was that great, Manchester United wouldn't have let him go. They wanted Thierry Henry but weren't able to get him. Arsenal knew how good he was, so naturally they didn't want to help strengthen one of their main rivals by letting him go. That wouldn't be smart. Ronaldo and Raul from Real Madrid were also mentioned in the papers as potential transfer targets.

Bringing in thirteen new players so rapidly is asking for trouble and eventually problems arose. Some footballers Ranieri bought weren't any better than the ones he already had. Finally, the manager saw the light and realized for example that Adrian Mutu and Hernan Crespo just couldn't work together. They were not a good pairing. In the beginning I played with Adrian Mutu and that went very well. Then I was replaced by Hernan Crespo, but that didn't work at all. Both Crespo and Mutu are good players, but are not suited to the hustle and bustle of the English league.

The season started with an away game at Liverpool. On 17 August 2003 we won 2–1 at Anfield and I scored one of the goals. Later I heard that the new chairman had landed in his own Boeing at John Lennon Airport. I thought that was special. That guy really had a lot of money. He also owned a few big yachts. We saw one of them up close, in the harbour at Monaco, but we didn't go inside. It made sense to me. I mean, you don't show off your house to everybody, there is no boss who does that.

I started the season by scoring five goals in four games. We won our second game, against Leicester City, although I didn't score there. On 30 August 2003 we played at Blackburn Rovers where the game finished in a 2–2 draw with me contributing one goal. A week later we beat Spurs 4–2, and again I scored one goal. I got another in a 5–0 win over Wolverhampton Wanderers and the only goal of the game in a home win over Aston Villa. It was all going well and we were top of the league. We were still in first place in December after taking thirty-five points from fourteen matches. Arsenal were one point behind us. Despite taking the early lead, we were overtaken by Arsenal by the end of the season. They became champions while we finished in second place.

We even reached the semi-finals of the Champions' League after beating Arsenal in the quarter-finals. At the beginning of the season the chairman had promised us £50,000 per player if we reached the semi-finals. On 24 March 2004 we met Arsenal at home, but the game ended in a 1–1 draw. It wasn't really a good result. Due to an injury I wasn't able to play that game. On 6 April we set off to Highbury for the return. We knew we had to score at least once in order to reach the semi-finals. Ranieri selected me to start the game. We played quite well, winning 2–1. Everybody was of course overjoyed. In the changing room the atmosphere was exuberant. Abramovich came to join us and was laughing really loudly. When he entered the room Adrian Mutu joked with him, saying, 'Come on man, Come on. Double the bonus, for fun!' Everybody looked at the chairman to see his reaction. And he said, 'OK. I will double it then.' Indeed, at the end of the month, instead of the promised £50,000 there was £100,000 in our bank accounts. I went on holiday with that bonus, and gave my whole family an extra treat.

A few months before, around December, Peter Kenyon had come from Manchester United to take over Trevor Birch's job as chief executive. We never thought Peter Kenyon would do it but he succumbed to the offer.

I was disappointed to hear Marcel Desailly announce his departure on 18 November 2003. I thought he was a very special colleague and a very good footballer. The arrival of the nineteen-year-old Arjen Robben was announced halfway through January, after the PSV chairman Harry van Raay confirmed that they and Chelsea were discussing the transfer. It wasn't long before I heard that I also could leave. I would much rather have not heard that announcement as I would have been very happy to stay.

In the 2004–05 season Adrian Mutu had some bad publicity after traces of cocaine were found in his blood. He was sacked immediately. I hadn't noticed that he was using drugs. I think his problem was his attitude. He was a handsome but spoiled fellow and in Romania he was treated like a king. I'm sure he was able to get any girl he wanted in Romania, and had always been spoiled there. At Chelsea, on the other hand, it didn't go so well for him, and he really had to fight in order to keep his place in the team. For some people it goes right, for others it goes wrong. As he had always been spoiled he had little discipline or strength and couldn't fight temptation.

As someone who plays sport at such a high level and still has his right mind, I'm of the opinion that you can hold him responsible for his actions. Someone like that should know better. He should know what's right and what's not. Perhaps the club didn't have him under control, and let it all happen. Maybe the fact that he didn't really fit in the team that well didn't help him. The same can be said for Mark Bosnich. However, Chelsea couldn't afford to just fire somebody like that. Part of the reason why Mutu could be fired was that he was a difficult person to handle. If John Terry or Frank Lampard had got themselves into the same kind of trouble, Chelsea Football Club would have had a problem. But everybody could accept that Mutu would be sacked. It was a simple thanks and goodbye with a lot of money attached. Nobody talks about Mark Bosnich and Adrian Mutu at Chelsea anymore. The bad things of the past are simply forgotten. That's the way it works.

I thought they were right to punish Mutu. It doesn't matter what kind of drugs he used, because I'm convinced that they are all bad. What kind of message are we giving youngsters who look up to us, and who want to become footballers themselves if we take drugs? If he hadn't been punished, children might think that things like that are tolerated and that you can get away with them. I thought he was a good colleague and he has never done anything bad to me, but I honestly think that his punishment was too light. I think he should have been punished much more harshly. He did something that was prohibited. He should have used his common sense.

I also read in the papers that some of the players have started acting like pop stars. However, I never knew that they were also writing about my earrings! I have had these earrings for two years now. Apparently there was an article in some magazine or newspaper saying that I bought these earrings for £6,000. There are diamonds inside, so they are expensive but they didn't cost me £6,000. They actually cost me £7,500 each, meaning I have £15,000 worth of jewellery hanging from my ears. I don't care if people know how expensive they are, but I do want to show them that they are something beautiful.

If there is something I really want, and I can afford it, I buy it. Why shouldn't I? I rightfully earned that money, and why else should I work? I love watches, and I spend a lot of money on them too. There will always be things I will spend a lot of money on. Clothes are one such item. I don't care if something is a little expensive, as long as the quality is good. The same goes for furniture. I have a modern taste, and I love warmth. You should be able to tell that the owner is living in the house just by looking at the furniture.

Now I can look back on the great time I had at Chelsea. I think I did relatively well at the Bridge, although you should never be satisfied. It could always have been better. Recently someone placed a list in front of me of the players who have been the Chelsea top scorer of the season over the past ten years. I was on it three times, which felt good. In 1996 it was John Spencer with thirteen goals, in 1997 Gianluca Vialli with nine goals, in 1998 Gianluca Vialli and Tore André Flo with eleven, in 1999 Gianfranco Zola with thirteen, in 2000 Tore André Flo and Gustavo Poyet with ten, in 2001 Jerrel Hasselbaink with twenty-three, in 2002 Jerrel Hasselbaink with twenty-three, in 2003 Gianfranco Zola with fourteen, in 2004 Jerrel Hasselbaink with thirteen and in 2005 Frank Lampard with thirteen. Don't get me wrong, I think Frank Lampard is more than a fantastic footballer, but I think that at a club like Chelsea it should never be a midfielder who becomes top scorer. To me it merely means that the forwards didn't do their job.

The fact that I only scored thirteen goals in my fourth and final season with Chelsea was because of the ever-changing tactics of the manager. I started the year off well, playing in partnership with Adrian Mutu and that was working out, despite the fact that he is quite an egocentric player. It was understandable of course that he would be a little selfish as he had to prove that he was worth his transfer fee. The problem, however, was that we had thirteen new players, and all thirteen wanted to prove themselves and so they all made that little extra effort. And they all made the step in their own direction, and not necessarily to the team's benefit. That was why we didn't function all that well and never really became a team. At the same time it was why the guys who had been playing there for some time already, such as Frank Lampard, John Terry, Eidur Gudjohnsen, and William Gallas, had a fantastic season. These guys could now play freely since they didn't need to prove themselves anymore. They had already done so and were not concerned with what kind of impression they made.

We wanted to become champions, but Claudio Ranieri kept on telling us, 'We have a new squad, take it easy, the team has to grow first.' I think he told the press the exact same thing in order to relieve us of some of the pressure. The fans and press, however, expected more from us than the manager did. Every one of the players wanted to go for the title but Ranieri didn't always put his best footballers on the field. Instead, he wanted to be friends with everybody. That wasn't always possible with thirteen new players. He thought he could employ twenty-five players who all deserved to start matches but it didn't work. In the end, he saw the light himself, and eventually fell back on the guys who had done it for him the previous season. He should have never bought so many new players. By doing so, he lost the respect of the guys who had already played for several seasons.

The previous season we had finished in fourth place. It made sense to strengthen the squad, since a team needs continuous improvement in order to become champions. Getting four new players is a lot, but taking on *thirteen* is like signing your own death sentence. Jose Mourinho got it right. He let a few go and he took on a few new ones, but not nearly as many as Ranieri. Damien Duff was one such real reinforcement, and so was Claude Makelele.

Not every acquisition turned out to be a good signing, probably because the players weren't so hungry to win anymore. I think that's why Juan Sebastian Veron and Hernan Crespo, at least the first time round, didn't work out. Adrian Mutu appeared very eager and I personally thought he was a good buy. The trouble was that he wanted the whole team to be built around him. He was used to that back in Romania. It was partly due to his divorce that he went off the rails. He had trouble dealing with it, but then again he always had problems in his private life. It was in his character. He loved to party until very late. I often went out to parties with him, together with Mario Melchiot. The only difference between Mutu and us was that Mario and I would go home at around 3 am. That was late too, but it didn't affect us on the pitch. While we went home, Mutu would stay on, more often than not surrounded by several beautiful women. He just did whatever he liked. He partied until dawn and didn't give a damn that his activities would be all over the papers the next day.

I was also regularly photographed, but never with a girl. Of course, I was also dating at that time, but I didn't need that to be all over the papers. I always made sure I left the nightclub by myself, while my date would either leave ten minutes before or ten minutes after me. That way nobody knew anything. I would have been very embarrassed if my private life had been all over the papers, but Mutu just didn't care. It didn't interest him. He was simply a fun guy to party with. One time he took us to his nightclub in Romania, arranging a private jet for the trip. When we arrived in the country, we didn't even need to show our passports. We were escorted by police to our hotel. At the hotel there were cars waiting for us and more police to take us to the club. The next day we flew back to London, once again in a private jet.

If I had known Mutu was taking drugs I would not have been close to him. He is a nice guy, but I don't want to hang out with that kind of person. It's not that I'm afraid that I would ever be seduced into taking drugs myself. In my youth I saw more than enough of what drugs can do to you. I knew enough guys who used or sold drugs. Still, it's the same with children. After insisting 100 times a child will still say no, but the next time he isn't feeling right and is ready to try it out. That's what I am really afraid of; that if I'm ever down for some reason, that I'll succumb to trying it out. That'll be the end. I don't even want the opportunity to be seduced, and if friends of mine put themselves in that position I break off the contact immediately. I don't like drugs at all. I've had friends who I hung out with day-in day-out, and if you saw what drugs did to them, you wouldn't believe it. Several of those guys have died, although I don't know whether if that was down to overdoses or other reasons. They were strong men. I am a strong man, so I wonder: at what moment did they start taking drugs? At what moment would I start taking them? I don't know, and that's why it's just better to stay away from drugs altogether.

I still speak to Mutu occasionally, but there is more distance now. These days he is playing for Juventus, and he is back in the Romanian national team. I'm glad things are going well for him again.

I have hired a private jet only once in my life. We were playing a pre-season friendly with Middlesbrough in Rostock, Germany. I had to be in London that same evening for the birthday party of a girl I was seeing at the time, and so I hired a plane to fly me back. It cost me about 5,000 euros, but I thought it was well worth it. There were only two pilots (and unfortunately not two stewardesses for me alone!), and it was a seven-seater. I insisted on it being a proper plane. By that I mean a real jet, because I will never again get into a propeller-engined plane, no matter how much you pay me.

Once I was in one of those that almost exploded in the air. On 30 August 1998 I was travelling with the Leeds United team after we had played a match in London against West Ham. We lost 2–0 and then travelled to Stansted in order to fly to Leeds/ Bradford airport in a chartered plane. There were about fifty people on the aircraft so it was packed. Only George Graham had stayed behind in London – I think he was staying with friends or family. We had only just taken off when suddenly we heard 'Boom! Boom!' I had no idea what had happened. I was sitting next to the aisle and looked around me but I couldn't see anything. Robert Molenaar was sitting next to me in the window seat, close to the right wing. The propeller on that side had exploded. He said to me in Dutch, 'Jerrel, I see fire! The engine

is on fire!' I said, 'What?' and together we yelled 'Vuur! Vuur!'
It took us a few moments before we remembered we were in
England, after which we shouted 'Fire! Fire!'

The pilot ordered everyone to stay calm and said that he was
going to attempt an emergency landing. To be honest, I wasn't
so comfortable with that word 'attempt'. In the meantime, I
saw my whole life flash before me. All the shit I pulled when I
was young, but also the fun things. I thought about my daughter Ghislaine, about my mother and my family. Everything was
going through my head.

Robert Molenaar nudged me and said, 'It's getting pretty
warm here now.' I said, 'Shit, you're right!' Fortunately I was
relatively calm then, and so was Robert. Then the plane began
lurching to one side because the pilot was trying to turn in
order to make an emergency landing back at Stansted. I didn't
know what to think, but the chairman was going crazy. Peter
Ridsdale was shouting, 'Where is my son? Where is my son?'
He started running like a madman up and down the aisle. His
son was about fourteen years old and was sitting quietly in his
seat. Everybody was telling Ridsdale, 'Calm down! Sit down
and be calm.' Really, out of all of us, he was panicking the
most.

We ended up making a successful landing at Stansted, not on
the runaway, but on the grass. In order to get out we had to
open the emergency exit on top of the left wing, but it wouldn't
open. We started to panic again, especially because the right
engine was still on fire. Pictures of the burning plane appeared
in the papers the next day. Fortunately the fire engines arrived
very quickly. After a struggle, the assistant manager David

O'Leary was able to open the door. Once the door was open, we saw someone sprint away from the fuselage. Robert and I looked at each other wondering, who was that? It turned out to be the pilot. He had got out first and was sprinting like a dog. Later he received a special award from the club for saving us. Despite the difficult and challenging situation, he had managed to put us back on the ground in one piece.

We still had to get out of the plane. Some went back to look for their belongings, but I was thinking, 'To hell with my bag ...' I jumped out and raced away. I think I've never been so quick. Fortunately everyone was all right. Some passengers got sprained ankles from jumping down from a height, but fortunately no one was seriously hurt. After that, we had to wait at the airport for a few hours. The ground staff asked us whether we wanted to fly again or return by bus back to Leeds. 'Back to the aeroplane ... are you crazy? Put us on the bus right now, I don't care if it takes us three hours. I'm definitely not boarding a plane again!' Not much later I started flying again, but I am still apprehensive during take-off and landing.

In the spring of 2004 I scored another hat-trick. The best part of it was that it was on my birthday, 27 March. I didn't even play the whole game, just the last thirty minutes. The match against Wolverhampton Wanderers ended 5–2 to us after we had been 2–1 down. Then I was put on the pitch, and it turned out I could score after all. I scored the last three goals of the game to make it a truly memorable day.

We should have won the Champions' League that year. On 20 April we played the first leg of the semi-final away to Monaco. Claudio Ranieri made a big tactical mistake there. Monaco led

1–0 thanks to a goal by Dado Prso, who was able to outjump Mario Melchiot at a free-kick in the seventeenth minute and head the ball in. Melchiot received a yellow card early in the game, and in a way he was lucky since he could easily have been sent off for the challenge. Within five minutes Hernan Crespo made the equalizer. Not much later he even had a chance to make the score 2–1 but his shot went over the bar. Normally you would say that a 1–1 draw in an away game is a good result. It means that a 0–0 result at home could be enough to go through to the next round. However, after the break our manager made a critical mistake – he replaced Jesper Gronkjaer with Juan Sebastian Veron. The Argentinian had just got back into shape, but it was his first match in four months. He had only trained with us for three weeks, so why would you then let him come on in the most important match of the season? Ranieri had once again lost his head. He wanted to win so badly that he forgot that 1–1 would have been a perfectly good result. In the fifty-second minute Claude Makelele went down after being shoved by Zikos, and ref Urs Meier immediately showed the Monaco player a red card. At that moment I thought we should be able to hold them. However, Ranieri then substituted a defender for an attacker. He put me on and took off Melchiot. Even though Mario had got a yellow card already, he was smart enough not to get himself a second one. I had to play on the right wing, which surprised me but I could do nothing but obey orders. A little while later Robert Huth came on for Scott Parker, but that didn't help matters either – the team was now completely unbalanced. It must have been because of the yellow card that Ranieri took Mario off, but I was stunned. I understood nothing about his tactics anymore, and it seemed as if our manager had gone totally berserk.

It all went wrong in the last fifteen minutes. Morientes scored to make it 2–1 twelve minutes from time and then Shabani Nonda made things worse for us by making it 3–1. Makelele received a yellow card which meant that he could not play in the return match on 5 May 2004. After the match, the manager immediately had a talk with Abramovich, probably about what had gone wrong in the game. When he came to our hotel later he didn't look very happy.

Two weeks later the return game was played at Stamford Bridge. Before the season I had told the press that if we didn't make the final it would be our own fault. There was no way we should lose to this Monaco team. For me it would be equally wrong if I wasn't in the starting line-up. Fortunately, this time the manager agreed with me.

At this time stories started appearing in the papers that Celtic wanted to take me on loan the following season. But my focus was on the upcoming Monaco tie. The return game at Stamford Bridge started well. I agreed with the setup the manager had put in place on the pitch. Our team consisted of: Carlo Cudicini, Mario Melchiot, Willam Gallas, John Terry, Wayne Bridge, Jesper Gronkjaer, Geremi, Frank Lampard, Joe Cole, myself and Eidur Gudjohnsen. That meant that there were five changes from the previous match. In the meantime Jose Mourinho was walking around London together with Pini Zahavi and his agent Jorge Mendez. I thought that the coach of Porto hadn't just come to spy on us, although it would be either Didier Deschamps' Monaco or us in the final against his Porto team.

The papers were writing more and more about that he would be the successor to Claudio Ranieri. Moreover, Mourinho had also allegedly been spotted in conversation with Peter Kenyon.

We started the game off very well. In no time we were 2–0 ahead, which would have been enough to carry us into the final. Their keeper Flavio Roma first blocked two good chances, one from me and one from Frank Lampard. Jesper Gronkjaer put us ahead with a cross-shot. Lampard subsequently made it 2–0. The prize of reaching the finals was once again within reach. However, just before the break Hugo Iberra made it 2–1. Even though he scored using his hand, the goal stood. Mario Melchiot could have fouled him to prevent him from scoring, but he didn't. Mario was really sharp and concentrating on his game. He knew that if he got another yellow card, he would miss the final. However, I can't believe that was the reason for him being hesitant with Iberra. If it was me I would have risked another yellow card in the interest of the team. That's part of professional sport.

Shortly before that goal, both Joe Cole and Jesper Gronkjaer had good opportunities to increase our lead. In the second half I was replaced by Hernan Crespo. It was a real disappointment since I hadn't been able to score. But the worst part was that Monaco equalized to make it 2–2 when Morientes scored after an hour. We still had half an hour to go but it was to no avail. We were all distraught in the dressing room after the game, with nobody saying a word. Everyone was shattered. We had come so close. I knew that it was probably the closest I would get to a Champions' League final and now it wasn't going to happen. According to the Monaco coach, Didier Deschamps, we had spent too much of our energy in the first half. Had we reached the final, I think we would have done well against Porto. This time it just wasn't meant to be.

I'm not the type to ask what if, but I'm convinced the constant shifting of players in and out of our team wasn't good. Claudio Ranieri is a nice man, and I've always had a good relationship with him. I just disagreed with some of his methods. For one, he managed a big club but he never put pressure on the squad. He did, however, put negative pressure on us by having us stay very quiet in the dressing room. He didn't want any noise in the dressing room before a match. During the break nobody would say a word. Here in England it is normal that before a game you have some music on, you make some noise and you kick the ball around a bit. Ranieri, on the other hand, wanted us to be calm and quiet. He would even take the ball away from us. For away games, he wanted us to be very quiet on the way to the ground. We couldn't even turn on any music. We were allowed Walkmans, but only with the volume turned down. The older players in the squad, Zola, Poyet, Wise, Gudjohnsen, Desailly and I, always sat at the back of the coach, joking and fooling around. If we were laughing a little too loudly, Ranieri would turn around and look at us scornfully. Sometimes it was so bad that he sent his assistant manager Angelo to the back of the bus. Angelo would then sit next to us and make us be quiet and concentrate on the match. It was ridiculous! Concentration came on the pitch. Before the game it was more important that we could relax a bit. After the match he didn't care about the noise.

I have seen Ranieri very angry several times. He often got

angry because we were picking on Roberto Sassi. He also got cross with me for that. I didn't always take the initiative in picking on Sassi, far from it, but I was an eager participant. That Sassi was a complete nutter. He seemed to think that we were in some kind of detention camp. It was abnormal how hard he made us work.

Ranieri once got angry because the group hadn't done something he wanted, and he had convinced himself that we were pulling his leg. 'You want me to get the sack? I don't care. I'll take the money. Then I'll go and sit on the beach with a big cigar.' He probably felt that we had deserted him. Probably he also wanted to make something clear to us. I think the pressure from above was enormous. Stories that circulated about the English national manager being his most likely successor certainly contributed to that. However, he should have made it clear that he didn't need any more new players. Ranieri should have listened less to those at the top while showing more understanding and support for his squad, especially towards those players who had been at Chelsea for some time already.

All transfer business was taken care of by Pini Zahavi. The chairman is coincidentally also Jewish, so I presume that created an extra bond between the two of them. Zahavi talked with all the clubs, but also with all the players' agents. He is very important for arranging transfers. If Chelsea want to do business that way, then that's fine by me. It just costs a little extra, because the players' agents also want to make some profit on the deal, and they are not giving away discounts just because Zahavi is also involved. The courting of Eriksson took quite some time. Only after he was spotted entering the house of

Peter Kenyon did the rumours stop. I think Eriksson had agreed to take the job, but when he was caught at Kenyon's house it became impossible. It would have been very difficult for him to leave the English national team for Chelsea. Perhaps it would have been possible after the 2006 World Cup, but probably not before. Mourinho is now doing a fantastic job, so Eriksson probably isn't required anymore. I'm sure Mourinho will be there for some time.

I saw Jose Mourinho once at the club. It was at the end of the season, and I already knew that I was going to leave. Humphry Nijman had spoken with Peter Kenyon. There were rumours that I would leave in December 2003 but as far as I know that was never discussed. I didn't have to leave then, I still had one-and-a-half-years to go on my contract. However, I just wanted to play football and be important to the team. I no longer felt like that at Chelsea. Jose Mourinho had new ideas and wanted to attract some new players too. It made sense. I was thirty-two years old then and had reached an age at which only a handful of players are able to carry on at the top. Roy Keane, Alan Shearer, Tony Adams and Dennis Bergkamp were or are such players. For others, like me, we have to be realistic.

Of course, it would have been fantastic if Mourinho had come to me and said, 'I want you in the team. You are not going to play every game, but I want you as my permanent reserve, with a chance of being in the starting line-up, meaning that, if someone is injured, I can put you on the pitch.' If he had told me that I would have stayed. Instead he took on Didier Drogba and Arjen Robben, among others. For those guys their first season wasn't easy. In England, technical skills alone are not enough. You also need character. I have the feeling that I could definitely have delivered the same as Drogba did in the 2004–05 season. On the other hand, it wasn't an easy first season for him. He was bought for £24 million and that brings huge pressure to perform well. That's also something you need to be able to handle. Some players need a bit more time for that. I suspect Jose Mourinho misjudged me. I think he thought that Jimmy is thirty-two or thirty-three years old. I can't just say anything to him anymore and I also can't just put him aside. I suspect he entertained those kinds of thoughts and that he didn't want any such problems in the group. That's probably why he decided it was better to let me go. However, I also heard later that he had spoken with several people who know me well, and that he more or less found out deep into the season what sort of character I really was.

In any case, he did well. He helped the team to win the league, something that hadn't happened to Chelsea for fifty years. He is simply very special. Also, it works the way he does it. I would have loved to have been part of it myself, not just because they became champions, but mostly because I heard from others that he is a very different type of manager to Ranieri. That's what I would have liked to experience myself. It shouldn't take anything away from my present manager at Middlesbrough. Steve McClaren is also top class. He is a very different man to Ranieri, and treats his players very differently too. McClaren gives us a lot of free time and lets us make our own decisions on the pitch. His training sessions are fantastic, and there is simply nothing negative to say about him. However, Chelsea is still the club to which my heart belongs. At Chelsea

I left of my own will under very good circumstances, while receiving the appreciation I lacked when I left Leeds United. I was fortunate to experience that appreciation once more during a match at Stamford Bridge, when this time I was playing for Middlesbrough.

After the season was over I went with friends and my brother to Surinam and Barbados. During the holiday I didn't know yet where I would be signing my new contract. I only found that out in August 2004.

Over the last few years I have also been about four or five times to Dubai, and two years ago I even bought a house on the Palm, a man-made peninsula in the shape of a palm tree. My house is located on one of the leaves. It is a lot of fun there. It takes about six to seven hours to fly there from England but it is comfortably warm and relaxed the whole year round. I still have to take care of a few things there, but two years ago I also bought a holiday house there with five bedrooms. The house there has a private beach with its own jetty. In 2009 the construction will be finished, and by that time I will have retired, I guess in about two or three seasons. Then, I can go for about two to three months to Dubai every year. It's a great place for snorkelling and diving as well, but I haven't done that yet. First I must conquer my fear. I'm afraid that I'll encounter a big fish, such as a shark or something, and start panicking. I should go with someone who isn't scared. If I have another girlfriend, I will go diving with her, and then try to conquer my fear. It's not my world, but I would like to explore under the sea.

10 Tales at the Riverside

It was disappointing to hear from Peter Kenyon that Chelsea were looking to get rid of me. He didn't tell me directly of course, instead letting Humphry Nijman know that several clubs had expressed an interest in me and that we were free to talk to them. That made the message clear enough: Chelsea didn't want to keep me, and they probably already had plans for someone to take my place – either a new acquisition or someone already at the club. I still had a contract for one more season with them, but they weren't going to make me sit that out in London. I was free to leave.

PSV's manager, Guus Hiddink, enquired about the possibility of me joining his club. I would have loved to work with him but Eindhoven was not an option to me as I didn't want to return to Holland yet, and certainly not as a footballer. Of course, that doesn't mean that I wasn't very flattered by the 2004–05 Champions' League semi-finalist's interest in me.

There was interest from other foreign leagues as well. Sporting Lisbon were interested, as were Betis Sevilla, where Serra Ferrer, the former manager of Barcelona, was now manager. In

2004–05 they finished fourth in the Primera Liga, qualifying for the preliminaries of the Champions' League. Levante also called to discuss a possible move there, and in England Charlton, Everton and Fulham all made enquiries. However, those clubs weren't involved in European football, and that was something I definitely wanted.

AC Milan also called for me, but I wasn't interested. Sure, they are one of Europe's best football clubs, but after thinking about it for a while I decided against it. The same goes for Sporting Lisbon. The reason I didn't choose another foreign adventure was that I really preferred to continue playing in England. I'm actually not so fond of Italy. I know that AC Milan is a fantastic club, but the type of football they play there, as well as the country itself, just doesn't appeal to me. The emphasis on defence in Serie A doesn't do anything for me. Another important point to consider was that they always have a lot of great forwards competing for a place. Last summer, they even managed to sign Christian Vieri from Inter, their big rival. I would love to have played with Andrei Shevchenko, but I wouldn't have been certain of a place in the team and I still want to spend a lot of time on the pitch. I suspect I would not have been offered a lot of playing time had I joined Milan. It was nonsense to suggest that I turned them down because I would have had problems adjusting to life there. In fact, I think I am actually rather good at adapting, and I am able to do so rather quickly.

I can imagine people thinking that I was crazy to choose Middlesbrough, a club playing European football for the very first time, instead of a giant like AC Milan. Granted, the difference is big. If I had been twenty-five years old, I would probably have chosen Milan. Joining Middlesbrough also meant that I hadn't let money make up my mind, because I could have earned more with AC Milan. In any case, if I was just interested in earning money, I might as well have gone to Turkey. The real decisive factor was that I wanted to stay in England.

The move to Middlesbrough began with my agent sending a message to my holiday home in Dubai, asking me if I was interested in going there. At that moment it was already clear that whatever happened I would be leaving Chelsea. When I called Humphry back, he told me that Steve McClaren, Middlesbrough's manager, had called him to ask if I would be willing to move to his club. Before making my decision I asked Humphry about the merits of moving to Middlesbrough. He told me about the club's ambitious growth plans. An hour later, I was talking to Steve McClaren myself for the very first time. He sounded very sure of himself and of his plans, and told me which other players would be joining, and who had already come. It was a good initial talk, but I wasn't yet 100 per cent convinced. It meant that I would have to leave London, although because of my two years in Leeds United, I had a pretty good idea of what life would be like in the north of England.

Several days later George Boateng called me. He told me that Steve McClaren had asked him to call me up and find out if there was a realistic chance that I would join them. Boateng, who was already playing with Middlesbrough, told me very openly that the club could really become a top team if I joined them. He also told me that there was already a good group there, consisting of a mix of young talent and experienced players such as

Stewart Downing, Gareth Southgate and Mark Viduka and that the training facilities were excellent. In fact, everything was perfect there according to George. The only thing missing, he said, was my signature. I then told him that I would travel to Middlesbrough to hear more.

In my first face-to-face talk with Steve McClaren he made it clear that he already knew that I was a true striker but was keen to find out what kind of person I was. He then made it clear that he was eager to have me in his team. After the personal talks the more business-like formalities commenced between Humphry Nijman and the Middlesbrough management.

In the end I chose 'Boro' because of the overall shape of the club. As they had won the League Cup for the first time they were going to be playing European football. I was also familiar with the many positive stories about the manager. He was on several clubs' wish lists, as well as the FA's one for Sven-Goran Eriksson's successor. When I arrived at Middlesbrough, he was already Eriksson's assistant. Before that he had been Sir Alex Ferguson's assistant for two-and-a-half years at Manchester United. There were rumours that if Ferguson left Manchester United, McClaren would have a very good chance of succeeding him.

Boudewijn Zenden was loaned to Middlesbrough by Chelsea for the 2004–05 season. 'Bolo' told me that training at Boro was a 100 per cent improvement on Claudio Ranieri's training regime at Chelsea. He also told me that another Dutchman, the national team player Michael Reiziger, would be joining from Barcelona. I asked him about all the good things I had heard about McClaren, and they were all confirmed. I decided I wanted to have fun again with football, and play in as many games as possible. I really didn't want another season at Chelsea, where everybody just had to wait to see if they were playing. Tinkerman Ranieri had made a mess of things there. His methods hadn't improved the team one bit.

I was very happy with the new acquisitions at Middlesbrough. Chairman Steve Gibson had taken some big risks, and they had paid off. Under his command, the club had been steadily growing, while the arrival of Steve McClaren in the summer of 2002 had provided the club with a real boost.

Middlesbrough FC was founded in 1876 and played its first game in 1877 at Old Archery Road in Albert Park. In 1879 the club started playing at Breckom Hill and three years later they moved again, this time to Linthorpe Road. In 1889 the club turned professional for a little while but quickly returned to the amateur ranks where they easily won the FA Cup for amateurs. Four years later Middlesbrough turned professional once again, and in 1899 they joined Division Two. In 1903 the club moved again, this time to Ayresome Park. Ever since then they have played mainly in either the first or second division, but during the 1966–67 season they were even relegated to the third division. In 1993 Middlesbrough became one of the founding members of the Premier League, but they were relegated after one season. Two years later the club moved to the Riverside Stadium, which can hold 34,500 people. The club's record attendance is therefore likely to remain 53,596, a figure achieved in 1949. In 1997 the club reached both the League and FA Cup Final, but lost in both. To top the season off, they were also relegated to the first division once again.

In my first season the club achieved all my targets for the year. We qualified for European football, again in the UEFA Cup, which says a lot about the quality of the team. I also felt that with the right new players, we would even have a chance of qualifying for the Champions' League the following season. For now, the target is to achieve fourth or fifth place. I think that should be possible, especially when you take into account all the bad luck we had with injuries last season.

One thing I really like about Steve McClaren is that he gives the young players a fair chance. James Morrison has an excellent chance of breaking through and Stewart Downing is already usually in the starting line-up. In that sense I think the club can look forward to a good future. It's comparable to my second year at Leeds United, where the youth players were also given many opportunities. It's a very positive thing for a football club to have a good youth team.

My introduction at Middlesbrough wasn't as big a deal as the one at Atlético Madrid. For most of the fans it came as a total surprise as almost nobody knew about my pending arrival. Many people didn't expect me to move to Middlesbrough as I had a contract for another season with Chelsea. I was allowed to leave on a free transfer, which was very generous of the Blues. It was a beautiful gesture, and it gave me a great sense of appreciation for the years I played with them. It was wonderful.

I signed the contract with a good salary attached, but even in my own book I am not going to reveal how much I earn. I have already divulged a lot about myself, but I will not talk about money. Footballers almost never talk about their income.

Journalists are the ones interested in how much we earn. The only thing I will say is that the salary they offered me for two seasons was good enough for us not to have to negotiate for very long. I signed my contract on 7 July 2004.

The team had just started their pre-season training. We trained at our own facilities, rather than going away to a training camp, as was the case at Chelsea. It was fine with me. I was actually happy not to have to go to Roccaporena, as you can well imagine. Even though we stayed at home, I missed nothing. The Rockcliff Park training complex is simply perfect. It has everything you need for football training. It even has all the facilities you want when recuperating after injury. Chelsea have now built themselves a new training ground, but the one at Middlesbrough is certainly a lot better than the old one at Chelsea.

After four years I finally had a spell of perfect pre-season training. We worked hard – thank God we spent a lot of time working with the ball. At Middlesbrough we do about ten per cent of the physical training that was expected at Chelsea.

Steve McClaren didn't make it to the absolute top as a player, partly because injury forced him to retire from the professional game aged twenty-seven in 1988. Before ending his playing career at Oxford he had played for Derby County, Hull, and Bristol City. After he stopped playing, he coached the reserves at Oxford. He then had a coaching post at Derby County before moving to Manchester United. Every now and then McClaren likes to join in during training. I can't tell if he was a very good player, but he is still fanatically keen. He is also surrounded by a good group of support staff. He has an assistant trainer, Steve Harrison, and a coach purely for the attackers,

Steve Round. Our goalkeeper-trainer, Paul Barron, is one of England's best. But no matter who else is there, Steve McClaren is the boss. Steve Round, who we call Roundie, was a top-level player himself. He is still young, only thirty-six, but after he damaged his knee he was unable to carry on playing. Fortunately, we don't have a Roberto Sassi walking around at Middlesbrough. Our physical trainer is also not as whacko as Sassi was; Chris Barnes likes to keep things simple. The training routines are, in fact, much more varied than at Chelsea.

Even though we didn't have a pre-season training camp abroad, we did play friendly matches against foreign teams, such as the one against Hansa Rostock in Germany when I hired a private jet. We may have lost that match, but look what happened. Hansa ended up relegated while we qualified for the UEFA Cup again!

Our first league match, on 14 August 2004 was a derby against Newcastle United, the club of Bobby Robson, Alan Shearer, and Patrick Kluivert. We should have won that home match, but it ended in a 2–2 draw. I was able to score the last goal of the game after a nice pass from Boudewijn Zenden. He went past a defender on the left and provided the perfect cross. However, I needed my hand to get the ball into the net. Fortunately, the referee didn't notice it and so the goal counted. The fact that my hand touched the ball was, however, clearly visible from the television pictures. When I was interviewed right after the match I said that I didn't exactly remember what I had done, but whatever it was I definitely hadn't done it on purpose. It had been a reflex. The ball had gained speed, and because the pitch was wet I couldn't properly push myself off from the ground. I was already low, and so I went with my head first. It was, as Maradona had said, 'the hand of God'.

Unfortunately, Sir Bobby Robson was fired a few weeks later. That was a ridiculous decision. That man had achieved so much not only for his club, but also for England. I know he would never have stopped on his own account, that much was clear. He was a legend in England. Sir Bobby Robson rightfully deserves a statue. There were rumours that he couldn't win over Kieron Dyer and a few of the other young players, but I'm personally not so sure about that even though I don't know the real reasons behind his dismissal. In Holland he was manager of PSV twice, but he never got as much appreciation there as he deserved. The Dutch are always very critical about everything. They usually only see the negative aspects, while they have forgotten the fact that he made PSV national champions.

For me it was a good thing that I was able to score in my first game. One week later I also scored against Arsenal, but that single goal was not enough as we lost 5–3 at Highbury. The match went well to start with and at one point we were even ahead 3–1. But then Thierry Henry went to work in the second half which is why we lost in the end. Although we had suffered an unfortunate defeat, it was already clear to me that we would have a very good year. The only unlucky thing was that many guys, such as Mark Viduka, Michael Reiziger, George Boateng and Gaizka Mendieta were unavailable because of injury, for weeks, sometimes months.

Three days after the Arsenal game, we were back in London again, this time to play Fulham who we beat 2–0. I didn't have any part in the goals, however. After a 2–1 home victory over

Crystal Palace on 28 August the fans also started to believe that it would be a good season. During that match at the Riverside, I scored my third goal of the season. Again, it felt good. One week later we won again and by the same score when we took on Birmingham City and my good friend Mario Melchiot. The next match we lost though, 1–0 to Everton at Goodison Park.

A few days later Chelsea came to play us. My old team-mates beat us 1–0. It was a game with very few scoring opportunities. It was strange having to play against all the familiar faces. During the game I clashed with John Terry. In a challenge for the ball, his leg was high, while I had put my head a bit low. It was an unnecessary hit. I'm sure he didn't mean to kick me, but his foot was much higher than it needed to be, and so I got the full impact of it in my face. I needed seven stitches. After the game, John came to our dressing room to apologize. I warned him half-jokingly, 'You know that you'll get this one back some time, eh?' And he said, 'Yes, I know. I've known you for a while now.'

I hadn't spoken with any of my ex-Chelsea team-mates before the game. What can you say under such circumstances? More-over, I never speak with opponents before a match, I only do so once I'm on the pitch. This time I only exchanged a few words with Geremi and Eidur Gudjohnsen, asking them how they were doing. I also shook hands with the doctor, physio and the assistant manager.

I had psyched myself up with the idea that this should be my game. I wanted to show Chelsea that they had let me go one year too early, but unfortunately none of those plans material-ized. Afterwards, I didn't speak to many people, except for John

Terry. As I had just had seven stitches in my head, I wasn't really up for social conversation.

The following match, I felt better again. The stitches were no longer bothering me and I was able to score another hat-trick in a 4–0 win against Blackburn Rovers. I scored the first, third and fourth goals while George Boateng scored the second one. All the goals came in the second half. We won so easily partly because Tugay had to leave the pitch after getting two yellow cards in the first thirty minutes. After that game it took a while – until 6 December – before I scored my next goal. In the meantime we played against Portsmouth, Charlton Athletic, Bolton Wanderers, West Bromwich Albion, Liverpool and Tottenham Hotspur, but it wasn't until the Manchester City game that I was able to find the net again. We beat them 3–2. Not scoring for six matches was quite frustrating, but it didn't help me having to play with a different partner up front each time.

In the meantime we also played European football. Our first opponents in the UEFA Cup were Banik Ostrava, the Czech champions. They had been eliminated during the Champions' League preliminaries by Bayer Leverkusen, but we found out soon enough that they were no match for us either. We beat them 3–0, thanks to one goal from me and two from Mark Viduka. Two weeks later, we boarded a plane for Middlesbrough's first-ever official away European match. It ended in a 1–1 draw. Not only was it a very special day for the club, it was also a proud moment for Chairman Steve Gibson. For me, on the other hand, it was just another game that had to be won.

The format of the competition was such that once you reached the second round, you were in a group with four other clubs. In total there were eight groups. We were in group E along with Egaleo, Villareal, Lazio and Partizan Belgrade. Our first game was against the Greek team, Egaleo, on 21 October which we won 1–0. A few days later we played against Coventry City in the Carling Cup, beating them 3–0. I didn't play in that game, probably because the manager wanted to save me for upcoming matches. On 4 November we won our UEFA Cup home game against Lazio 2–0. One week later, on 10 November, we were eliminated from the Carling Cup, the competition the club had won the previous year, by Liverpool, losing 2–0 at Anfield. Ten days later, however, Liverpool came to us for a league game and this time we won 2–0. It was clear then that Liverpool v Middlesbrough would remain a close call for the rest of the season.

After we had won our first two group matches in the UEFA Cup, we lost our third one, 2–0 to the Spanish side Villareal. However, I didn't play in that game. Our fans had clearly become really excited about the UEFA Cup, since at least 4,000 of them travelled to watch us play in the Costa Blanca. It turned out that Villareal's advance to the Cup would only be halted in the semi-finals by my former Dutch club AZ Alkmaar. On 15 December we won our fourth and last UEFA Cup match in group E, beating Partizan Belgrade 3–0. We had done enough to qualify for the last sixteen.

We were also performing reasonably well in the league. We drew at Southampton, I scored when we beat Aston Villa 3–0, we lost 2–0 against Birmingham City and we won our last match of 2004 when we beat Norwich City 2–0 on 28 December.

On 1 January 2005 Manchester United came to the Riverside,

winning 2–0. That game, however, had little effect on my mind. I was more anxious about our midweek match against Chelsea at the Bridge on 4 January. I was very worried about how the Chelsea fans would react. It turned out to be a very special match for me however, as the fans were truly fantastic. I was presented with a medal by Chelsea for my long-standing dedication to the club, which made me feel really appreciated for the efforts I had put in when I played for them. The tribute was made even more memorable because one of my closest friends at Chelsea, Eidur Gudjohnsen, presented me with the medal on the field. I was really honoured.

At the same time it felt a little strange, because I was used to being yelled at whenever I returned to play at my other English former club, Leeds United. This time it was the opposite. It meant a lot to me, it still does. We lost the game 3–0, but I considered that I had won a victory for myself. I was very nervous before that match, but as in other cases, I was able to sleep well the night before. I had called a few guys before to find out which players would be in the Chelsea line-up. For one, I was interested to know if John Terry would be playing. I still owed him something from our little incident at the Riverside. Geremi told me that he would be playing, which, as you can imagine, was a great relief to me!

I confronted him several times during that match at Stamford Bridge. I wasn't going to kick him into hospital, no, but I did try to bring back a few memories of our little aerial collision in Middlesbrough. Fortunately, we were able to laugh about it even a short time after the match. That was good, it's the way it should be.

The manager gave me permission to stay in London in order to have a drink with a few old friends, so I went out with Eidur and some other friends from London. We went to The Funky Buddha, a club popular among celebrities and footballers. You don't have to be a member, but it is difficult to get in. Guess who I met there? John Terry! We shared a joke about still trying to get even over a small personal incident that afternoon. However, I noticed that he was having some problems walking. It was because I had hit him in an aerial clash that wasn't completely accidental. We both jumped up, and my foot hit his thigh. He had quite a number of scratches on his leg and subsequently had some problems walking. It turned out that I had given him a dead leg.

I had warned him beforehand that something like that could happen, saying that I still hadn't forgotten about my stitches. During the first half I went to find him. He knew me through and through, so he was aware that I would try to get even before the end of the match.

When he was young John Terry could also be quite rough at times during training. When I signed with Chelsea he was still a young lad – I think he must have been something like seventeen or eighteen years old at the time. That year he was allowed to train with the first team for the first time. During his very first training session he kicked the shit out of me. He gained a lot of respect from me then. In a way, I admired the fact that he was already doing that sort of thing to an expensive new acquisition like me. He also understood the way I think and work. I don't normally complain about that sort of thing, but I just had to say something about it.

He knew I would get him back for our clash earlier in the

season, and that then it would be over; scores would be settled, nothing more nothing less. It was a mental fight that we were involved in, and this time I won on points. It wasn't a knockout, since he didn't have to leave the pitch. However, he had to be treated, and afterwards he had some difficulty running. Even so, that same evening, at The Funky Buddha, we were able to have a big laugh about it.

We had limited Cup success that season. In the third round of the FA Cup, played in early January, we won 2–1 against Notts County. One round later we were up against Manchester United, who beat us 3–0 at Old Trafford. The Cup was over for us for another year.

After Chelsea our next league game was against Everton. We drew 1–1 with them on 16 January. A week later I scored again, twice this time, in a game against Norwich City that ended 4–4. At one point we were ahead 4–1, but still managed to drop two valuable points. In the meantime it had become clear that there were only three clubs in the Premiership who were significantly stronger than us: Arsenal, Chelsea and Manchester United. Although Everton, Liverpool and Bolton Wanderers also finished ahead of us at the end of the season, all of us were at a similar level.

Everton were lucky in that they played against us when we were going through a bad spell. Nonetheless, the 1–1 draw at home and the 1–0 defeat at Goodison did suggest that we were of similar strength. Before the away game we had made our European debut against Banik Ostrava on the Thursday and then had to play against Everton on the Sunday. They, on the other hand, weren't playing any European football, which in my view made a considerable difference for that match. For Everton it was a unique season. They finished in fourth place in the Premiership, ahead of the Champions' League winners Liverpool. That hadn't happened in eighteen years. The previous season they had only finished seventeenth, narrowly missing relegation. To me, that says a lot about their manager. It was acknowledged by the other coaches as well, as can be deduced from the fact that David Moyes was voted manager of the year, ahead of Jose Mourinho at Chelsea and Rafael Benitez at Liverpool.

From a European perspective things went well. On 17 February we visited Graz AK in Austria. The game ended in a 2–2 draw, even though we took the lead twice during the game. Boudewijn Zenden made it 1–0 and I scored to make it 2–1 later on. One week later they came to Middlesbrough. Even though 1–1 would have been good enough for us to go through, we beat them 2–1. The Austrians went into a 1–0 lead before James Morrison scored the equalizer and in the second half I scored the winning goal.

We didn't win a lot of league matches during February. On the first day of the month we lost 2–1 against Portsmouth. We managed to beat Blackburn 1–0 at home four days later, but that was to be our only league victory that month. We drew 0–0 against Bolton Wanderers on 12 February and on 27 February Charlton Athletic held us 2–2 at home. One week later we lost 2–0 to Aston Villa. On Thursday 10 March we played Sporting Lisbon in the UEFA Cup quarter-finals. They had knocked out Feyenoord, which was a disappointment as I would love to have played in Rotterdam, even if it were just for my brother-in-law, who is a big Feyenoord fan.

Sporting had a good team, and they beat us 3–2 at the River-side. After the break they scored three goals in twenty minutes. Thanks to goals from Joseph Desire Job and Chris Riggott we still had a chance in the return match. However, I would not be travelling to Portugal as a sprained knee was giving me prob-lems. Previously I'd been offered injections to numb the pain of an injury during a match, but this time I'd had enough. Never-theless I was very annoyed that I couldn't play because Portugal is an important country to me. It was there where people first noticed me, and it was there where I was given the chances denied to me even in my own country.

We lost 1–0 in Lisbon and were therefore eliminated from the tournament. The Portuguese team went on to reach the final, losing to CSKA Moscow in their own stadium.

Three days later we lost 3–1 at home against Southampton. It was their first away victory of the season. It seemed that our players weren't completely mentally recovered from our defeat in Lisbon and the long journey home. We then won 1–0 at Crystal Palace but lost at home to Arsenal by the same score. That was an unnecessary defeat, since I missed a very good chance against the Gunners. On Tuesday 19 April we drew 1–1 with Fulham. With just a few minutes left I won a penalty kick after keeper Van der Sar floored me. In hindsight, we were lucky to get a point as I think the penalty was a present from the referee as the collision happened just outside the box. Edwin was very angry with the referee afterwards. We won our next game easily, beating West Brom 4–0, with me scoring one goal. We then drew 0–0 against Newcastle. I had a good chance, but somehow I couldn't take it. We might have won, but the Magpies also had a good chance right before the final whistle.

We then had another draw, 1–1 against Liverpool. Steven Gerrard scored with a beautiful long-distance shot from about thirty-five yards that went in just under the crossbar. The match against Liverpool was like a final for us, as we were both competing for a UEFA Cup place for the following season. Getting one point at Liverpool was good, but one week later we faced another rival for Europe, Tottenham Hotspur. We had to win in order to keep them below us. Fortunately we did so, beating them 1–0 thanks to a goal by George Boateng early on in the game. Martin Jol's team dominated the match, but we created the best chances.

It wasn't until the end of the very last game of the season that we knew if we would be playing European football again. It was a difficult period for me. I wasn't scoring as much as I should. I was getting chances, but I wasn't taking them. I definitely had my mind on the matches, but at the same time I was also busy working on my house in Harrogate. I had been doing renovating work there, and this went on for months on end. It was one misfortune after the other, and yet I wanted to take care of everything myself. I wanted to decide myself what work should take place and how it should be done. In hindsight, all those worries about the house probably affected my performance on the pitch. I was getting quite stressed out.

Our biggest match of the season was on Sunday 15 May, at the City of Manchester stadium. We needed at least a draw against Manchester City. If we lost then Stuart Pearce's club would take the final UEFA Cup place. We left for Manchester the day prior to the match. It turned out to be one of the most exciting games of my career. It contained everything. After twenty-three minutes I scored from a free-kick from about twenty-five yards to put us in the lead. In fact, the free-kick had had to be retaken. The first time Bolo passed the ball poorly, a bit too nonchalantly, but luckily the City players ran in too fast so referee Styles told me to start again. This time Bolo wanted to shift the ball to me again, but I pushed him away telling him, 'Get out of here! I want you next to the wall, so that the keeper can't see the ball.' Fortunately he walked away this time. I hit the ball perfectly, curving it inward at the very last moment, and David James was beaten.

I received many compliments about my shot afterwards. Everybody I met on the street talked to me about it. Friends and family called up and sent me text messages. I didn't know whether it would be considered the goal of the season, but I hoped it would be a candidate for a place among the top ten. It was also a very important goal as it proved to be our ticket to the UEFA Cup.

After one minute of the second half, Manchester City equalized through Kiki Musampa which put the game back on a knife edge. I could feel the tension on the pitch, and it was nerve-wracking. Their manager Stuart Pearce even replaced the midfielder Claudio Reyna five minutes from time with the reserve goalie Nicky Weaver so that David James could join the attack. It was odd, he even went away to put on a different jersey. They wanted to confuse us, I'm sure, and it almost worked. In fact, it did work. In injury time they were awarded a penalty kick after a goalmouth scramble. Had that gone in then Manchester

City would be playing in Europe, but instead Robbie Fowler's penalty was smothered by Mark Schwarzer to his left. I felt sorry for Robbie. I don't wish upon anybody the feeling you go through when you miss such an ideal chance in such an important match in the very last minute.

How exactly he felt, nobody knows. You can only imagine. I didn't talk to him after the match. It's better to leave people alone. I didn't think he took the penalty badly, it's just that Mark made a very good save. He was the deserving hero of Middlesbrough. At moments like that football is such a beautiful thing, it captures all the emotions known to man.

There was no special celebration at the club that evening, but the next day we all went for dinner. It was our planned goodbye dinner for the 2004–05 season. Afterwards we could go on holiday. On evenings like that you meet the whole board and all the employees of the club. I like such parties. I don't know the chairman Steve Gibson that well as we don't see each other very often, but I do know that he looks after things brilliantly at the Riverside. He doesn't interfere with the manager and remains in the background. He makes clear what the budget for new acquisitions is, and that's it. He doesn't do strange, extravagant things, he is a well-respected and a capable businessman. The chairman is doing well, and the club is getting bigger and bigger. The structure is strong, and there are good and capable people at this club.

Mr Gibson is there for all of our home games, but he doesn't show up in the dressing room after a match. He also sometimes comes along for away games. On our last match of the season in Manchester he was there, but even then he didn't come to the dressing room afterwards. He maintains a very clear dividing line which makes life easier for everyone.

For me 2004–05 was a good season. There is no reason for me to leave Middlesbrough. I had hoped Boudewijn Zenden would remain with us, but he chose to go to Liverpool. This coming season I will be joined up front by the twenty-two-year-old Nigerian striker Yakubu Aiyegbeni. The former Portsmouth forward is an important acquisition for the club. Just like me, he also scored thirteen goals last season. Thierry Henry was again top scorer with twenty-five goals. I was in fourth place, together with Jermain Defoe and Yakubu, but behind Andy Johnson from Crystal Palace with twenty-one goals, and Robert Pires from Arsenal with fourteen goals.

Fortunately, Middlesbrough also have some promising young talent at the club. Stewart Downing is improving daily. He has something extra that stands out. He can accelerate well, his movements are good and his left foot is excellent. He only has to work on the mental side of the game. Especially here in England, you have to be able to stand up to your marker. He sometimes lacks the necessary aggression, and so he has to work on that a little bit more. He is still a little intimidated at times and opponents know how to take advantage of that. Once he conquers that fear, he can easily be a top player for club and country.

Everyone is talking about Stewart Downing, and rightly so, but my personal favourite is Tony McMahon because in many aspects he is just like me. He is still young, and very comfortable with the ball. He is a good passer, but when he has to tackle or subdue somebody he can do that as well. He is almost the complete player. He still acts the celebrity a little bit, but at that age it's okay. I also admire James Morrison. He is a midfielder, very quick and with a sound technique. He is a shrewd fellow, and knows no fear.

They are three young talents that can grow to become excellent players. It's very important for the club to have those three. They act as an example to other young footballers. You don't have to be a star player from overseas in order to become famous in England. You can see the English youth fighting back and getting into teams. It's happening at every club. I often work with these guys during training. I treat Stewie a little rougher than the others because that's what he needs. I'm telling him to get tough, and he understands me now. If everybody keeps on babying him, he won't learn.

The idea of becoming an assistant coach to Guus Hiddink or Louis van Gaal when I stop playing still appeals to me. I notice I enjoy working with the younger players, but honestly I really don't know what I'll do when I retire. The most important thing for me is to play for Middlesbrough, bring them the success they deserve and enjoy the game. After that, who knows.

Career Statistics

Jerrel Hasselbaink

Date of birth	27 Mar 1972
Nationality	Netherlands
Place of birth	Paramaribo
Current club	Middlesbrough
Previous clubs	Telstar, AZ, Neerlandia/SLTO, Campomaiorense, Boavista, Leeds United, Atletico Madrid, Chelsea
Int. debut	27 May 1998 against Cameroon (D 0-0)
Caps	23
Cap goals	9

Domestic League Summary

Season	Club	Competition	Country
1990/1991	Telstar	Eerste Divisie	NED
1991/1992	AZ	Eerste Divisie	NED
1992/1993	AZ	Eerste Divisie	NED
1993/1994	Neerlandia/SLTO	(Amateurs)	NED
1994/1995	Neerlandia/SLTO	(Amateurs)	NED
1995/1996	SC Campomaiorense	I Divisão	POR
1996/1997	Boavista FC	I Divisão	POR
1997/1998	Leeds United	Premier League	ENG
1998/1999	Leeds United	FA Premiership	ENG
1999/2000	Atlético Madrid	Primera División	ESP
2000/2001	Chelsea	FA Premiership	ENG
2001/2002	Chelsea	FA Premiership	ENG
2002/2003	Chelsea	FA Premiership	ENG
2003/2004	Chelsea	Barclaycard FA Premiership	ENG
2004/2005	Middlesbrough	Barclaycard FA Premiership	ENG

Totals

Debuts

Telstar	27 Oct 1990	VVV v Telstar	2-0
AZ	17 Aug 1991	AZ v Excelsior	3-1
Leeds United	09 Aug 1997	Leeds United v Arsenal	1-1
Atlético Madrid	22 Aug 1999	Atlético Madrid v Rayo Vallecano	0-2
Netherlands	27 May 2000	Netherlands v Cameroon	0-0
Chelsea	19 Aug 2000	Chelsea v West Ham United	4-2
Middlesbrough	14 Aug 2004	Middlesbrough v Newcastle United	2-2

List of honours

Domestic Cup [1]	1997 Boavista FC (3-2 vs Benfica)

Personal honours

Topscorer Premier League	1999 (equal with Michael Owen)
	2001

Level	Matches	Goals
2	4	0
2	26	2
2	9	0
1	31	12
1	29	20
1	33	16
1	36	18
1	34	24
1	35	23
1	35	23
1	36	11
1*	30	12
1	36	13
	374	**174**

Transfers

Year	Transfer	Sum	
1996	Campomaiorense to Boavista	250,000 Euro	(550,000 guilders)
1997	Boavista to Leeds United	2.7 million Euro	(6 million guilders)
1999	Leeds United to Atlético Madrid	18.1 million Euro	(40 million guilders)
2000	Atlético Madrid to Chelsea	24.1 million Euro	(53 million guilders)
2004	Chelsea to Middlesbrough	Free	

International matches

Datum	Competition	Match		Result
27 May 1998	Friendlies	Netherlands	Cameroon	0-0
01 Jun 1998	Friendlies	Netherlands	Paraguay	5-1
05 Jun 1998	Friendlies	Netherlands	Nigeria	5-1
13 Jun 1998	-Wc-	Netherlands	Belgium	0-0
25 Jun 1998	-Wc-	Netherlands	Mexico	2-2
18 Aug 1999	Friendlies	Denmark	Netherlands	0-0
23 Feb 2000	Friendlies	Netherlands	Germany	2-1
26 Apr 2000	Friendlies	Netherlands	Scotland	0-0
15 Nov 2000	Friendlies	Spain	Netherlands	1-2
24 Mar 2001	WCQ UEFA	Andorra	Netherlands	0-5
28 Mar 2001	WCQ UEFA	Portugal	Netherlands	2-2
25 Apr 2001	WCQ UEFA	Netherlands	Cyprus	4-0
02 Jun 2001	WCQ UEFA	Estonia	Netherlands	2-4
15 Aug 2001	Friendlies	England	Netherlands	0-2
01 Sep 2001	WCQ UEFA	Rep. of Ireland	Netherlands	1-0
05 Sep 2001	WCQ UEFA	Netherlands	Estonia	5-0
10 Nov 2001	Friendlies	Denmark	Netherlands	1-1
13 Feb 2002	Friendlies	Netherlands	England	1-1
27 Mar 2002	Friendlies	Netherlands	Spain	1-0
21 Aug 2002	Friendlies	Norway	Netherlands	0-1
07 Sep 2002	ECh Qual.	Netherlands	Belarus	3-0
16 Oct 2002	ECh Qual.	Austria	Netherlands	0-3
20 Nov 2002	Friendlies	Germany	Netherlands	1-3

Totals

All the above statistics provided courtesy of infostradasports.com as at 31 July 2005.

Basis	In	Goals	Yt(R2y)	Rt(R2y)
	X	0	0 (0)	0 (0)
	X	1	0 (0)	0 (0)
X		1	0 (0)	0 (0)
X		0	0 (0)	0 (0)
	X	0	0 (0)	0 (0)
X		0	0 (0)	0 (0)
	X	0	0 (0)	0 (0)
X		0	0 (0)	0 (0)
X		1	0 (0)	1 (0)
X		1	0 (0)	0 (0)
X		1	0 (0)	0 (0)
X		1	0 (0)	0 (0)
X		0	0 (0)	0 (0)
	X	0	0 (0)	0 (0)
	X	0	0 (0)	0 (0)
	X	0	0 (0)	0 (0)
X		1	0 (0)	0 (0)
	X	0	0 (0)	0 (0)
X		0	0 (0)	0 (0)
	X	0	0 (0)	0 (0)
	X	1	0 (0)	0 (0)
	X	0	0 (0)	0 (0)
	X	1	0 (0)	0 (0
11	**12**	**9**	**0 (0)**	**1 (0)**

Personal statistics

Match

27 Oct 1990	1. Div.	VVV	Telstar	2-0
24 Nov 1990	1. Div.	Telstar	RBC	1-1
01 Dec 1990	1. Div.	FC Dordrecht'90	Telstar	2-0
08 Dec 1990	1. Div.	Telstar	Helmond Sport	0-4
17 Aug 1991	1. Div.	AZ	Excelsior	3-1
21 Aug 1991	1. Div.	Telstar	AZ	4-2
24 Aug 1991	1. Div.	AZ	Go Ahead Eagles	3-0
28 Aug 1991	1. Div.	AZ	VCV Zeeland	2-0
31 Aug 1991	1. Div.	Eindhoven	AZ	1-1
04 Sep 1991	1. Div.	AZ	TOP	3-1
07 Sep 1991	1. Div.	Helmond Sport	AZ	3-2
14 Sep 1991	1. Div.	AZ	BV Veendam	2-1
23 Nov 1991	1. Div.	VCV Zeeland	AZ	0-3
01 Dec 1991	1. Div.	AZ	Cambuur Leeuwarden	4-1
07 Dec 1991	1. Div.	Excelsior	AZ	0-5
14 Dec 1991	1. Div.	AZ	Telstar	1-1
11 Jan 1992	1. Div.	AZ	Eindhoven	0-2
18 Jan 1992	1. Div.	TOP	AZ	0-1
25 Jan 1992	1. Div.	AZ	Helmond Sport	1-2
05 Feb 1992	1. Div.	Go Ahead Eagles	AZ	3-1
08 Feb 1992	1. Div.	Cambuur Leeuwarden	AZ	1-0
15 Feb 1992	1. Div.	AZ	SC Heerenveen	0-0
22 Feb 1992	1. Div.	SC Heracles	AZ	0-0
07 Mar 1992	1. Div.	AZ	FC Zwolle	0-0
15 Mar 1992	1. Div.	Haarlem	AZ	0-2
04 Apr 1992	1. Div.	AZ	BVV Den Bosch	0-0
11 Apr 1992	1. Div.	Wageningen	AZ	0-1
18 Apr 1992	1. Div.	AZ	NEC	1-2
20 Apr 1992	1. Div.	AZ	Emmen	2-0
25 Apr 1992	1. Div.	RBC	AZ	0-0
12 Sep 1992	1. Div.	AZ	Haarlem	2-2
03 Oct 1992	1. Div.	AZ	RBC	1-2
13 Mar 1993	1. Div.	RBC	AZ	2-0

Compl.	In	Out	G	P	Ass	Yt(R2y)	Rt(R2y)	O. G.
X			0	0	0	1 (0)	0 (0)	0
	X		0	0	0	0 (0)	0 (0)	0
		X	0	0	0	1 (0)	0 (0)	0
X			0	0	0	0 (0)	0 (0)	0
X			1	0	0	1 (0)	0 (0)	0
X			0	0	0	0 (0)	0 (0)	0
X			0	0	0	1 (0)	0 (0)	0
X			0	0	0	0 (0)	0 (0)	0
X			0	0	0	0 (0)	0 (0)	0
		X	0	0	0	0 (0)	0 (0)	0
		X	0	0	0	0 (0)	0 (0)	0
	X		0	0	0	0 (0)	0 (0)	0
X			0	0	0	0 (0)	0 (0)	0
		X	0	0	0	0 (0)	0 (0)	0
X			1	0	0	0 (0)	0 (0)	0
X			0	0	0	0 (0)	0 (0)	0
		X	0	0	0	0 (0)	0 (0)	0
X			0	0	0	0 (0)	0 (0)	0
		X	0	0	0	0 (0)	0 (0)	0
X			0	0	0	0 (0)	0 (0)	0
X			0	0	0	0 (0)	0 (0)	0
	X		0	0	0	0 (0)	0 (0)	0
X			0	0	0	0 (0)	0 (0)	0
		X	0	0	0	0 (0)	0 (0)	0
X			0	0	0	1 (0)	0 (0)	0
	X		0	0	0	0 (0)	0 (0)	0
	X		0	0	0	0 (0)	0 (0)	0
		X	0	0	0	0 (0)	0 (0)	0
	X		0	0	0	0 (0)	0 (0)	0
	X		0	0	0	0 (0)	0 (0)	0
		X	0	0	0	0 (0)	0 (0)	0
	X		0	0	0	0 (0)	0 (0)	0
	X		0	0	0	0 (0)	0 (0)	0

Match

27 Mar 1993	1. Div.	Helmond Sport	AZ	2-3
03 Apr 1993	1. Div.	AZ	TOP	0-1
12 Apr 1993	1. Div.	VVV	AZ	4-1
01 May 1993	1. Div.	SC Heerenveen	AZ	3-2
08 May 1993	1. Div.	AZ	Telstar	1-2
14 May 1993	1. Div.	FC Zwolle	AZ	0-0
09 Aug 1997	Prem.	Leeds United	Arsenal	1-1
27 May 1998	Friendlies	Netherlands	Cameroon	0-0
01 Jun 1998	Friendlies	Netherlands	Paraguay	5-1
05 Jun 1998	Friendlies	Netherlands	Nigeria	5-1
13 Jun 1998	-Wc -	Netherlands	Belgium	0-0
25 Jun 1998	-Wc -	Netherlands	Mexico	2-2
24 Aug 1998	Prem.	Leeds United	Blackburn Rovers	1-0
29 Aug 1998	Prem.	Wimbledon	Leeds United	1-1
08 Sep 1998	Prem.	Leeds United	Southampton	3-0
12 Sep 1998	Prem.	Everton	Leeds United	0-0
15 Sep 1998	UEFA	Leeds United	CS Marítimo	1-0
19 Sep 1998	Prem.	Leeds United	Aston Villa	0-0
26 Sep 1998	Prem.	Tottenham Hotspur	Leeds United	3-3
03 Oct 1998	Prem.	Leeds United	Leicester City	0-1
17 Oct 1998	Prem.	Nottingham Forest	Leeds United	1-1
20 Oct 1998	UEFA	AS Roma	Leeds United	1-0
25 Oct 1998	Prem.	Leeds United	Chelsea	0-0
31 Oct 1998	Prem.	Derby County	Leeds United	2-2
03 Nov 1998	UEFA	Leeds United	AS Roma	0-0
08 Nov 1998	Prem.	Leeds United	Sheffield Wednesday	2-1
14 Nov 1998	Prem.	Liverpool	Leeds United	1-3
21 Nov 1998	Prem.	Leeds United	Charlton Athletic	4-1
29 Nov 1998	Prem.	Manchester United	Leeds United	3-2
05 Dec 1998	Prem.	Leeds United	West Ham United	4-0
14 Dec 1998	Prem.	Leeds United	Coventry City	2-0
20 Dec 1998	Prem.	Arsenal	Leeds United	3-1
26 Dec 1998	Prem.	Newcastle United	Leeds United	0-3
29 Dec 1998	Prem.	Leeds United	Wimbledon	2-2
09 Jan 1999	Prem.	Blackburn Rovers	Leeds United	1-0

Compl.	In	Out	G	P	Ass	Yt(R2y)	Rt(R2y)	O. G.
	X		0	0	0	0 (0)	0 (0)	0
	X		0	0	0	0 (0)	0 (0)	0
	X		0	0	0	1 (0)	0 (0)	0
X			0	0	0	0 (0)	0 (0)	0
	X		0	0	0	0 (0)	0 (0)	0
X			0	0	0	0 (0)	0 (0)	0
X			1	0	0	0 (0)	0 (0)	0
	X		0	0	0	0 (0)	0 (0)	0
	X		1	0	0	0 (0)	0.(0)	0
	X		1	0	0	0 (0)	0 (0)	0
		X	0	0	0	0 (0)	0 (0)	0
	X		0	0	0	0 (0)	0 (0)	0
X			1	0	0	0 (0)	0 (0)	0
X			0	0	0	0 (0)	0 (0)	0
X			0	0	0	0 (0)	0 (0)	0
X			0	0	0	0 (0)	0 (0)	0
X			1	0	0	0 (0)	0 (0)	0
X			0	0	0	0 (0)	0 (0)	0
X			1	0	0	0 (0)	0 (0)	0
X			0	0	0	1 (0)	0 (0)	0
		X	0	0	0	0 (0)	0 (0)	0
		X	0	0	0	0 (0)	0 (0)	0
		X	0	0	0	1 (0)	0 (0)	0
		X	0	0	0	0 (0)	0 (0)	0
X			0	0	0	1 (0)	0 (0)	0
X			1	0	0	0 (0)	0 (0)	0
X			2	0	0	0 (0)	0 (0)	0
X			1	0	0	0 (0)	0 (0)	0
X			1	0	0	0 (0)	0 (0)	0
X			1	0	0	1 (0)	0 (0)	0
X			0	0	0	1 (0)	0 (0)	0
X			1	0	0	0 (0)	0 (0)	0
X			1	0	0	0 (0)	0 (0)	0
X			0	0	0	0 (0)	0 (0)	0
X			0	0	0	0 (0)	0 (0)	0

Match

16 Jan 1999	Prem.	Leeds United	Middlesbrough	2-0
30 Jan 1999	Prem.	Southampton	Leeds United	3-0
13 Feb 1999	FA Cup	Leeds United	Tottenham Hotspur	1-1
17 Feb 1999	Prem.	Aston Villa	Leeds United	1-2
20 Feb 1999	Prem.	Leeds United	Everton	1-0
01 Mar 1999	Prem.	Leicester City	Leeds United	1-2
10 Mar 1999	Prem.	Leeds United	Tottenham Hotspur	2-0
13 Mar 1999	Prem.	Sheffield Wednesday	Leeds United	0-2
20 Mar 1999	Prem.	Leeds United	Derby County	4-1
03 Apr 1999	Prem.	Leeds United	Nottingham Forest	3-1
12 Apr 1999	Prem.	Leeds United	Liverpool	0-0
17 Apr 1999	Prem.	Charlton Athletic	Leeds United	1-1
25 Apr 1999	Prem.	Leeds United	Manchester United	1-1
01 May 1999	Prem.	West Ham United	Leeds United	1-5
05 May 1999	Prem.	Chelsea	Leeds United	1-0
11 May 1999	Prem.	Leeds United	Arsenal	1-0
16 May 1999	Prem.	Coventry City	Leeds United	2-2
18 Aug 1999	Friendlies	Denmark	Netherlands	0-0
22 Aug 1999	Primera	Atlético Madrid	Rayo Vallecano	0-2
28 Aug 1999	Primera	Real Sociedad	Atlético Madrid	4-1
12 Sep 1999	Primera	Atlético Madrid	Celta de Vigo	1-2
16 Sep 1999	UEFA	Atlético Madrid	Ankaragücü	3-0
19 Sep 1999	Primera	Real Zaragoza	Atlético Madrid	1-1
26 Sep 1999	Primera	Atlético Madrid	Racing Santander	2-0
03 Oct 1999	Primera	RCD Espanyol	Atlético Madrid	3-1
12 Oct 1999	Primera	Atlético Madrid	Alavés	1-0
17 Oct 1999	Primera	Real Betis	Atlético Madrid	2-1
21 Oct 1999	UEFA	Atlético Madrid	Amica Wronki	1-0
24 Oct 1999	Primera	Atlético Madrid	Real Valladolid	3-1
30 Oct 1999	Primera	Real Madrid	Atlético Madrid	1-3
04 Nov 1999	UEFA	Amica Wronki	Atlético Madrid	1-4
07 Nov 1999	Primera	Atlético Madrid	Numancia	2-2
20 Nov 1999	Primera	Athletic Bilbao	Atlético Madrid	4-2
23 Nov 1999	UEFA	VfL Wolfsburg	Atlético Madrid	2-3
28 Nov 1999	Primera	Atlético Madrid	Deportivo La Coruña	1-3

Compl.	In	Out	G	P	Ass	Yt(R2y)	Rt(R2y)	O. G.
X			0	0	0	0 (0)	0 (0)	0
X			0	0	0	0 (0)	0 (0)	0
X			0	0	0	0 (0)	0 (0)	0
X			2	0	0	1 (0)	0 (0)	0
	X		0	0	0	1 (0)	0 (0)	0
		X	0	0	0	0 (0)	0 (0)	0
X			0	0	0	0 (0)	0 (0)	0
X			1	0	0	0 (0)	0 (0)	0
X			1	0	0	0 (0)	0 (0)	0
X			1	0	0	0 (0)	0 (0)	0
X			0	0	0	0 (0)	0 (0)	0
		X	0	0	0	0 (0)	0 (0)	0
		X	1	0	0	1 (0)	0 (0)	0
		X	1	0	0	0 (0)	0 (0)	0
X			0	0	0	0 (0)	0 (0)	0
X			1	0	0	1 (0)	0 (0)	0
X			0	0	0	0 (0)	0 (0)	0
		X	0	0	0	0 (0)	0 (0)	0
X			0	0	0	0 (0)	0 (0)	0
X			0	0	0	1 (0)	0 (0)	0
X			0	0	0	0 (0)	0 (0)	0
		X	1	0	0	0 (0)	0 (0)	0
X			1	0	0	0 (0)	0 (0)	0
X			1	0	0	0 (0)	0 (0)	0
X			1	0	0	0 (0)	0 (0)	0
X			1	0	0	0 (0)	0 (0)	0
X			0	0	0	0 (0)	0 (0)	0
X			0	0	0	0 (0)	0 (0)	0
X			1	0	0	0 (0)	0 (0)	0
		X	2	0	0	0 (0)	0 (0)	0
		X	1	0	0	0 (0)	0 (0)	0
X			1	0	0	0 (0)	0 (0)	0
X			1	1	0	0 (0)	0 (0)	0
X			1	0	0	1 (0)	0 (0)	0
X			0	0	0	1 (0)	0 (0)	0

Match

05 Dec 1999	Primera	Málaga CF	Atlético Madrid	2-3
09 Dec 1999	UEFA	Atlético Madrid	VfL Wolfsburg	2-1
12 Dec 1999	Primera	Atlético Madrid	Valencia CF	1-2
19 Dec 1999	Primera	FC Barcelona	Atlético Madrid	2-1
22 Dec 1999	Primera	Atlético Madrid	Real Oviedo	5-0
05 Jan 2000	Primera	Sevilla FC	Atlético Madrid	2-1
09 Jan 2000	Primera	Atlético Madrid	RCD Mallorca	1-0
15 Jan 2000	Primera	Rayo Vallecano	Atlético Madrid	1-1
23 Jan 2000	Primera	Atlético Madrid	Real Sociedad	1-1
06 Feb 2000	Primera	Atlético Madrid	Real Zaragoza	2-2
13 Feb 2000	Primera	Racing Santander	Atlético Madrid	2-1
20 Feb 2000	Primera	Atlético Madrid	RCD Espanyol	1-1
23 Feb 2000	Friendlies	Netherlands	Germany	2-1
02 Mar 2000	UEFA	Atlético Madrid	RC Lens	2-2
05 Mar 2000	Primera	Atlético Madrid	Real Betis	0-0
09 Mar 2000	UEFA	RC Lens	Atlético Madrid	4-2
12 Mar 2000	Primera	Real Valladolid	Atlético Madrid	1-0
18 Mar 2000	Primera	Atlético Madrid	Real Madrid	1-1
02 Apr 2000	Primera	Atlético Madrid	Athletic Bilbao	1-2
08 Apr 2000	Primera	Deportivo La Coruña	Atlético Madrid	4-1
16 Apr 2000	Primera	Atlético Madrid	Málaga CF	2-2
26 Apr 2000	Friendlies	Netherlands	Scotland	0-0
29 Apr 2000	Primera	Atlético Madrid	FC Barcelona	0-3
07 May 2000	Primera	Real Oviedo	Atlético Madrid	2-2
13 May 2000	Primera	Atlético Madrid	Sevilla FC	1-1
19 May 2000	Primera	RCD Mallorca	Atlético Madrid	1-2
19 Aug 2000	Prem.	Chelsea	West Ham United	4-2
22 Aug 2000	Prem.	Bradford City	Chelsea	2-0
27 Aug 2000	Prem.	Aston Villa	Chelsea	1-1
06 Sep 2000	Prem.	Chelsea	Arsenal	2-2
09 Sep 2000	Prem.	Newcastle United	Chelsea	0-0
14 Sep 2000	UEFA	Chelsea	FC St. Gallen	1-0
17 Sep 2000	Prem.	Chelsea	Leicester City	0-2
23 Sep 2000	Prem.	Manchester United	Chelsea	3-3
28 Sep 2000	UEFA	FC St. Gallen	Chelsea	2-0

Compl.	In	Out	G	P	Ass	Yt(R2y)	Rt(R2y)	O. G.
X			2	0	0	0 (0)	0 (0)	0
		X	1	0	0	0 (0)	0 (0)	0
X			1	0	0	0 (0)	0 (0)	0
X			1	1	0	1 (0)	0 (0)	0
X			2	0	0	0 (0)	0 (0)	0
X			1	0	0	0 (0)	0 (0)	0
X			1	1	0	0 (0)	0 (0)	0
X			0	0	0	0 (0)	0 (0)	0
X			1	0	0	0 (0)	0 (0)	0
X			2	1	0	0 (0)	0 (0)	0
X			0	0	0	1 (0)	0 (0)	0
X			1	0	0	1 (0)	0 (0)	0
	X		0	0	0	0 (0)	0 (0)	0
X			2	0	0	1 (0)	0 (0)	0
X			0	0	0	1 (0)	0 (0)	0
X			1	0	0	0 (0)	0 (0)	0
X			0	0	0	1 (0)	0 (0)	0
X			0	0	0	0 (0)	0 (0)	0
X			1	0	0	0 (0)	0 (0)	0
X			1	0	0	0 (0)	0 (0)	0
		X	0	0	0	0 (0)	1 (0)	0
		X	0	0	0	0 (0)	0 (0)	0
X			0	0	0	0 (0)	0 (0)	0
X			1	0	0	0 (0)	0 (0)	0
X			0	0	0	0 (0)	0 (0)	0
		X	0	0	0	0 (0)	0 (0)	0
X			1	1	0	0 (0)	0 (0)	0
		X	0	0	0	0 (0)	0 (0)	0
		X	0	0	0	1 (0)	0 (0)	0
X			1	0	0	0 (0)	0 (0)	0
X			0	0	0	0 (0)	0 (0)	0
X			0	0	0	1 (0)	0 (0)	0
		X	0	0	0	1 (0)	0 (0)	0
		X	1	0	0	0 (0)	0 (0)	0
X			0	0	0	0 (0)	0 (0)	0

Match

Date	Comp.	Home	Away	Score
01 Oct 2000	Prem.	Chelsea	Liverpool	3-0
14 Oct 2000	Prem.	Sunderland	Chelsea	1-0
21 Oct 2000	Prem.	Chelsea	Coventry City	6-1
28 Oct 2000	Prem.	Chelsea	Tottenham Hotspur	3-0
04 Nov 2000	Prem.	Southampton	Chelsea	3-2
12 Nov 2000	Prem.	Chelsea	Leeds United	1-1
15 Nov 2000	Friendlies	Spain	Netherlands	1-2
18 Nov 2000	Prem.	Charlton Athletic	Chelsea	2-0
25 Nov 2000	Prem.	Everton	Chelsea	2-1
03 Dec 2000	Prem.	Chelsea	Manchester City	2-1
26 Dec 2000	Prem.	Ipswich Town	Chelsea	2-2
01 Jan 2001	Prem.	Chelsea	Aston Villa	1-0
13 Jan 2001	Prem.	Arsenal	Chelsea	1-1
20 Jan 2001	Prem.	Chelsea	Ipswich Town	4-1
31 Jan 2001	Prem.	Chelsea	Newcastle United	3-1
03 Feb 2001	Prem.	Leicester City	Chelsea	2-1
10 Feb 2001	Prem.	Chelsea	Manchester United	1-1
03 Mar 2001	Prem.	Coventry City	Chelsea	0-0
07 Mar 2001	Prem.	West Ham United	Chelsea	0-2
17 Mar 2001	Prem.	Chelsea	Sunderland	2-4
24 Mar 2001	WCQ UEFA	Andorra	Netherlands	0-5
28 Mar 2001	WCQ UEFA	Portugal	Netherlands	2-2
31 Mar 2001	Prem.	Chelsea	Middlesbrough	2-1
07 April 2001	Prem.	Derby County	Chelsea	04
14 Apr 2001	Prem.	Chelsea	Southampton	1-0
17 Apr 2001	Prem.	Tottenham Hotspur	Chelsea	0-3
21 Apr 2001	Prem.	Chelsea	Charlton Athletic	0-1
25 April 2001	WCQ UEFA	Netherlands	Cyprus	4-0
28 Apr 2001	Prem.	Leeds United	Chelsea	2-0
05 May 2001	Prem.	Chelsea	Everton	2-1
08 May 2001	Prem.	Liverpool	Chelsea	2-2
19 May 2001	Prem.	Manchester City	Chelsea	1-2
02 Jun 2001	WCQ UEFA	Estonia	Netherlands	2-4
15 Aug 2001	Friendlies	England	Netherlands	0-2
19 Aug 2001	Prem.	Chelsea	Newcastle United	1-1

Compl.	In	Out	G	P	Ass	Yt(R2y)	Rt(R2y)	O. G.
		X	1	0	0	0 (0)	0 (0)	0
		X	0	0	0	0 (0)	0 (0)	0
X			4	1	0	0 (0)	0 (0)	0
X			2	1	0	0 (0)	0 (0)	0
X			0	0	0	0 (0)	0 (0)	0
X			0	0	0	0 (0)	0 (0)	0
		X	1	0	0	0 (0)	1 (0)	0
		X	0	0	0	0 (0)	0 (0)	0
		X	0	0	0	0 (0)	1 (0)	0
X			1	0	0	0 (0)	0 (0)	0
		X	0	0	0	0 (0)	0 (0)	0
		X	1	0	0	0 (0)	0 (0)	0
X			0	0	0	0 (0)	0 (0)	0
X			1	1	0	0 (0)	0 (0)	0
X			0	0	0	0 (0)	0 (0)	0
X			1	0	0	0 (0)	0 (0)	0
X			1	0	0	0 (0)	0 (0)	0
X			0	0	0	0 (0)	0 (0)	0
X			1	0	0	0 (0)	0 (0)	0
X			0	0	0	0 (0)	0 (0)	0
X			1	0	0	0 (0)	0 (0)	0
		X	1	1	0	0 (0)	0 (0)	0
X			0	0	0	0 (0)	0 (0)	0
X			1	0	0	0 (0)	0 (0)	0
X			0	0	0	0 (0)	0 (0)	0
X			1	0	0	0 (0)	0 (0)	0
		X	0	0	0	1 (0)	0 (0)	0
		X	1	0	0	0 (0)	0 (0)	0
X			0	0	0	1 (0)	0 (0)	0
X			2	0	0	0 (0)	0 (0)	0
X			2	0	0	1 (0)	0 (0)	0
X			1	0	0	1 (0)	0 (0)	0
		X	0	0	0	0 (0)	0 (0)	0
	X		0	0	0	0 (0)	0 (0)	0
X			0	0	0	0 (0)	0 (0)	0

Match

25 Aug 2001	Prem.	Southampton	Chelsea	0-2
01 Sep 2001	WCQ UEFA	Republic of Ireland	Netherlands	1-0
05 Sep 2001	WCQ UEFA	Netherlands	Estonia	5-0
08 Sep 2001	Prem.	Chelsea	Arsenal	1-1
16 Sep 2001	Prem.	Tottenham Hotspur	Chelsea	2-3
23 Sep 2001	Prem.	Chelsea	Middlesbrough	2-2
30 Sep 2001	Prem.	Fulham	Chelsea	1-1
13 Oct 2001	Prem.	Chelsea	Leicester City	2-0
18 Oct 2001	UEFA	Hapoel Tel Aviv	Chelsea	2-0
21 Oct 2001	Prem.	Leeds United	Chelsea	0-0
24 Oct 2001	Prem.	West Ham United	Chelsea	2-1
28 Oct 2001	Prem.	Derby County	Chelsea	1-1
01 Nov 2001	UEFA	Chelsea	Hapoel Tel Aviv	1-1
04 Nov 2001	Prem.	Chelsea	Ipswich Town	2-1
10 Nov 2001	Friendlies	Denmark	Netherlands	1-1
18 Nov 2001	Prem.	Everton	Chelsea	0-0
24 Nov 2001	Prem.	Chelsea	Blackburn Rovers	0-0
01 Dec 2001	Prem.	Manchester United	Chelsea	0-3
05 Dec 2001	Prem.	Chelsea	Charlton Athletic	0-1
09 Dec 2001	Prem.	Sunderland	Chelsea	0-0
16 Dec 2001	Prem.	Chelsea	Liverpool	4-0
23 Dec 2001	Prem.	Chelsea	Bolton Wanderers	5-1
26 Dec 2001	Prem.	Arsenal	Chelsea	2-1
29 Dec 2001	Prem.	Newcastle United	Chelsea	1-2
01 Jan 2002	Prem.	Chelsea	Southampton	2-4
20 Jan 2002	Prem.	Chelsea	West Ham United	5-1
30 Jan 2002	Prem.	Chelsea	Leeds United	2-0
02 Feb 2002	Prem.	Leicester City	Chelsea	2-3
09 Feb 2002	Prem.	Aston Villa	Chelsea	1-1
13 Feb 2002	Friendlies	Netherlands	England	1-1
02 Mar 2002	Prem.	Charlton Athletic	Chelsea	2-1
06 Mar 2002	Prem.	Chelsea	Fulham	3-2
13 Mar 2002	Prem.	Chelsea	Tottenham Hotspur	4-0
16 Mar 2002	Prem.	Chelsea	Sunderland	4-0
24 Mar 2002	Prem.	Liverpool	Chelsea	1-0

Compl.	In	Out	G	P	Ass	Yt(R2y)	Rt(R2y)	O. G.
X			1	0	0	0 (0)	0 (0)	0
	X		0	0	0	0 (0)	0 (0)	0
	X		0	0	0	0 (0)	0 (0)	0
		X	1	1	0	0 (0)	1 (0)	0
X			2	1	0	0 (0)	0 (0)	0
X			2	0	0	1 (0)	0 (0)	0
X			1	0	0	0 (0)	0 (0)	0
		X	1	1	0	0 (0)	0 (0)	0
		X	0	0	0	0 (0)	0 (0)	0
X			0	0	0	0 (0)	0 (0)	0
X			1	0	0	0 (0)	0 (0)	0
X			1	0	0	1 (0)	0 (0)	0
X			0	0	0	1 (0)	0 (0)	0
X			0	0	0	0 (0)	0 (0)	0
X			1	1	0	0 (0)	0 (0)	0
X			0	0	0	0 (0)	0 (0)	0
X			0	0	0	0 (0)	0 (0)	0
		X	1	0	0	0 (0)	0 (0)	0
X			0	0	0	1 (0)	0 (0)	0
X			0	0	0	0 (0)	0 (0)	0
		X	1	0	0	0 (0)	0 (0)	0
X			1	0	0	0 (0)	0 (0)	0
X			0	0	0	0 (0)	0 (0)	0
		X	0	0	0	0 (0)	0 (0)	0
X			1	0	0	0 (0)	0 (0)	0
		X	2	0	0	0 (0)	0 (0)	0
X			0	0	0	0 (0)	0 (0)	0
X			2	0	0	0 (0)	0 (0)	0
X			0	0	0	0 (0)	0 (0)	0
	X		0	0	0	0 (0)	0 (0)	0
X			0	0	0	0 (0)	0 (0)	0
X			0	0	0	0 (0)	0 (0)	0
		X	3	0	0	0 (0)	0 (0)	0
X			0	0	0	0 (0)	0 (0)	0
X			0	0	0	0 (0)	0 (0)	0

Match

27 Mar 2002	Friendlies	Netherlands	Spain	1-0
30 Mar 2002	Prem.	Chelsea	Derby County	2-1
01 Apr 2002	Prem.	Ipswich Town	Chelsea	0-0
06 Apr 2002	Prem.	Chelsea	Everton	3-0
10 Apr 2002	Prem.	Blackburn Rovers	Chelsea	0-0
20 Apr 2002	Prem.	Chelsea	Manchester United	0-3
17 Aug 2002	Prem.	Charlton Athletic	Chelsea	2-3
21 Aug 2002	Friendlies	Norway	Netherlands	0-1
23 Aug 2002	Prem.	Chelsea	Manchester United	2-2
28 Aug 2002	Prem.	Southampton	Chelsea	1-1
01 Sep 2002	Prem.	Chelsea	Arsenal	1-1
07 Sep 2002	ECh Qual.	Netherlands	Belarus	3-0
11 Sep 2002	Prem.	Blackburn Rovers	Chelsea	2-3
14 Sep 2002	Prem.	Chelsea	Newcastle United	3-0
19 Sep 2002	UEFA	Chelsea	Viking FK	2-1
23 Sep 2002	Prem.	Fulham	Chelsea	0-0
28 Sep 2002	Prem.	Chelsea	West Ham United	2-3
03 Oct 2002	UEFA	Viking FK	Chelsea	4-2
06 Oct 2002	Prem.	Liverpool	Chelsea	1-0
16 Oct 2002	ECh Qual.	Austria	Netherlands	0-3
19 Oct 2002	Prem.	Manchester City	Chelsea	0-3
26 Oct 2002	Prem.	Chelsea	West Bromwich Albion	2-0
03 Nov 2002	Prem.	Tottenham Hotspur	Chelsea	0-0
16 Nov 2002	Prem.	Chelsea	Middlesbrough	1-0
20 Nov 2002	Friendlies	Germany	Netherlands	1-3
23 Nov 2002	Prem.	Bolton Wanderers	Chelsea	1-1
30 Nov 2002	Prem.	Chelsea	Sunderland	3-0
07 Dec 2002	Prem.	Everton	Chelsea	1-3
14 Dec 2002	Prem.	Middlesbrough	Chelsea	1-1
21 Dec 2002	Prem.	Chelsea	Aston Villa	2-0
26 Dec 2002	Prem.	Chelsea	Southampton	0-0
28 Dec 2002	Prem.	Leeds United	Chelsea	2-0
01 Jan 2003	Prem.	Arsenal	Chelsea	3-2
11 Jan 2003	Prem.	Chelsea	Charlton Athletic	4-1
18 Jan 2003	Prem.	Manchester United	Chelsea	2-1

Compl.	In	Out	G	P	Ass	Yt(R2y)	Rt(R2y)	O. G.
X			0	0	0	0 (0)	0 (0)	0
X			0	0	0	1 (0)	0 (0)	0
X			0	0	0	0 (0)	0 (0)	0
		X	2	0	0	0 (0)	0 (0)	0
X			0	0	0	0 (0)	0 (0)	0
X			0	0	0	1 (0)	0 (0)	0
		X	0	0	0	0 (0)	0 (0)	0
	X		0	0	0	0 (0)	0 (0)	0
		X	0	0	0	1 (0)	0 (0)	0
		X	0	0	0	0 (0)	0 (0)	0
	X		0	0	0	0 (0)	0 (0)	0
	X		1	0	0	0 (0)	0 (0)	0
X			0	0	0	0 (0)	0 (0)	0
	X		0	0	0	0 (0)	0 (0)	0
X			1	0	0	0 (0)	0 (0)	0
X			0	0	0	0 (0)	0 (0)	0
X			1	1	0	0 (0)	0 (0)	0
		X	0	0	0	0 (0)	0 (0)	0
		X	0	0	0	0 (0)	0 (0)	0
	X		0	0	0	0 (0)	0 (0)	0
X			1	0	0	0 (0)	0 (0)	0
X			1	0	0	0 (0)	0 (0)	0
		X	0	0	0	0 (0)	0 (0)	0
	X		0	0	0	0 (0)	0 (0)	0
	X		1	0	0	0 (0)	0 (0)	0
	X		1	0	0	1 (0)	0 (0)	0
X			1	0	0	0 (0)	0 (0)	0
		X	1	0	0	1 (0)	0 (0)	0
		X	0	0	0	0 (0)	0 (0)	0
		X	0	0	0	0 (0)	0 (0)	0
X			0	0	0	0 (0)	0 (0)	0
	X		0	0	0	0 (0)	0 (0)	0
X			0	0	0	0 (0)	0 (0)	0
X			1	1	0	0 (0)	0 (0)	0
		X	0	0	0	0 (0)	0 (0)	0

Match

01 Feb 2003	Prem.	Chelsea	Tottenham Hotspur	1-1
08 Feb 2003	Prem.	Birmingham City	Chelsea	1-3
22 Feb 2003	Prem.	Chelsea	Blackburn Rovers	1-2
01 Mar 2003	Prem.	Newcastle United	Chelsea	2-1
08 Mar 2003	FA Cup	Arsenal	Chelsea	2-2
16 Mar 2003	Prem.	West Bromwich Albion	Chelsea	0-2
22 Mar 2003	Prem.	Chelsea	Manchester City	5-0
25 Mar 2003	FA Cup	Chelsea	Arsenal	1-3
05 Apr 2003	Prem.	Sunderland	Chelsea	1-2
12 Apr 2003	Prem.	Chelsea	Bolton Wanderers	1-0
19 Apr 2003	Prem.	Aston Villa	Chelsea	2-1
21 Apr 2003	Prem.	Chelsea	Everton	4-1
26 Apr 2003	Prem.	Chelsea	Fulham	1-1
03 May 2003	Prem.	West Ham United	Chelsea	1-0
11 May 2003	Prem.	Chelsea	Liverpool	2-1
17 Aug 2003	Prem.	Liverpool	Chelsea	1-2
23 Aug 2003	Prem.	Chelsea	Leicester City	2-1
30 Aug 2003	Prem.	Chelsea	Blackburn Rovers	2-2
13 Sep 2003	Prem.	Chelsea	Tottenham Hotspur	4-2
16 Sep 2003	Ch. League	Sparta Praha	Chelsea	0-1
20 Sep 2003	Prem.	Wolverhampton	Chelsea	0-5
27 Sep 2003	Prem.	Chelsea	Aston Villa	1-0
01 Oct 2003	Ch. League	Chelsea	Besiktas	0-2
05 Oct 2003	Prem.	Middlesbrough	Chelsea	1-2
14 Oct 2003	Prem.	Birmingham City	Chelsea	0-0
18 Oct 2003	Prem.	Arsenal	Chelsea	2-1
25 Oct 2003	Prem.	Chelsea	Manchester City	1-0
01 Nov 2003	Prem.	Everton	Chelsea	0-1
22 Nov 2003	Prem.	Southampton	Chelsea	0-1
30 Nov 2003	Prem.	Chelsea	Manchester United	1-0
06 Dec 2003	Prem.	Leeds United	Chelsea	1-1
09 Dec 2003	Ch. League	Besiktas	Chelsea	0-2
13 Dec 2003	Prem.	Chelsea	Bolton Wanderers	1-2
17 Dec 2003	Carl. Cup	Aston Villa	Chelsea	2-1
26 Dec 2003	Prem.	Charlton Athletic	Chelsea	4-2

Compl.	In	Out	G	P	Ass	Yt(R2y)	Rt(R2y)	O. G.
	X		0	0	0	0 (0)	0 (0)	0
	X		1	1	0	0 (0)	0 (0)	0
X			1	0	0	0 (0)	0 (0)	0
X			0	0	0	0 (0)	0 (0)	1
X			0	0	0	0 (0)	0 (0)	0
X			0	0	0	0 (0)	0 (0)	0
		X	1	0	0	0 (0)	0 (0)	0
X			0	0	0	0 (0)	0 (0)	0
		X	0	0	0	0 (0)	0 (0)	0
X			0	0	0	0 (0)	0 (0)	0
	X		0	0	0	0 (0)	0 (0)	0
		X	1	0	0	0 (0)	0 (0)	0
X			0	0	0	0 (0)	0 (0)	0
	X		0	0	0	0 (0)	0 (0)	0
		X	0	0	0	1 (0)	0 (0)	0
	X		1	0	0	0 (0)	0 (0)	0
		X	0	0	0	0 (0)	0 (0)	0
X			1	1	0	0 (0)	0 (0)	0
X			1	0	0	1 (0)	0 (0)	0
	X		0	0	0	0 (0)	0 (0)	0
		X	1	0	0	0 (0)	0 (0)	0
X			1	0	0	0 (0)	0 (0)	0
	X		0	0	0	0 (0)	0 (0)	0
		X	0	0	0	1 (0)	0 (0)	0
		X	0	0	0	0 (0)	0 (0)	0
	X		0	0	0	1 (0)	0 (0)	0
		X	1	0	0	0 (0)	0 (0)	0
X			0	0	0	0 (0)	0 (0)	0
		X	0	0	0	0 (0)	0 (0)	0
	X		0	0	0	0 (0)	0 (0)	0
		X	0	0	0	1 (0)	0 (0)	0
X			1	0	0	0 (0)	0 (0)	0
	X		0	0	0	0 (0)	0 (0)	0
X			0	0	0	0 (0)	0 (0)	0
X			0	0	0	0 (0)	0 (0)	0

Match

11 Jan 2004	Prem.	Leicester City	Chelsea	0-4
18 Jan 2004	Prem.	Chelsea	Birmingham City	0-0
01 Feb 2004	Prem.	Blackburn Rovers	Chelsea	2-3
08 Feb 2004	Prem.	Chelsea	Charlton Athletic	1-0
11 Feb 2004	Prem.	Portsmouth	Chelsea	0-2
21 Feb 2004	Prem.	Chelsea	Arsenal	1-2
25 Feb 2004	Ch. League	VfB Stuttgart	Chelsea	0-1
28 Feb 2004	Prem.	Manchester City	Chelsea	0-1
13 Mar 2004	Prem.	Bolton Wanderers	Chelsea	0-2
27 Mar 2004	Prem.	Chelsea	Wolverhampton	5-2
03 Apr 2004	Prem.	Tottenham Hotspur	Chelsea	0-1
06 Apr 2004	Ch. League	Arsenal	Chelsea	1-2
10 Apr 2004	Prem.	Chelsea	Middlesbrough	0-0
17 Apr 2004	Prem.	Chelsea	Everton	0-0
20 Apr 2004	Ch. League	AS Monaco	Chelsea	3-1
25 Apr 2004	Prem.	Newcastle United	Chelsea	2-1
01 May 2004	Prem.	Chelsea	Southampton	4-0
05 May 2004	Ch. League	Chelsea	AS Monaco	2-2
14 Aug 2004	Prem.	Middlesbrough	Newcastle United	2-2
22 Aug 2004	Prem.	Arsenal	Middlesbrough	5-3
25 Aug 2004	Prem.	Fulham	Middlesbrough	0-2
28 Aug 2004	Prem.	Middlesbrough	Crystal Palace	2-1
11 Sep 2004	Prem.	Middlesbrough	Birmingham City	2-1
16 Sep 2004	UEFA	Middlesbrough	Baník Ostrava	3-0
19 Sep 2004	Prem.	Everton	Middlesbrough	1-0
25 Sep 2004	Prem.	Middlesbrough	Chelsea	0-1
16 Oct 2004	Prem.	Blackburn Rovers	Middlesbrough	0-4
21 Oct 2004	UEFA	Aigáleo Athinai	Middlesbrough	0-1
24 Oct 2004	Prem.	Middlesbrough	Portsmouth	1-1
30 Oct 2004	Prem.	Charlton Athletic	Middlesbrough	1-2
04 Nov 2004	UEFA	Middlesbrough	Lazio	2-0
07 Nov 2004	Prem.	Middlesbrough	Bolton Wanderers	1-1
14 Nov 2004	Prem.	West Bromwich Albion	Middlesbrough	1-2
20 Nov 2004	Prem.	Middlesbrough	Liverpool	2-0
25 Nov 2004	UEFA	Villarreal CF	Middlesbrough	2-0

Compl.	In	Out	G	P	Ass	Yt(R2y)	Rt(R2y)	O. G.
X			1	0	0	1 (0)	0 (0)	0
X			0	0	0	0 (0)	0 (0)	0
X			0	0	0	0 (0)	0 (0)	0
		X	1	1	0	0 (0)	0 (0)	0
	X		0	0	0	0 (0)	0 (0)	0
	X		0	0	0	0 (0)	0 (0)	0
	X		0	0	0	0 (0)	0 (0)	0
		X	0	0	0	0 (0)	0 (0)	0
X			0	0	0	0 (0)	0 (0)	0
	X		3	0	0	0 (0)	0 (0)	0
		X	1	0	0	0 (0)	0 (0)	0
		X	0	0	0	1 (0)	0 (0)	0
X			0	0	0	0 (0)	0 (0)	0
X			0	0	0	0 (0)	0 (0)	0
	X		0	0	0	0 (0)	0 (0)	0
	X		0	0	0	1 (0)	0 (0)	0
X			0	0	0	0 (0)	0 (0)	0
		X	0	0	0	0 (0)	0 (0)	0
X			1	0	0	0 (0)	0 (0)	0
X			1	0	0	0 (0)	0 (0)	0
X			0	0	0	0 (0)	0 (0)	0
X			1	0	0	0 (0)	0 (0)	0
X			0	0	0	0 (0)	0 (0)	0
			1	0	0	0 (0)	0 (0)	0
X			0	0	0	0 (0)	0 (0)	0
X			0	0	0	0 (0)	0 (0)	0
X			3	0	0	0 (0)	0 (0)	0
	X		0	0	0	0 (0)	0 (0)	0
X			0	0	0	0 (0)	0 (0)	0
X			0	0	0	0 (0)	0 (0)	0
		X	0	0	0	0 (0)	0 (0)	0
X			0	0	0	0 (0)	0 (0)	0
X			0	0	0	0 (0)	0 (0)	0
		X	0	0	0	0 (0)	0 (0)	0
	X		0	0	0	0 (0)	0 (0)	0

Match

28 Nov 2004	Prem.	Tottenham Hotspur	Middlesbrough	2-0
06 Dec 2004	Prem.	Middlesbrough	Manchester City	3-2
11 Dec 2004	Prem.	Southampton	Middlesbrough	2-2
18 Dec 2004	Prem.	Middlesbrough	Aston Villa	3-0
26 Dec 2004	Prem.	Birmingham City	Middlesbrough	2-0
28 Dec 2004	Prem.	Middlesbrough	Norwich City	2-0
01 Jan 2005	Prem.	Middlesbrough	Manchester United	0-2
04 Jan 2005	Prem.	Chelsea	Middlesbrough	2-0
16 Jan 2005	Prem.	Middlesbrough	Everton	1-1
22 Jan 2005	Prem.	Norwich City	Middlesbrough	4-4
29 Jan 2005	FA Cup	Manchester United	Middlesbrough	3-0
01 Feb 2005	Prem.	Portsmouth	Middlesbrough	2-1
12 Feb 2005	Prem.	Bolton Wanderers	Middlesbrough	0-0
17 Feb 2005	UEFA	Grazer AK	Middlesbrough	2-2
24 Feb 2005	UEFA	Middlesbrough	Grazer AK	2-1
27 Feb 2005	Prem.	Middlesbrough	Charlton Athletic	2-2
05 Mar 2005	Prem.	Aston Villa	Middlesbrough	2-0
10 Mar 2005	UEFA	Middlesbrough	Sporting CP	2-3
20 Mar 2005	Prem.	Middlesbrough	Southampton	1-3
02 Apr 2005	Prem.	Crystal Palace	Middlesbrough	0-1
09 Apr 2005	Prem.	Middlesbrough	Arsenal	0-1
19 Apr 2005	Prem.	Middlesbrough	Fulham	1-1
23 Apr 2005	Prem.	Middlesbrough	West Bromwich Albion	4-0
27 Apr 2005	Prem.	Newcastle United	Middlesbrough	0-0
30 Apr 2005	Prem.	Liverpool	Middlesbrough	1-1
07 May 2005	Prem.	Middlesbrough	Tottenham Hotspur	1-0
15 May 2005	Prem.	Manchester City	Middlesbrough	1-1

Totals

Compl.	In	Out	G	P	Ass	Yt(R2y)	Rt(R2y)	O. G.
X			0	0	0	0 (0)	0 (0)	0
		X	1	0	0	0 (0)	0 (0)	0
X			0	0	0	0 (0)	0 (0)	0
X			1	0	0	0 (0)	0 (0)	0
X			0	0	0	0 (0)	0 (0)	0
X			0	0	0	0 (0)	0 (0)	0
X			0	0	0	0 (0)	0 (0)	0
X			0	0	0	0 (0)	0 (0)	0
X			0	0	0	0 (0)	0 (0)	0
X			0	0	0	0 (0)	0 (0)	0
X			2	0	0	0 (0)	0 (0)	0
		X	0	0	0	0 (0)	0 (0)	0
X			0	0	0	0 (0)	0 (0)	0
X			0	0	0	0 (0)	0 (0)	0
X			1	0	0	1 (0)	0 (0)	0
X			1	0	0	0 (0)	0 (0)	0
X			0	0	0	0 (0)	0 (0)	0
X			0	0	0	0 (0)	0 (0)	0
X			0	0	0	0 (0)	0 (0)	0
X			1	0	0	0 (0)	0 (0)	0
X			0	0	0	1 (0)	0 (0)	0
X			0	0	0	0 (0)	0 (0)	0
X			0	0	0	0 (0)	0 (0)	0
X			1	0	0	0 (0)	0 (0)	0
X			0	0	0	1 (0)	0 (0)	0
X			0	0	0	0 (0)	0 (0)	0
X			0	0	0	0 (0)	0 (0)	0
X			1	0	0	0 (0)	0 (0)	0
210	**48**	**81**	**149**	**18**	**0**	**51 (0)**	**4 (0)**	**1**

Index